Reference-Dependent Preferences

Evelyn Stommel

Reference-Dependent Preferences

A Theoretical and Experimental Investigation of Individual Reference-Point Formation

Springer Gabler

Evelyn Stommel
Essen, Germany

Zugl. Dissertation Wissenschaftliche Hochschule für Unternehmensführung (WHU) – Otto Beisheim School of Management, Germany, 2012

ISBN 978-3-658-00634-1 ISBN 978-3-658-00635-8 (eBook)
DOI 10.1007/978-3-658-00635-8

The Deutsche Nationalbibliothek lists this publication in the Deutsche Nationalbibliografie; detailed bibliographic data are available in the Internet at http://dnb.d-nb.de.

Library of Congress Control Number: 2012952263

Springer Gabler

Printed on acid-free paper

Springer Gabler is a brand of Springer DE.
Springer DE is part of Springer Science+Business Media.
www.springer-gabler.de

Foreword

„I hate to lose more than I like to win". Are these words spoken by the famous tennis player Jimmy Connors not true for quite a few of us? This feeling is what theory describes as loss aversion, the tendency to overvalue losses relative to comparable gains – and a determinate violation of rational thinking. Prospect Theory was motivated by these failures of rational models to describe actual decision making in everyday life. Daniel Kahneman, one of the founders of Prospect Theory along with the late Amos Tversky, won the 2002 Nobel Prize in Economics, at least in part, for this work.

One of the most interesting features of Prospect Theory is that its predictions of when (and why) people will make decisions that differ from perfectly rational or normative decisions strongly depends on the reference point people use to evaluate outcomes. Unfortunately, Prospect Theory remains silent about what exactly the reference point is.

One can think about many possible reference points, such as the current status quo, historical status quo, social comparisons, expectations, or even ambitions. And one might find a whole array of theoretical reasons for all of them. But the question, why people make a variety of obviously bad decisions in daily life, can only be answered if we know more about exactly which reference point is used in cognitive processing. This has initiated a new empirical research stream in economics on what reference point people use in different decision situations. Unfortunately, this research is still in its infancy and there is a great need for more and above all substantial work in this area.

That is where the dissertation project by Evelyn Stommel comes into play. Its goal is to shed more light on three critical questions concerning reference points. Namely, (a) which information serves as reference points, (b) how reference points are cognitively formed, and (c) what factors influence the reference point formation.

The author has taken up these questions in an interesting and very innovative way. Using a set of unique experimental methods she demonstrates that expectations indeed play an important role in reference point adaptation, but with differing intensity in the domains of gains and losses. Furthermore, she shows that individual differences most likely have an effect on reference point preferences and deserve much more attention in future studies. Finally and perhaps most importantly, her results indicate that the same information and the same situation lead to different cognitive outcomes due to differing emotional processing of decision makers. Thus, one cannot refrain from contextual factors when trying to assess the formation of reference points.

With her thesis, Evelyn Stommel makes a valuable research contribution. It treats a current and very relevant subject at the right time. Not only is it based on a stringent theoretical foundation, but also on unique empirical analyses. This doctoral dissertation complements the recent scientific discussion and is highly recommended to everyone who wants to advance their knowledge on human decision making.

Prof. Dr. Andreas Hack

Acknowledgement

I have prepared this dissertation during my work as external doctoral student at the WHU – Otto Beisheim School of Management. Everyone who intends to write a dissertation knows, that this is hardly possible without the support of many persons. Bearing in mind the words of Adolf von Harnack who once said “Nothing can strengthen someone more than the confidence put in him“, I would like to express my thanks to all the people who have trusted and supported me.

I am very grateful to my doctoral advisor Prof. Andreas Hack for the scientific, content-related and personal first-class support he provided me. He gave me the necessary freedom for preparing this dissertation, contributing greatly to its completion with his valuable discussions and advice. I am indebted to Prof. Franz W. Kellermanns (University of Tennessee, Knoxville) for kindly and readily agreeing to prepare the second opinion and for making my stay in the USA possible. Furthermore I'm very grateful for his valuable advice with regard to statistical evaluation methods.

Thanks to Prof. Frauke Lammers (University of Bern) for the instructive discussions and the countless suggestions she provided during two empirical studies assisted by her. I also want to thank Prof. Kimberly Eddleston (Northeastern University, Boston) who invited me to spend a research visit at the Northeastern University in Boston. I thank her for the critical discussions, as well as for the valuable suggestions concerning theoretical embedding.

I owe thanks to Prof. Peter Witt (Bergische Universität Wuppertal) for permitting me to use parts of his lectures at the University for conducting experiments with students.

This dissertation has largely been prepared in tandem with work. I should therefore like to thank my employer, ThyssenKrupp, my superiors and colleagues for their support and encouragement. I am especially indebted to Dr. Jens Knöll, Dr. Uwe Stoklossa, Dr. Oliver Tietze and Mr. Konrad Wahnschaffe.

It would have been hardly possible to finish this dissertation without the support of my friends and family. Thanks to my friends for motivating me, and for taking my mind off things from time to time. My greatest debt is to my boyfriend

Dr. Pedram Faghfouri for his enduring and unconditional support and encouragement in every phase of my life. It is largely owing to his patience, confidence and his faith in me, that I have been able to finish this dissertation.

Finally I want to express my heartfelt gratefulness to my parents Peter and Maria Stommel and my sister Cordula. Not only the fact that they have followed the progress of this dissertation with great interest, but supported and relieved me whenever they could. I thank them with all my heart for their encouragement and their love. I dedicate this dissertation to them with deepest gratitude.

Dr. Evelyn Stommel

Table of Contents

List of Figures and Tables

List of Abbreviations

ANOVA	Analysis of variance
FMs	Family manager-owners
MWUt	Mann–Whitney U-test
NFMs	Non-family managers in family firms
OLS	Ordinary least squares
PMs	Non-family managers in public firms
ROA	Return on assets
ROE	Return on equity
VIF	Variance Inflation Factor

1 Introduction

> "Making decisions is like speaking prose – people do it all the time, knowingly or unknowingly. It is hardly surprising, then, that the topic of decision making is shared by many disciplines, from mathematics and statistics, through economics and political science, to sociology and psychology." (Kahneman & Tversky, 1984, p. 341).

Most of our daily decisions are made under uncertainty and risk – without complete information about all relevant aspects. We all make such decisions constantly, from the simplest "should I take my raincoat today?" to more serious examples, such as those on investment and portfolio decisions, holding of shares, insurance patterns, negotiation processes, or the next move of your counterpart in a conflict. Within these situations, the bounded rationality (Simon, 1976) of individuals and institutions towards risk and uncertainty is embedded. In light of the ongoing not yet survived economic crisis, catastrophes may result from the bounded rationality of decision makers.

The ideal of Mr. Spock of Star Trek as an individual who is completely rational is unrealistic for human beings. Our way of thinking is influenced by several biases resulting in irrational decisions and planning of our daily lives. For example, we suffer a strong tendency to weigh negative information more heavily than positive information in a wide range of contexts (Kahneman & Tversky, 1979; Kunda, 1999; Baron, 2004).

One of the core tasks of economics scholars is to create proper models that predict the real and most often bounded rationality of human behavior given certain incentives, preferences, and constraints. These models are evaluated by their success at explaining economic phenomena in an irrational world and at describing efficient solutions.

Behavioral economics explores the implications of the violations of rationality, with the goal of making economic theories more plausible by explaining and predicting behavior (Ho et al., 2006). It is a research discipline that integrates psychological insights into formal economic models. Fruitfully applied are the behavioral models in disciplines such as finance (Barberis & Thaler, 2003), marketing (Ho et al., 2006), and organizational behavior (Camerer & Malmendier,

2005). In the past 30 years, behavioral economics has changed from a niche topic to one that is well represented in all major international research journals.

The central theory underlying this doctoral thesis is prospect theory (Kahneman & Tversky, 1979), which is the "rational theory of irrational behavior" (Wakker, 2010, p. 2). Among behavioral economists, it was the first descriptive theory[1] that considered irrational behavior explicitly (Kahneman, 2003), and more than 30 years after its inception, "prospect theory is still the only theory that can deliver the full spectrum of what is required for decision under uncertainty, with a natural integration of risk and ambiguity" (Wakker, 2010, p. 2). Prospect theory has attracted much attention both from practitioners and from academics (e.g., Benartzi & Thaler, 1995; Barberis et al., 1998; Hirshleifer & Subrahmanyam, 1998). According to a study by Kim et al. (2006), Kahneman and Tversky (1979) has been the second most frequently cited paper in economies since 1970. Closely associated with this is the growing importance of behavioral aspects in decision theories, rewarded by the 2002 Nobel Prize in Economics to Daniel Kahneman.[2]

Prospect theory builds on the concept of subjective values – gains and losses defined in terms of a reference point (Baron, 2004). The key feature is this reference dependency – how an individual's perception of gains or losses (or success or failure) depends on a starting or reference point (e.g., the status quo). Individuals tend to include reference points in making their decisions in order to simplify the process of the utility maximization of choices. Several theoretical and empirical studies have evidenced that an individual's decision making is indeed reference point-dependent (Bleichrodt, 2007).

Reference points can generally be defined as any stimulus that "other stimuli are seen in relation to" (Rosch, 1975). Individuals constantly adapt a level of psychological dimension and find it to be neutral. "In a similar way, we adapt to the reduced light in a movie theater when we enter it – finding it not particularly dark after a few seconds – and then readapt to the much brighter light outside when we leave the theater – finding it not to be unusually bright after a few seconds" (Dawes, 2001, p. 195).

---

1 Economists traditionally conceptualize the individual as a "homo economicus", rational individual and unemotional utility maximizers.

2 His colleague Amos Tversky had already died, but it is broadly believed that he would have shared this honor.

Although reference-dependent preferences are well explored in the psychology research field, prospect theory takes the reference point only as a given fact and does not provide hypotheses for reference point formation in the economic context. Up to now, research on the nature of reference points in the economics literature is limited (Köszegi & Rabin, 2006). For instance, one of the most fundamental and most direct issues is the question "what serves as a reference point?" to which the answer has not yet been sufficiently and satisfactorily provided in the literature. Therefore, the focus of this dissertation is on what information serves as a reference point, what influences the use of one reference point over another, and how context characteristics, framings, emotions, feelings, and personality differences influence these reference points.

To provide new insights, I adopt an interdisciplinary research approach bundling methods from the distinct areas of economics and psychology. As Rabin (2002, p. 660) pointed out, "the idea that economists should incorporate behavioral evidence from psychology (...) is so fundamentally and manifestly good economics, that I am confident this line of research will have long-term influence in economics."

1.1 Motivation

A substantial body of research has already evidenced the importance of reference-dependent preferences. Reference points deserve this attention, because of their potential consequences on the evaluation and approach of decision making under risk and uncertainty.

Several studies have used the idea of reference points to explain suboptimal human behavior and decision making. An example is a field study in the mid-1990s of New York City taxicab drivers (Camerer et al., 1997). These cab drivers pay a fixed fee for 12 hours car renting and then keep all their revenues from their shifts. However, they can choose how long they want to work. Although the rational profit-maximizing approach would suggest working longer hours on good days (e.g., rainy days) and finishing early on bad days, Camerer et al. (1997) observed a different behavior. They showed that cab drivers set themselves a target earnings level for each working day as their reference points and treat shortfalls relative to that target earning as a loss. The study observed that cab drivers finish working whenever they reach their reference points, resulting in knocking off work early on good days and working longer on bad days.

Numerous articles in marketing journals have dealt with the topic of reference prices. Reference prices are standards against which the purchase price of a product or service is judged (Monroe, 1973; Mazumdar & Sinha, 2005). Thus, purchase decisions are based on the setting of reference prices. Therefore, marketing scientists and practitioners are interested in understanding how these reference points are built and manipulated.

Panel data analyses have provided evidence that prior price experiences, prices encountered on recent occasions, and prior promotional purchases are the most influential reference price factors. The results of these analyses have shown that, for instance, customers who are loyal to a few brands integrate the price experiences of only their favorite brands (Mazumdar & Sinha, 2005). Determinants such as price trends, current and anticipated economic conditions, the predictive signals of future prices, and household demographics seem to influence reference price formation as well (Winer, 1985; Mazumdar & Sinha, 2005). Studies have also provided insights into which kinds of stores (e.g., outlet, normal store), levels of provided services, or assortments offered in a store influence individual reference prices. "For example, the same price of a bottle of wine could be judged more favorably if it is sold in a specialty wine store than if it is sold in a discount wine store" (Mazumdar & Sinha, 2005, p. 87). Moreover, studies have already developed analytical models to assess the profit implications for companies when reference prices are included in the consumer demand function. For example, Greenleaf (1995) showed that reference price effects increase profits on promotions. He demonstrated how retailers may develop an optimal strategy for repeated promotions over time that maximizes the company's profits (Mazumdar & Sinha, 2005). For instance, this study showed that in the presence of reference price effects, the optimal strategy of a monopolist is to institute a cyclical (high-low) pricing policy. This and further studies with respect to pricing and promotional strategies demonstrate that reference prices are an important factor in managerial decisions.

In organizational studies, risk–return relationships (Bowman, 1980) have received a lot of attention. Fiegenbaum and Thomas (1988) summarized risk–return studies and used prospect theory to predict the non-linear relationships between risks and returns for companies (Lehner, 2000). Based on empirical tests by Fiegenbaum (1990), they showed that managers in firms with returns below a certain reference point are risk-seeking, which results in negative risk–return associations. This finding is very important in light of the fact that risky firms are related to lower performance (e.g., Bromiley, 1991). Fiegenbaum et al. (1996) argued that a firm's choice of a specific reference point may help it achieve strategic alignments, which might lead to improved performance and ideally even sustainable competitive advantage. Hence, an essential aspect for explaining these organizational behaviors is the reference point, which affects the outcomes of strategic decisions in firms.

This chapter proposes that insights into reference points help identify how individuals actually make and how they should make decisions to maximize their choice outcomes over several disciplines. However, the research community has not yet been able to provide appropriate and explicit advice on how individuals decide under uncertainty and risk.

1.2 Structure of the dissertation

This dissertation includes three parts and eight chapters. The first part deals with the theoretical foundations of descriptive decision theories under uncertainty and risk and presents the concept of reference-dependent preferences as the major research field. It also discusses research gaps and the research questions of this dissertation in order to provide a first step towards closing the identified gaps. The second part introduces the research approach and includes three experiments that investigate the research questions of this dissertation. The third part summarizes the key findings and discusses the main theoretical and practical implications.

More specifically, ***chapter 2*** introduces expected utility theory. In the next step, it discusses the anomalies and biases that it cannot explain, but with its widely accepted non-expected utility counterpart – prospect theory. After outlining prospect theory, it then concludes with the main limitation of prospect theory – the lack of insights into reference-dependent preferences.

Chapter 3 reviews the existing literature on reference-dependent preferences. For this purpose, a framework is developed. Within this framework, this chapter also introduces the main underlying research questions of this work. In order to provide a deeper understanding of reference-dependent preferences, key terms are defined, i.e., what constitutes a reference point, the process of the formation of a reference point, and factors influencing the formation of reference points.

Chapter 4 describes the research design and explains the methods used in the empirical studies. Specifically, these empirical studies rely on experimental approaches to identify the individual reference points of participants including their cognitive formation. The benefits and limitations of using experiments are also discussed. This chapter ends with a presentation of the statistical methods used to test the research questions of this dissertation.

Chapter 5 experimentally investigates the adaptation process of reference points. Specifically, the central purpose of this chapter is to explore the role of expectations on the magnitude of reference point adaptation in the domain of gains and losses over time. I perform univariate analysis in order to determine and compare the adaptation of reference points with expectations. Moreover, the results are theoretically discussed and, more importantly, the disappointment effect is presented as a new explanation for the observed results within reference point adaptation in the domain of losses.

Chapter 6 experimentally analyzes the individual differences that might determine the formation and adaptation of reference points. Specifically, for the first time, this chapter investigates to what extent personality differences affect reference point adaptation in the domains of gains and losses. In particular, it formulates hypotheses stating that personality traits affect the formation of reference points and that the impact in the domains of gains and losses differs. In the next step, univariate analyses are conducted to test these hypotheses. After presenting the results, the chapter ends with a discussion of the results and theoretical implications.

Chapter 7 experimentally analyzes the multiple reference points of different manager types by considering risk as information that might serve as a reference point. The central aim of this chapter is to extend the reference dependence literature. To my knowledge, for the first time it is argued that affects (i.e., emotions and feelings) seem to determine reference point formation. Based on affect theory, I formulate my hypotheses stating that even equal information and situations might lead to different degree of cognitive reference point formation based on the context-related affective expressions of managers. This chapter also investigates for the first time whether risk might be a further factor on reference points in multiple and dynamic reference point settings. Then, univariate and multivariate analyses are performed to test the hypotheses. The chapter ends with a discussion of the results as well as theoretical and practical implications.

Finally, ***chapter 8*** concludes with a summary of the main results and contributions of this dissertation. Based on the key findings of the studies presented, recommendations for further research are presented and implications for research and practice are discussed.

Part 1:
Literature review and research gaps

2 Theoretical basis

Until the end of the 1970s, the behavior of bounded rationality was believed to be chaotic and unsuited to modeling (Wakker, 2010). Until then, normative expected utility theory was seen to be the best describer of behavior (Friedman & Savage, 1948; Arrow, 1971). "Kahneman & Tversky's (1979) prospect theory provided a major breakaway. It was the first descriptive theory that explicitly incorporated irrational behavior in an empirically realistic manner (Kahneman, 2003, p. 1456), while at the same time being systematic and tractable" (Wakker, 2010, p. 2).

Following rank-dependent or cumulative functional utility, first proposed by Quiggin (1982) for decision under risk, and second by Schmeidler (1989) for decision under uncertainty, Tversky and Kahneman provided an improved version of prospect theory in 1992. Within this improved version, they combined the empirical insights of Kahneman and Tversky (1979) with the theoretical insights of Schmeidler (1989). From 1992 on, there thus exists broad agreement in the research community that utility theory is not an adequate descriptive model of decision making.

The next several chapters present decision making models under uncertainty and risk to understand how individuals make decisions. This chapter starts with a brief summary of expected utility theory and some apparent anomalies. Then, it will be shown how the most widely accepted non-expected utility counterpart – prospect theory – integrates these anomalies in descriptive patterns into an alternative theory, which then will be presented briefly. This chapter concludes with the main limitation of prospect theory – the constitution and formation of reference points.

For more details on prospect theory, see Kahneman and Tversky (1979, 1984). For the extended theory of risk (known probabilities such as flipping a coin) to uncertainty and ambiguity (unknown probabilities such as filing a lawsuit), see Tversky and Kahneman (1991, 1992) for riskless choices. For experiments that illustrate these effects, please see Kahneman et al. (1990, 1991).

2.1 Expected utility theory

"It is no exaggeration to consider expected utility theory the major paradigm in decision making since the Second World War. It has been used prescriptively in management science (especially decision analysis), predictively in finance and economics, descriptively by psychologists, and has played a central role in theories of measurable utility" (Schoemaker, 1982, p. 529).

The mathematical form of expected utility theory goes back to Bernoulli (1738, 1954), who wanted to explain the St. Petersburg paradox.[3] He suggested that individuals do not maximize expected utility by the expectation of their monetary outcomes, but rather by the expected value of these outcomes (Kahneman & Tversky, 1984). Modern foundations of the theory are more than 60 years old and extend prior works with the development of an axiomatic choice-theoretic foundation. The two best-received variations of the theory are subjective expected utility theory in the case of uncertainty and the von Neumann–Morgenstern theory in the case of risk. Von Neumann and Morgenstern (1944, 1947) firstly formalized the theory and Savage (1954) further developed the theory for risk by including the notion of subjective[4] probabilities.

Expected utility theory suggests that individuals make risky or uncertain decisions by comparing their expected utility values. These expected utility values are weighted prospects (mental anticipations, expectations) yielded by multiplying the utility values of uncertain and risky outcomes by their respective preferences or probabilities. In subjective expected utility theory, the probabilities are personal or subjective parameters that characterize the decision maker (Wakker, 2010), according to the expectation of their utility values. Individuals maximize expected values based on those probabilities.

The fundamental expected utility theory of von Neumann and Morgenstern (1944) consists of four general and simple assumptions that define a rational

---

3 St. Petersburg issue: Consider the following well-known game, which involves flipping a fair coin until the first head occurs. The payoff of this experiment depends on the number of immediate heads. The first immediate head gives \$2, and after each tail the payoff will double. Basically, after 19 tails is possible to be a millionaire. Interestingly, individuals were willing to pay just something around \$5 to play this game (Wakker, 2010).

4 For the contrast between objective and subjective probability, please see Fine (1973) and Fishburn (1986).

individual. It assumes that preference ordering over a given set of lotteries or gambles is complete, transitive, continuous, and independent.

Completeness axiom: This axiom assumes that decision makers (1) have well-defined preferences, (2) are able to choose between any two alternatives, and (3) are able to rank them all. Specifically, this means X is either preferred by an individual to Y (X>Y), or is indifferent between them by X~Y, or Y to X is preferred (Y<X).

Transitivity axiom: Transitivity assumes that decision makers also decide consistently. If an individual prefers forever X, Y, and Z with X>Y and Y>Z, decision makers must prefer X>Z.

Continuity axiom: The continuity assumption is needed to ensure that for any gamble some probabilities exist by which decision makers are indifferent between the best and worst alternatives. If a decision maker prefers X to Y and Y to Z (X>Y>Z), then there exists a possible combination of X and Z for which a decision maker is indifferent between X and Z and the gamble Y.

Independence axiom: The independence axiom implies that replacing a prospect in a mixture (X & Y) by another similar prospect Z does not affect the preference value of the mix (Wakker, 2010). Imagine that gamble X is weakly preferred to gamble Y if a compound gamble that yields X with probability q and the third gamble Z with the probability 1–q is weakly preferred to a compound gamble that yields Y with probability q and Z with probability 1–q, for any gamble Z. Therefore, the choice between X and Y is independent of the third one (Holt, 1986).

In sum, "the key characteristics of this general maximization model are: (1) a holistic evaluation of alternatives, (2) separable transformations on probabilities and outcomes, and (3) an expectation-type operation that combines probabilities and outcomes multiplicatively (after certain transformations)" (Schoemaker, 1982, p. 530). Thus, mathematical properties are additive and if the independence axiom is also satisfied utility is linear (Andreoni & Sprenger, 2011). In other words, if all four axioms are given, the decision maker is assumed to be rational and the preferences are able to be represented by a utility function.

Several variants of the expected utility model exist (e.g., certainty equivalence theory (DeFinetti, 1937; Schneeweiss, 1974; Handa, 1977), subjective expected utility (Ramsey, 1931; Savage, 1954; Edwards, 1955; Quiggin, 1982), subjectively weighted utility (Karmarkar, 1978)). Schoemaker (1982) provided an overview of these major expected utility variants. The alternatives depend on how utility is measured, what types of probability transformations are allowed, and how the outcomes are measured (Schoemaker, 1982). For further explanations and empirical examples, please see also, for instance, Wakker (2010).

2.2 Violations of expected utility theory and the need for an alternative theory

In a perfect world, expected utility theory would be ideal, as it provides exact measurements of utility and gives perfect predictions (Wakker, 2010). However, usually there exists the behavior of bounded rationality and biases, and thus it is not a reliable model for depicting human behavior. In particular, the non-linearity of preferences (Allais, 1953; Camerer & Ho, 1994), loss aversion behavior (Kahneman & Tversky, 1984), reference dependency (Kahneman & Tversky, 1979), framing effects (Tversky & Kahneman, 1986), and mental accounting (Thaler, 1999) cannot be sufficiently explained. The following chapter provides several behavioral phenomena of bounded rationality that violate the assumptions of expected utility theory.

Non-linear decision weights

Expected utility theory assumes that the decision maker's preferences over prospects are represented by linear responses to variations in probability and utility (Wakker, 2010). However, studies have shown non-linear preferences in choices (Allais, 1953; Machina, 1987; Camerer & Ho, 1991), and that the ideas of transitivity (X>Y and Y>Z, then X>Z) could be questioned (Tversky & Kahneman, 1986). For instance, the famous Allais paradox (Allais, 1953) shows that some behavior is better explained by utility functions that are non-linear. Imagine the following situation. Although the probabilities of winning a lottery are minuscule (.002; .001), most participants choose the prospect that offers the larger gain (3000; 6000), while in another lottery with substantial probabilities of winning

(.90; .45), people choose the prospect where winning is probable (3000; 6000).[5] Moreover, the following phenomena support the non-linearity of preferences.

Certainty effect

According expected utility theory, individuals should weight prospects by respective probabilities. However, individuals overweight outcomes that are considered to be certain relative to outcomes that are merely probable (Kahneman & Tversky, 1979). For instance, the Allais paradox (1953) for uncertainty shows that the difference between the probabilities of .99 and 1.00 has more impact on preferences than the difference between .10 and .11 (Tversky & Kahneman, 1992).

Source dependency

Besides the degree of uncertainty, a decision maker's preferences also depend on the source of uncertainty. "Ellsberg (1961) observed that people prefer to bet on an urn containing equal numbers of red and green balls, rather than on an urn that contains red and green balls in unknown proportions" (Tversky & Kahneman, 1992, p. 298). Moreover, individuals more often prefer a bet on an event in their fields of competence to a bet on a matched chance event even though the previous probability is ambiguous and the latter is clear (Heath & Tversky, 1991; Tversky & Kahneman, 1992).

Reference dependence and loss aversion

Utility theory considers the assumption that the outcomes of risky prospects are evaluated as final asset positions. However, there are overwhelming observations that suggest that decision makers are often more sensitive to how an outcome differs from some reference level than to the absolute level of the decision outcome itself (Rabin, 1997). In particular, several studies have provided evidence that decision outcomes are described as gains and losses to some subjective ref-

5 The "Allais paradox, can be interpreted as saying that when probability of a worst outcome are tiny (…), a person demands a huge increase in the probability of the best outcome to compensate for increasing the probability of the worst outcome by a little (..); but when the probability of the worst outcome is large (…), a person is more willing to accept an increase in the likelihood of the worst outcome to increase the probability of the best outcome (…)." (Rabin, 1997, p. 10).

erence level or reference point (e.g., Kahneman & Tversky, 1979; Camerer, 1998). According to the psychological analysis of value, reference levels play a role in determining preferences (Tversky & Kahneman, 1991). The following phenomena stress the salience of changes from reference points as the basics of human behavior:

Reflection effect

Individuals tend to be risk-averse over prospects involving gains, which is accompanied by risk-seeking behavior over prospects involving losses (Kahneman & Tversky, 1979). This implies that individuals prefer risk-averse behavior in the domain of gains, but risk-seeking behavior in the domain of losses in order to compensate for possible deficits. Of primary importance for the reflection effect is that outcomes are coded relative to a reference point (Schneider & Lopes, 1986). Moreover, experiments have shown that choices between prospects are not determined solely by the probability of final states but rather by perceived gains and losses compared with this reference point (Kahneman & Tversky, 2000).

Risk-seeking

Individuals tend to prefer small probabilities of winning a large prize to the expected value of that prospect (Tversky & Kahneman, 1992). In addition, risk-seeking occurs when individuals must choose between a secure loss and a substantial probability of a large loss (Tversky & Kahneman, 1992). Therefore, individuals simultaneously tend to (unknowingly) take unfair gambles to avoid risk (e.g., life insurance) and unfair gambles that increase risk (e.g., playing roulette).

Loss aversion

Loss aversion refers to the fact that losses loom larger than gains (Kahneman & Tversky, 1984). According to Kahneman and Tversky (1979, p. 279), "the aggravation that one experiences in losing a sum of money appears to be greater than the pleasure associated with gaining the same amount." Therefore, an individual's displeasure from monetary loss is greater than the pleasure from the same amount of gain (Rabin, 2002). This observed asymmetry between gains and losses is too extreme to be explained by transaction cost or income effects (Tversky & Kahneman, 1992) as expected utility theory is.

The difference between loss aversion and risk aversion refers to the behavior that decision makers are risk-averse for even small amounts of money. Tversky and Kahneman (1991) showed that decision makers evaluate moderate losses roughly twice as much as equal sized gains.

Endowment effect

Loss aversion is related to the endowment effect observed by Thaler (1980). Some studies have shown that purchasing and selling prices for the same good are often diverse (Kahneman et al., 1990). Once a decision maker owns a good, he/she immediately values it more than before he/she owned it (Rabin, 1997). Research has provided evidence that the selling price is generally much larger than purchase price (e.g., Kahneman et al., 1990). This is because decision makers treat the newly owned good as a part of their reference level and consider not having the good to be a loss, whereas decision makers without that good consider not having that good as remaining at their reference level (Rabin, 1997).

Disposition effect

Shefrin and Statman (1985) showed that as decision makers dislike losses more than they enjoy gains, and as they are more willing to gamble in the domain of losses (Montier, 2002), investors hold onto stocks that have lost value relative to their purchase prices too long and are eager to sell stocks that have increased in value (see also Weber & Camerer, 1998). However, the purchase price of a stock should actually not affect whether you decide to sell it or not.

This effect has also been observed in other settings such as the real estate market or in the context of stock options (Odean, 1998; Grinblatt & Keloharju, 2001; Genesove & Mayer, 2001). Odean (1998) found out that “when an investor in his sample sells shares, he has a greater propensity to sell shares of a stock that has risen in value since purchase rather than of one that has fallen in value” (see also Barberis & Xiong, 2009, p. 751).

Status quo bias

Samuelson and Zeckhauser (1988) referred to status quo bias as exaggerated preferences for the status quo. Thus, individuals tend to stick to their status quo situations. Decision makers seem to prefer the status quo to changes that involve losses, even when losses are coupled with gains in other dimensions (Rabin, 2002). Knetsch (1989) demonstrated status quo bias by giving one group of students candy bars and another group mugs. After a while, the students had the opportunity to trade their gifts – a mug for a candy bar or vice versa. Interestingly, 90 percent of both students groups chose not to trade.

Framing effect and mental accounting

A further challenge to the general model of rational choice consists of the dependence of choices on the description and interpretation of decision problems. Specially, this includes:

Framing

The rational theory of choice assumes that equivalent formulations of a choice problem should result in the same preference order (Arrow, 1982). However, there exists empirical evidence that variation in the framing of options results in systematically different preferences (Tversky & Kahneman, 1986). Hence, the way a decision problem is presented influences the choices, even given the same data (see, for instance, the phenomenon discovered by Allais, 1953).

Heuristics of choice

Individuals use a variety of heuristic procedures within complex decision situations in order to simplify the evaluation of choices. For example, heuristic procedures include computational shortcuts, editing operations, such as the elimination of common components, and imitating non-essential differences (Tversky, 1969). Moreover, the heuristics of choice depend on the formulation of the problem, the method of elicitation, and the context of choice (Tversky & Kahneman, 1992). For instance, Wang's (2008) findings highlight the importance of interpersonal affect-based heuristics in the context of predicting public choices.

Mental accounting: integration and segregation

Thaler's (1985) idea of mental accounting described the procedure that individuals organize decisions and outcomes by integrating some and segregating others, often violating standard economic theory (Kahneman & Tversky, 2000). This implies that individuals may control their own rewards by choosing to close or to keep mental accounts open. Hence, mental accounting refers to the cognitive process of how individuals keep track of where their money is going and keep spending under control (Thaler, 1999). An additional effect that considers closing and keeping an account is the sunk cost effect. Although following expected utility theory the historical cost should not affect the rational decision maker's best choice, experiments provide evidence that costs that have already been sunk are indeed integrated into decision choices.

Conclusion

Based on these behaviors of bounded rationality, there is consensus in the research community that utility theory as commonly interpreted and applied is not an adequate descriptive model (i.e., the prediction and explanation of actual behavior – what individuals actually do). It is rather a normative model (i.e., what individuals should do) of an idealized decision maker and not a description of the behavior of real people (Tversky & Kahneman, 1986).

Many alternative descriptive models of choices have been proposed in response to this challenge (see, for instance, Machina, 1987; Camerer, 1989). However, there is general agreement that prospect theory is the most promising alternative. Prospect and cumulative prospect theory[6] (Kahneman & Tversky, 1979; Tversky & Kahneman, 1992), motivated by the failures of the rational model, explains loss aversion, risk-seeking, and non-linear preferences, incorporates framing processes, and accommodates source preferences (Tversky & Kahneman, 1992). This could help better understand the violations mentioned above and other phenomena.

---

6 In 1992, Tversky and Kahneman (1992) presented an updated version of prospect theory called cumulative prospect theory. The new version still incorporates a value function and a probability weighting function. However, they applied the idea of Quiggin (1982) by considering non-linear rank-dependent weighting probability assessments as opposed to individual probabilities in order to include non-linear preferences.

2.3 Prospect theory

The most cited paper in *Econometrica* is on Kahneman and Tversky's prospect theory, the most important revision of subjective expected utility theory. The theory was founded by the two psychologists in 1979. It is an extension of the classical decision-theoretical perspective by predicting individual choices, even in cases in which expected utility theory is violated.

Prospect theory has two main features compared with expected utility theory. First, decision choices are based on gains and losses rather than a reference point in contrast to expected utility theory, in which decision choices are based on the probabilities of the final asset (Benartzi & Thaler, 1995). The key observation is that decision making begins by identifying a reference point (e.g., current wealth state, aspiration level), from which people tend to be risk-averse for gains and risk loving for losses. Prospect theory replaces the traditional utility function for wealth with an S-shaped function that shows changes in wealth rather than levels of wealth. Changes in wealth are defined by positive and negative changes to a reference point. Therefore, whether an individual perceives an outcome as a gain or as a loss depends on how the reference point is coded.

Second, the value and weighting functions are non-linear in the probabilities, while the utility function assumes linear probabilities. Prospect theory assumes choice consequences and that probabilities (which are replaced by decision weights) influence the evaluation of choices, and therefore the decision process. In prospect theory, decision weights are defined as a reflection of the impact of events on the overall attractiveness of a choice. Hence, they are monotonic (function that preserves the given order), but not necessarily linear (Schoemaker, 1982). Furthermore, prospect theory provides specific assumptions on how these consequences and decision weights will be transformed into subjective amounts. For instance, it allows different decision weighting for gains and losses. Hence, risk attitudes can be different for losses from those for gains in every respect (Wakker, 2010).

Although prospect theory was developed with the help of hypothetical gambles (for an overview of the experiments, see Levin et al., 1998), their predictions are not limited to behavior under laboratory conditions. The theory is supported in the domains of stock markets, labor economics, consumer goods and choices, macroeconomists, and insurance (Camerer, 1998). In addition, it is not limited to financial patterns (Kühberger et al., 1999).

The three key elements of prospect theory are (1) the distinction between two phases on the decision process, namely framing and valuation (Tversky & Kahneman, 1992); (2) the essential S-shaped value function to determine the outcome's apparent value; and (3) the weighting function in which the value of each outcome is multiplied by a decision weight. The following sections introduce the phase model of decision making and describe the properties of the value and weighting function.

2.3.1 Cognitive decision process

Prospect theory differentiates between two phases in the decision process: a first phase of editing/framing and a second phase of evaluation.

First phase

The decision problem is mentally and cognitively analyzed in this phase, which often results in simpler presentations of prospects (Kahneman & Tversky, 1992). "It includes the identification of the options available to the actor, the possible outcomes or consequences of each, and the values and probabilities associated with each of these outcomes" (Levy, 1992a, p. 179). Moreover, the individual organizes and reformulates the options to simplify subsequent choices. The major operations that transform outcomes and probabilities are the following:

Coding: As described above, people perceive decision outcomes as gains and losses compared with an individual subjective reference point. This reference point might be determined, for instance, by the current asset position or expectation. The location of that reference point and the consequent coding of outcomes as gains or losses are also influenced by the formulation of the decision problem (Kahneman & Tversky, 1979).

Combination: Individuals seem to simplify prospects by combining the probabilities associated with identical outcomes. For instance, the prospect (200, .25; 200, .25) is reduced to (200, .50) (Kahneman & Tversky, 1979).

Segregation: Individuals tend to segregate riskless choice components from the risky ones within a decision choice. For instance, a decision maker will segregate the secure win in this lottery (400, .7; 100, .3), resulting in a secure payment of 100 plus a 70 percent chance to win an additional 300.

Simplification: Individuals prefer to simplify prospects by rounding probabilities or outcomes. Moreover, they seem to discard extremely unlikely prospects and outcomes.

Detection of dominance: Individuals seem to search for dominant alternatives that will be rejected without further evaluation. Dominant alternatives are options that based on a comparison with other choice alternatives are evaluated to be worse in all features and thus can be discarded directly. "Dominance is both simpler and more compelling than cancellation and transitivity" (Tversky & Kahneman, 1986, p. 5253).

Cancellation: Cancellation describes the case in which identical components of different choices are eliminated if any state yields to the same outcome regardless of one's choice. For instance, in the case of the two prospects (400, .0; -100, .8) and (400, .2; -200, .8), the 80 percent probability of making a loss of 100 can only be compared with the 80 percent probability of making a loss of 200.

Depending on the structure of the offered prospect and format of the display, the operations and approached editing processes are likely to vary (Kahneman & Tversky, 1979). In particular, the same decision choices might be edited in different ways depending on the context in which they appear (Tversky & Kahneman, 1986). Moreover, the treatment of the process is likely to be informal and incomplete. Furthermore, the decision frames of an individual are controlled partly by the formulation of the problem by its norms, habits, and personal characteristics (Tversky & Kahneman, 1981).

Second Phase

After the decision problem has been edited, the individual assesses the value of each prospect and chooses accordingly the decision choice that will obtain him/her the highest subjective value. The outcomes and associated probabilities in each edited prospect are interpreted according to a subjective value function and to a probability weighting function, which are described below.

2.3.2 *Value function*

The value function is the essential feature of prospect theory, which is based on experimental studies. Kahneman and Tversky (1979) conducted experimental studies to indicate that preferences are typically given by an S-shaped value function V (x) (to distinguish it from the utility function). This function emphasizes that the drivers of value are changes in wealth rather than final states of wealth.

The prospect value function possesses three important properties:

First Property – the reference point

Individuals derive utility functions from gains and losses relative to a reference point. This reference point symbolizes the comparison, as the focus of prospect theory is on changes in outcome levels relative to a reference point, while traditional utility theory assumes that decision makers derive utility from absolute wealth or the consumption of a prospect. The reference point is coded during the framing phase. This coding influences preference because of the characteristic differences in the valuation of losses and gains. This implies that individuals might accept an option in one situation, but might reject it in another, depending on the reference point.

Second Property – the S-Shaped function

The value function is S-shaped (see Figure 1) and concave for gains above the reference point and convex for losses below the reference point. This shape implies that decisions are risk-averse for gains but risk-seeking for losses. This curvature displays the psychophysical principle of diminishing impact that the marginal value decreases with size, for losses as well as for gains. This means that slight changes nearer the reference point have more impact on decisions than corresponding changes further from the reference point. The difference between winning \$10 and winning \$15 is subjectively perceived as larger than, for in-

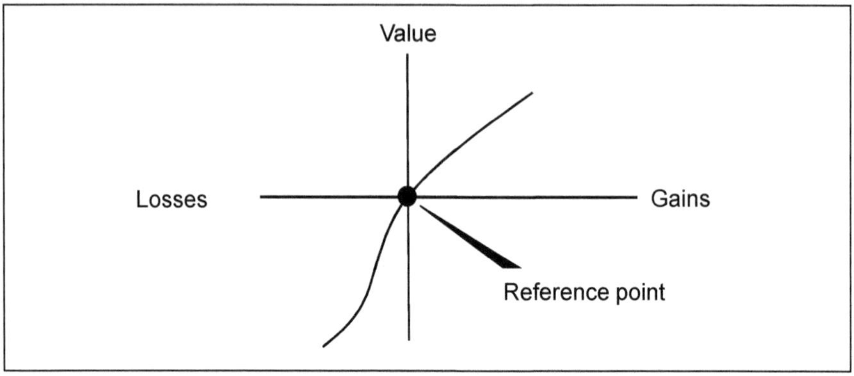

Figure 1: Hypothetical value function.
Source based on Kahneman and Tversky (1979, p. 279), slightly adjusted.

stance, winning $500 instead of winning $505, although the objective difference ($5) is identical (Tversky & Kahneman, 1981).

Third property – Steeper function in loss domain

Moreover, the value function is steeper in the domain of losses than in the domain of gains. Hence, the effect of a unit of loss compared with the reference point is assigned greater value than that of a unit of gain of an objectively identical amount. This greater aversion to losses than appreciation of gains reflects the principle of loss aversion[7] (Kahneman & Tversky, 1979). As the prospect of losses hurts more, individuals are likely to take greater risks to avoid a possible loss than to ensure a possible gain. This also explains why the framing of a decision in terms of gains or losses may have an effect on decision making, as individuals do not prefer choices that are framed as losses compared with the reference point.

In sum, in all of these illustrated properties, the reference point plays a major role. The value function describes how individuals evaluate potential losses and gains. In the simple case of a continuous outcome variable that monotonically increases in value (e.g., salary), the reference points separate the domain into regions of desirable (gains) and undesirable outcomes (losses).

---

7 For instance, status quo bias and the endowment effect can be explained by loss aversion (for more details, please see Kahneman et al., 1991; Camerer, 1998).

2.3.3 Weighting function

Besides the value function, Kahneman and Tversky additionally transformed probabilities using a probability weighting function. The definition of typical weighting functions (every individual has his/her own weighting function) draw upon empirical studies (Tversky & Kahneman, 1992). Kahneman and Tversky (1979, p. 280) argue that probabilities are decision weights that measure "the impact of events on the desirability of prospects and not merely the perceived likelihood of these events." Moreover, decision weights can be influenced by factors such as ambiguity about the level of uncertainty or risk (Kahneman & Tversky, 1979).

The main modification between decision weights and probabilities is based on the considered principle of diminishing sensitivity, which formulates the weighting function as well. The function applies the tendency of individuals to overweight low probabilities and to underweight moderate and large probabilities. "For example, an increase of .1 in the probability of winning a given price has more impact when it changes the probability from .9 to 1.0 or from 0 to .1, than when it changes the probability of winning from .3 to .4 or from .6 to .7. Diminishing sensitivity, therefore, gives rise to a weighting function that is concave near 0 and convex near 1" (Tversky & Kahneman, 1992, p. 303). These properties result in an inverse S-shaped function.

Furthermore, the weighting function also implies that individuals behave in a risk-seeking manner in the case of highly uncertain winning probabilities. For instance, individuals choose option B in this game: A = 45 percent chance of winning $6,000 compared with B = 90 percent chance of winning $3,000. This is a typical example for risk-averse behavior in the gain domain. However, if this game includes two low probabilities, individuals choose the opposite option: C = 1 percent chance of winning $6,000 compared with D = 2 percent chance of winning $3,000. Although, identical to the first example (winning $6,000 is half as large as the chance of winning $3,000), its impact on one's decision is not, because most individuals choose option C in this case (Kahneman & Tversky, 1979). Therefore, individuals choose the riskier option. This phenomenon helps explain why individuals gamble even in the case of very low probability events (e.g., lottery tickets).

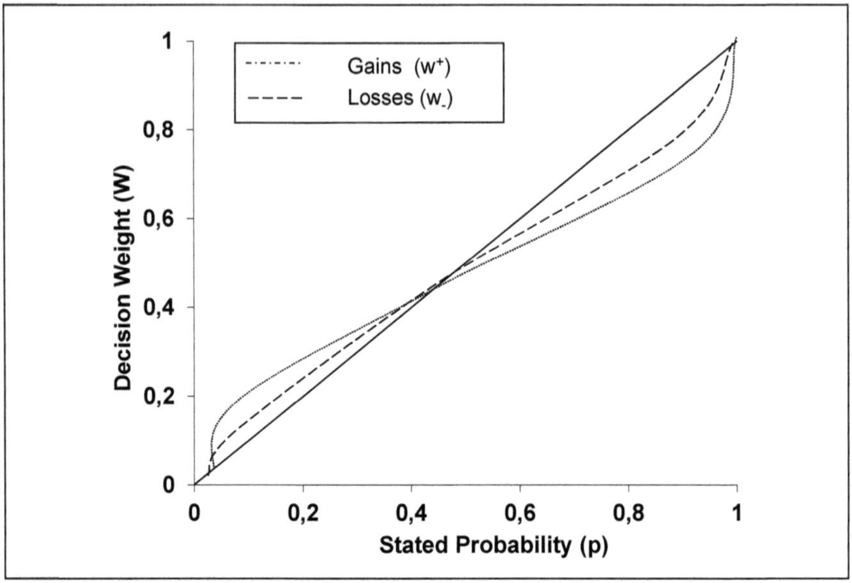

Figure 2: Weighting function for gains and for losses based on median estimations. Source: Tversky and Kahneman (1992, p. 310)

These psychological phenomena lead to a non-linear function of probability. Unlike utility functions, the properties of the weighting function, as Prelec (1998) pointed out, are characterized by a single property concavity, and functions that are:

1) Regressive, intersecting the diagonal from above,
2) Asymmetric, with a fixed point at about 1/3,
3) S-shaped concave at an initial interval and convex beyond that, and
4) Reflective, assigning equal weight to a given loss probability as to a given gain probability.

To conclude, the weighting function (see Figure 2) shows that individuals overweight low probabilities and underweight moderate and high probabilities in the case of positive as well as negative prospects. Further, individuals are insensitive to probability differences in the mid-range (Tversky & Kahneman, 1992), which

Table 1: Fourfold pattern of risk attitudes.
Source: Based on Tversky and Kahneman (1992)

	Low probabilities	Moderate to high probabilities
Gains	Risk-seeking	Risk-averse
Losses	Risk-averse	Risk-seeking

means that objective probability and subjective feelings are the same. Moreover, risk aversion for gains is more pronounced than risk-seeking for losses for moderate and high probabilities. This is shown in the slightly more curved weighting function for gains.

The combination of value and weighting functions results in prospect theory's fourfold risk pattern (see Table 1): risk-averse behavior in the domain of gains for moderate and high probabilities and in the domain of losses for low probabilities; and risk-seeking behavior in the domain of losses for moderate and high probabilities and in the domain of gains for low probabilities.

2.4 Main limitation of prospect theory

Up to now, prospect theory has been the best-performing and most-confirmed descriptive and empirical model for decision making under risk and uncertainty (Wakker, 2010). Numerous empirical studies in the laboratory (e.g., Fishburn & Kochenberger, 1979; Levin et al., 1998) as well as in the field (e.g., Camerer, 1998) have verified its major tenets.

For instance, a laboratory experiment has shown that negotiators bargaining over losses seem to make fewer concessions and more often fail to reach an agreement than negotiators bargaining over gains (loss aversion) (Bazerman et al., 1985). Another experiment has shown that individuals hold onto lost prospects once an investment in money, effort, or time has been made (loss aversion) (Arkes & Blumer, 1985).

Field settings have also evidenced prospect theory. For instance, Shea (1995) and Bowman et al. (1999) investigated a teacher's annual earnings and showed that when there is sufficient income uncertainty, a teacher resists dropping consumption in response to bad news about future income and that this resistance is greater than the resistance to growing consumption in response to good news (loss aversion, reflection effect). Further, Benartzi and Thaler (1995) applied prospect theory to understand why stocks outperform bonds (loss aversion), while Jullien and Salanie (2000) used it to explain favorite-longshot bias in horse races (overweight low probabilities in the domain of losses).

As mentioned above, support can also be found in a wide variety of disciplines as sociology, psychology, political science, medicine, and many areas within economics such as stock markets, international relations, labor economics, insurance, and consumer consumption (Wakker, 2010).

As presented, one of the two main features that distinguishes prospect theory from expected utility and rank-dependent utility theory is that choices are based on gains and losses compared with a reference point. This new component, namely reference-dependent preferences, is a different concept to those that have existed so far. "It depends on aspects of framing and entails, I think, a bigger deviation from rationality than probability weighting" (Wakker, 2010, p. 234). Gains and losses can only be defined relative to a reference point, and thus it is crucial to assess how choices are evaluated and decisions made. The following example illustrates the importance of understanding the reference point. Imagine someone on a winning streak; however, he/she will be more risk-averse if he/she frames the choice in terms of initial assets rather than total assets at the time of each new bet (Levy, 1992a). Based on the framing and editing of outcomes in terms of a reference point and the asymmetric treatment of gains and losses, the identification of the reference point is critical (Levy, 1992a).

The reference point as the major tenet has been demonstrated by a number of substantial empirical studies (McNeil et al., 1982; Levin et al., 1985; Tversky & Kahneman, 1986; Fleishman, 1988; Camerer, 1998). Several other authors have also highlighted the prominent role of reference points in the evaluation of outcomes and the explanation of phenomena such as status quo bias (Samuelson & Zeckhauser, 1988; Hartman et al., 1991; Johnson et al., 1993), default preferences (Johnson et al., 1993), disposition effect (Odean, 1998; Genesove & Mayer, 2001), or endowment effect (Thaler, 1980; Kahneman et al., 1990; Loewenstein & Kahneman, 1991). For example, Odean (1998) showed that the purchase price of a stock, although it should not matter much for the decision to sell it, plays an important role in the explanation of the so-called disposition effect.[8]

Despite the essential role of reference points, prospect theory usually assumes that a reference point has already been determined and is fixed (Wakker, 2010). Therefore, prospect theory has little to say on what exactly a reference point is or on how one is formed and determined (Fershtman, 1996; Köszegi & Rabin, 2006). This is a main weakness of the theory. "If too much liberty is left concerning the choice of reference points, then the theory becomes too general and is almost impossible to refute empirically. It does not then yield valuable predictions" (Wakker, 2010, p. 245). A missing insight of the theory is, for instance, the fact that individuals adapt their reference points faster to recent gains than to recent losses (Tversky & Kahneman, 1991; Arkes et al., 2008). This missing piece limits the ability to use preferences in economic applications (Fershtman, 1996).

Up to now, no theory has specified reference-dependent preferences. However, a new stream of literature has developed that only focuses on reference-dependent preferences. This stream is still in its infancy. Reference points are a subjective concept and they solely depend on the decision maker. In addition, intrapersonal decision making is not directly observable. This may lead to a lack of research on reference points.

As the literature shows that reference points are an important factor in explaining risk behavior and in predicting economic phenomena, any advances to the understanding of the evolution and determination of reference point formation are of particular importance for further economic research. The prediction of decision making under uncertainty and risk requires insights into the evolution of reference-dependent preferences (Bleichrodt et al., 2001; Schmidt, 2003). Therefore, this dissertation only focuses on the research stream of reference-dependent preferences and critical variable reference points. In particular, this project highlights the information that serves as reference points, the process of reference point formation, and the factors that influence this process.

This dissertation does not deal with further critical aspects of prospect theory. For instance, there are many violations of fundamental properties, "such as weak

8 The disposition effect is the tendency to sell assets that have gained in value (winners) and keep assets that have lost value (losers).

ordering and monotonicity. Such violations concern biases and heuristics (Tversky & Kahneman 1974; Gigerenzer 1991)" (Wakker, 2010, p. 350). Levy and Levy (2002a, b) posited that prospect theory's S-shaped value function is incorrect. Based on choice experiments, they suggested that the value function is convex for gains and concave for losses, implying a reverse S-shape in contrast to the inverse S-shape assumed by prospect theory. Schmidt et al. (2008) discussed the violation that the reference points from which prospects are evaluated are assumed to be certainties. They argued that "if reference points are interpreted as endowments or status quo positions, these theories cannot be applied to problems in which a decision maker is endowed with a lottery and has the opportunity to sell or exchange it" (Schmidt et al., 2008, p. 204).

This dissertation deals with neither the reality and systematic violations of probabilities nor rank-dependence (for an overview, see Starmer, 2000). For instance, Baltussen et al. (2006) studied a variant of Levy and Levy's (2002a) experiment. They observed that a probability weighting function that was much more linear for gains than that observed in other studies and more curved for losses than for gains, contrary to previously reviewed studies (Wu & Markle, 2007). Payne (2005) investigated choice patterns for mixed gambles and observed inconsistencies with cumulative prospect theory, demonstrating that decision makers sometimes use a heuristic of selecting the mixed gamble with the highest probability of a gain. Wu (1994) observed systematic violations of the ordinal independence axiom, which is necessary for cumulative prospect theory (Tversky & Kahneman, 1992). He assumed that if an outcome probability pair is common to both gambles, it is cancelled when the commonality is transparent.

This dissertation only focuses on the reference-dependent topic and aims to help advance the theoretical and empirical literature in the following directions. First, the purpose of this dissertation is to specify more accurately what information constitutes the reference point. Second, it aims to detail the process of reference point formation. Third, it provides more insights into the factors that influence the process of reference point formation. The next chapter reviews prior research and identifies research gaps and research questions. The second part of this dissertation then presents the empirical investigations, which shed light on the defined research gaps.

3 Reference-dependent preferences

The reference point as a neutral point, dividing two relative sides of a scale into the domains of gains and losses, has long been observed and investigated in many psychological domains (e.g., Nowlis & Nowlis, 1956; Peeters & Czapinski, 1990). The perception of such a neutral point accompanies us in our daily lives. For example, according to Wakker (2010), if we experience warmth, there exists a specific neutral point at which we feel neither hot nor cold. "The stimuli that generate a neutral experience may be different in different contexts" (Wakker, 2010, p. 240) or may be different among individuals and attributes (Tversky & Kahneman, 1981). Therefore, this dissertation understands the reference point as a subjective point.

In the economics literature, Bateman et al. (1997) conducted an experimental test of the reference dependence theory and broadly confirmed the prediction of a subjective reference point.[9] The concept of reference point dependent preferences has been adapted to several research fields, especially marketing and behavioral finance. For instance, the assessment of individual risk attitudes is important for various domains of managerial and financial decision making (e.g., for mergers and fusions, see Baker et al., 2009), for market and product developments (Winer, 1986; Kalyanaram & Winer, 1995; Kim et al., 2002), and for the domains of personnel selection or placement (Hack & Lammers, 2008). Lately, emerging research into neuroscience has been developing, too (e.g., Schultze & Dickinson, 2000; Knutson & Peterson, 2005).

However, research on the nature of reference points in the economics literature is limited (Köszegi & Rabin, 2006). The following chapter presents an overview of the state of research and emphasizes some research gaps to be investigated in subsequent sections. More specifically, this chapter presents a conceptual framework to review the reference-dependent preferences literature. After explaining the most important prior research, it provides directions for further research for every part of the defined conceptual framework. It then con-

---

9 Other proponents of theories of reference-dependent preferences include Samuelson and Zeckhauser (1988); Benartzi and Thaler (1995), and Myagkov and Plott (1997).

cludes with a brief summary of the identified research gaps and the development of the empirical research questions of this doctoral project.

3.1 State of the art

To review the main published articles on reference-dependent preferences and related topics, a framework is offered that includes the findings of the most important theoretical and empirical results of A and A+ articles (based on the German VHB-JOURQUAL Ranking, cf. Hennig-Thurau et al., 2003) in the economics literature. The most important journals were *Management Science, Organizational Behavior and Human Decision Processes, Journal of Finance, Quarterly Journal of Economics, Strategic Management Journal, Journal of Consumer Research, American Economic Review, Journal of Financial Economics*, and *Administrative Science Quarterly*.

The framework consists of three parts: constitution of reference points, reference point formation, and determinants of reference point formation. The reference-dependent preferences literature has been developing in several independent steps. In the first step, (1) researchers have explored which information might serve as reference points. Recently (2), they have generated findings by investigating the cognitive process of reference point formation, and (3) they have considered the theories and ideas of factors that affect the cognitive process of reference point formation.

Table 2: Conceptual framework of the literature review

1 Constitution of reference points	2 Reference point formation	3 Determinants of reference points
Question: What serves as reference points?	Question: How the reference point is formed?	Question: What influences the forming of reference points?
• status quo • aspiration level / goals • expectations • others	• cognitive processing • multiple reference points • integration / segregation • adaptation of reference points	• framing • individual differences • context / environment

3.1.1 *Constitution of reference points*

This chapter provides an overview of what kind of information within a decision task might serve as a reference point. The question "what serves as a reference point?" is the most fundamental and directly related research question in the literature stream of reference-dependent preferences (De Meza & Webb, 2007).

Although Kahneman and Tversky (1979) suggested that several factors such as status quo, social norms, and aspirations levels might determine the reference point, it is little known what exactly a reference point is (Köszegi & Rabin, 2006). As prospect theory does not offer hypotheses (Kahneman, 1992; Lehner, 2000), most studies have taken the reference point as given. In the 1990s, the first papers were published that investigated what kind of information might serve as a reference point (e.g., Neale & Bazerman, 1991, Kühberger, 1998; Thaler, 1999; Heath et al., 1999). In the following, the theoretical ideas and empirical results of different disciplines are reviewed, mainly from finance, marketing, and organizational research.

Historical or recent status quo

Theoretical results

In the initial phase of investigations, the reference point was usually taken as the individual historical or recent level of wealth, level of income, price, negotiation offer, or performance (Wakker, 2010). For instance, in financial situations the reference price was mostly assumed to be the past purchase price of a financial asset (Shefrin & Statman, 1985). In addition, the well-known paper by Bateman et al. (1997) tested a set of predictions derived from the loss aversion hypothesis of the theory of reference-dependent preferences by assuming that the reference point is given by the current endowment positions of individuals. The authors took these status quos for granted, as they often provide the most salient reference points (Brickman, 1975; Samuelson & Zeckhauser, 1988) within a decision task.

Samuelson and Zeckhauser (1988) presented several reasons why the status quo might be the most salient piece of information. "Faced with new options, decision makers often stick with the status quo alterative, for example, to follow customary company policy, to elect an incumbent to still another term in office, to purchase the same product brands, or to stay in the same job" (Samuelson & Zeckhauser, 1988, p. 8). The individual may retain the status quo out of convenience, habit or inertia, policy (company or government), or custom, or because of fear or conservatism. Moreover, the decision maker's past choice may have become known to others, and many real-world decisions are made by a person acting as part of an organization or group, which may exert additional pressures on status quo choices. Samuelson and Zeckhauser (1988) designed a series of decision making experiments to test for status quo effects. They confirmed that decision makers display a significant status quo bias across a range of decisions. Their results thus suggested that status quo serves as a salient reference point within decision tasks.

The status quo as a reference point was also used to study models of choices. For instance, Masatlioglu and Ok (2005) introduced a model in which the default alternative serves as a status quo option. They also considered a risk-free setting in which the status quo serves also as a reference point. They explored the normative aspects of reference dependence to propose a rational choice theory that allows for the presence of a status quo bias. In this spirit, Sagi's (2006) model of reference-dependent preferences over risky settings and Sudgen's (2003) model of reference-dependent subjective expected utility theory are also based on the assumption that the status quo serves as a reference point.

Empirical results

Weber and Camerer (1998) found support for the disposition effects for two assumptions about reference points: the initial purchase price and the previous stock price. This effect could be explained by the idea that people value gains and losses relative to a reference point, which was treated by the initial purchase price of shares.[10] A study of loss aversion in the housing market (Genesove & Mayer, 2001) also assumed that the reference point of a seller would be the status quo. This study and studies of stock trading (Odean, 1998) have found that agents are less likely to sell assets that have incurred losses than assets that have incurred gains. Prospect theory describes this behavior by assuming that inves-

[10] Their findings clearly support the disposition effect results of Shefrin and Statman (1985), and Ferris et al. (1988).

tors treat each asset as a separate decision using the purchase price as a reference point.

Using a formal framework, Chen and Rao (2002) demonstrated in several studies that an individual's reference point is dynamic. In particular, they showed that individuals update their reference points within a series of events to the current price level, which results in the suggestion that the recent status quo serves as a reference point. Heyman et al. (2004) evaluated the pleasure that individuals derive from a sequence of outcomes by arguing that pleasure is evaluated relative to an individual's reference point. The authors investigated whether the historical or the recent status quo is used more often for the evaluation of pleasure. They provided evidence that the recent status quo tends to dominate.

Arkes et al. (2008) directly tested a reference point adaptation from a historical to a recent status quo in response to payoff outcomes in experimental settings in the domain of securities trading. They asked subjects what stock price today would generate the same utility for them as a previous stock price that increased from the initial purchase price. This question allowed them to calculate directly the reference point under the assumptions that the purchase price serves as the initial reference point and that the value function remains stable over time. They also showed that the historical purchase price, as the subjective reference point in the context of stock investments, shifts closer to the recent stock price.

Aspirations level/Goal

Theoretical results

Although the historical or current status quo often serves as a reference point, Kahneman and Tversky (1979, p. 286) acknowledged that "there are situations in which gains and losses are coded relative to an expectation or aspiration level that differ from the status quo." The general concept of an aspiration level or goal is an old idea in theories of decision making (for an overview, see the comprehensive review by Locke and Latham, 1990). As a result, several studies have investigated goals and aspiration levels[11] – the objects of one's effort – as information that may serve as a reference point.

---

11 Aspiration level is defined as a point on an individual's scale of the utility of his/her goals (Becker & Siegel, 1958).

In the organizational literature, the perspective that organizations set goals or aspiration levels and compare their actual performances with these goals is common (Payne et al., 1980; Mezias, 1988). Like prospect theory, the theories of aspiration level effects predict that decisions under uncertainty and risk depend on whether performance is above or below some target level (Mezias, 1988). Studies have shown that the firm's performance relative to the aspiration level defines the organization's perception of success and failure (Cyert & March, 1963; Lant & Mezias, 1990, 1992) and that aspirations adjust upward in response to favorable feedback and downward in response to unfavorable feedback. March (1988) and March and Shapira (1987) argued that the reference point is a function of an aspiration level and a critical survival point. Managers tend to show more risk-seeking behavior when faced with the failure to meet their targets than when their targets are secure (March & Shapira, 1987).

Furthermore, other theories have considered aspiration levels in their modeling. For instance, Lopes (1987) assumed in her security potential/aspirations theory that choice options are evaluated based on their probabilities of reaching a goal. This theory incorporates aspiration levels as a further factor in the choice process that act as a point in the value function.[12]

Empirical results

Payne et al. (1980) used the value function to explain the effects of aspirations. They were the first to investigate empirically the effect of given aspiration levels on decision making under risk. The results confirmed the impact of an aspiration level on risky choice behavior, as changes in wealth are evaluated relative to an aspiration level, with gains (losses) being defined as a change in wealth above (below) the aspiration level, where risk preference is a mixture of risk-seeking for losses and risk aversion for gains. Sullivan and Kida (1995) argued that corporate managers typically operate in a decision environment that has managerial performance targets. Therefore, a performance target represents an important individual reference point in managerial decision making besides managers' current levels of performance. They showed that both reference points are con-

---

[12] Lopes and Oden (1999) used aspiration level as a reference point in the security potential/aspirations theory and showed that the model operates on the probability of achieving aspiration levels.

sidered when evaluating risky options, which confirmed the results presented by Payne et al. (1980) that alternatives above a performance target result in risk avoidance.

Lant (1992) found empirical support that aspiration levels are frequently key variables in organizational decision behavior. Her results suggested that aspiration level formation is well described by a history-dependent process. In other words, individuals learn about a system more by examining past experience with achieved goals than by predicting the future. In a marketing field study, Greve (2002) provided theoretical and empirical evidence that historical aspiration levels can be updated with different speeds. Focus on current performance leads to quickly adjusting aspiration levels where historical performance has a low weight, while a focus on past performance leads to slowly adjusting performance levels where the current performance has a low weight.[13]

Using field data, Camerer et al. (1997) suggested that New York cab drivers use a daily income target as a reference point and stop working after that target has been achieved. They observed that income targeting is an extreme form of loss aversion with the target income level as a reference point. More recently, a field analysis of dyad-level data in the US food processing industry supported the notion that the direction of a company's strategic change is formed by its aspiration level, performance level, and the performance gap between it (Park, 2007).

Heath et al. (1999) described with respect to a motivational problem that goals in terms of values rather than expectations explain how people react to their performances. "If goals are reference points, then people who set goals will sometimes feel worse about their performance even when they perform better" than expected (Asgary & Levy, 2009, p. 389). They argued that goals serve as reference points not only after an outcome has occurred but also before and during decision making.

---

13 Van Osch et al. (2006) pointed out that goals are mostly set for the near future. Therefore, the adoption of goals as reference points is more apparent for outcomes in the near than in the remote future.

Expectations

Theoretical results

As mentioned above, Kahneman and Tversky suggested that expectations might serve as reference points besides the status quo, goals, or aspiration level. Goal setting theories refer to the effort of achieving objectives. Once a goal has been accepted, individuals try hard until that goal is achieved or until they decide to give up on that goal (Locke, 1968). This is in contrast to expectancy theory, which refers to individuals that choose an effort level that they believe will lead to a valued outcome (Vroom, 1964). Although goals differ from expectations (Klein, 1991), anticipated goals affect the expectations (i.e., the expectation that goals could be achieved) of future outcomes, indicating a role of expectations in reference point formation (Hack & Lammers, 2011). Moreover, expectations play an important role in everyday life where the decision maker has no control over the outcome, while goals play a role in environments in which the decision maker has control over the outcome. For those reasons, expectations have been considered to serve as reference points as well (Kahneman & Tversky, 1979; Kahneman et al., 1986).

Several authors have also taken expectations as a given reference point (e.g., Van den Bos & Van Prooijen, 2001; Kivetz, 2003). For example, an intrinsic motivations study by Kivetz (2003) proposed that the level and intrinsic interest of effort have a predictable effect on preferences towards the tradeoff between the probability and magnitude of rewards. To analyze the characteristics of the required effort stream, he made the simple assumption that effort requirements create an expectation for reward (i.e., a reference point).

Some recent theoretical models are built on the assumption that expectations are the main servants of reference points. Köszegi and Rabin (2006, 2007, 2009) devolved a well-known model of reference-dependent preference[14] theory, which formalizes for the first time the idea of recent expectations as reference points. They argued that the general interpretation of the reference point as a status quo comes from contexts in which people expect to maintain the status quo (i.e., status quo bias). However, when expectations and the status quo are different,

[14] The model ties together neoclassical consumption utility with the gain/loss utility of Kahneman and Tversky (1979).

they believed that equating the reference point with expectations generally makes better predictions. By applying their model, they theoretically showed, for instance, that workers are less likely to continue work if income earned is unexpectedly high and not if their target income (aspiration level) is obtained (Camerer et al., 1997).

Empirical results

By investigating expectations as reference points, empirical research can be divided into direct and indirect approaches (Hack & Lammers, 2011). The indirect approach assumes that decision makers have risk preferences according to a value function, while the direct approach asks decision makers to rate their satisfaction levels with a certain outcome. Specifically, the indirect approach assumes that a risk-seeking behavior implies that a decision outcome is likely to be in the loss domain relative to an individual's reference point and vice versa. By rating the subject's satisfaction with certain outcomes, the direct approach directly estimates his/her utility given an outcome. In order to do so, subjects need to be able to assess their satisfaction degrees (Hack & Lammers, 2011).

1) Indirect empirical approach

In marketing studies, several researchers have processed expected reference prices as the distillation of various prior experiences and predictions into a single expectation with which actual decision outcomes can be compared (e.g., Tryon, 1994; Ordóñez, 1998). For example, the price-expectancy model proposed by Ordóñez (1998) defines the expected price as a function of subjective values. According to the model, consumers evaluate products by comparing the actual price with a reference or expected price. Winer (1986) found empirical support for a brand choice model in which the reference price is formed by rational expectations given past prices. The results indicated that based on the reference price, consumer brand choice decisions were strongly affected by discrepancies between expected and observed prices at the point of purchase.

Besides the marketing literature, expectations as reference points also play an important role in the human resource management literature. For example, Bartol and Martin (1998) provided empirical evidence that expectations have quantifiable behavioral consequences. They showed that the gap between expected and actual wages is predictive of subsequent turnover (Hack & Lammers, 2011). In a recent experiment, Abeler et al. (2011) examined the effect of an expectation-based model of reference-dependent preferences on the provision of effort. By employing a real effort experiment in a non-risky choice, they observed that expectations play a role in reference point formation: if expectations are high, participants work longer and earn more money than if expectations are low. A panel analysis by Post et al. (2008) showed that risk aversion decreases after earlier expectations have been shattered by unfavorable outcomes. This observed behavior can be explained if previous expectations serve as a reference point (Hack & Lammers, 2011).

Following Köszegi and Rabin (2006), Crawford and Meng (2011) constructed a model with targets for hours as well as income, both determined by rational expectations. The authors used data on New York City cap drivers' labor supply to test the theory of Köszegi and Rabin. They estimated the rational expectation about a driver's wage by the average wage earned per weekday. They found clear evidence for reference dependence, with the probability of stopping work strongly influenced by realized income (but not hours) when the realized wage is higher than expected, and by hours (but not income) when the wage is lower than expected.[15]

2) Direct approach

Several authors have examined the impact of expected outcomes on satisfaction with actual outcome (Hack & Lammers, 2011). By applying counterfactual thinking,[16] researchers have shown that identical outcomes can produce different emotional experiences (Kahneman & Miller, 1986; Baron, 1994) based on disappointment and regret aversions. Following disappointment and regret effects (Loomes & Sugden, 1986; Bell, 1985), decisions are partly based on the tendency to make choices in such a way as to minimize the future experience of disappointment or regret. Based on these assumptions, Mellers et al. (1997, 1999) showed within lottery decisions that unattained outcomes in a lottery affect self-reported emotions. Surprising gains are more elating than expected ones and surprising losses are more disappointing than expected ones. Medvec et al. (1995)

15 Yogo (2008) also applied this theory.

16 Thinking about how things could have turned out differently, to imagine what could have been.

observed a comparable result for satisfaction among Olympic medalists.[17] Both studies found that individuals' emotional responses to events are influenced by their thoughts about "what might have been."

A field study in the medical literature (Chapman, 2000) provided empirical evidence that expectations influence preferences. In three questionnaire experiments in specific health domains, the author assessed decision makers' preferences and expectations for health sequences. The preferred length of the health sequence was based on tracked expectations about how the sequences would realistically occur and which one would improve over time.

Hack and Lammers (2011) found additional empirical support within indirect and direct approaches for the influence of expectations on reference points. All their findings were consistent across both approaches. More importantly, similar to Arkes et al. (2008) they were the first to examine directly the role of expectations in the adaptation of reference points in the domain of gains. Their experiment suggests that a decision maker considers expectations when making a decision, as they observed a lower (higher) reference point adaptation by individuals when expectations are higher (lower) in the decision task.

Others

Different disciplines have discussed and tested other information that might also serve as a reference point within decision tasks under risk and uncertainty. A few ideas are presented in the following.

Social comparison and social preferences

Some researchers have theoretically discussed the importance of social comparison to evaluate one's outcome relative to a counterpart's outcome. These have pointed out that social comparisons may serve as reference points and alter the perceived value of an outcome (Kahneman & Miller, 1986; Boles & Messick, 1995; Novemsky & Schweitzer, 2004; Park, 2007). Similar studies have assumed that social preferences may serve as reference points for individuals (Fehr & Schmidt, 1999; Bolton & Ockenfels, 2000). Social preferences typically assume

---

17 Breiter et al. (2001) found support for the hypothesis that expectations-based counterfactuals affect reactions to outcomes in a neuroscientific setting.

that people are not just motivated by their own payoffs, but also care about payoffs to (relevant) others.

In an empirical study, Fiegenbaum and Thomas (1988) and Fiegenbaum (1990) used the industry's median return as a firm's reference point. Their assumption was based on studies by Frecka and Lee (1983) and Lev (1969), which used the industry mean at a point in time to show that firms adjust performance and financial ratios to the industry average in the previous period (Lehner, 2000). Lehner (2000) also found empirical support that the industry median is a valid representation of reference level for the significant properties of firms. He obtained his results from the COMPUSTAT database for the period 1972–1991 based on 876 firms from 14 industries.

Historical peaks

By empirically testing the disposition effect, Gneezy (2005) found that his experimental data were best described by assuming that participants use the historical peak as a reference level. Within a field study, Annaert et al. (2008) empirically confirmed disposition behavior when historical peak prices are used as reference points, while no disposition effect was observed when average, first, last, or highest purchase prices served as reference points. A further field study (Baker et al., 2009) used past peak prices as reference points or judgmental anchors in valuing targets effects on several aspects of merger and acquisition activities, including offer prices, deal success, market reaction, and merger waves.

Norms and ideals

Following Kahneman (1992) and Kahneman and Miller (1986), norms or ideals may also compete for attention as reference points within a decision task. In an empirical study of family business research, Gómez-Mejía et al. (2007) defined the family manager's reference points as its socioemotional wealth,[18] arguing that family firms are willing to take risks in order to preserve their socioemotion-

[18] Socioemotional wealth refers to (Gómez-Mejía et al., 2007; Zellweger et al., 2011): exercise authority, the satisfaction of the need for belonging, affect and intimacy, the preservation of family values through the business, the conservation of the family dynasty, the fulfillment of family obligations based on blood ties rather than on strict criteria of competences, and the opportunity to be altruistic to family members.

al wealth. Hence, socioemotional wealth might be a salient reference point in the decision situations of family managers.

Self-esteem

A qualitative marketing study (Gau & Viswanathan, 2008) assumed that self-esteem serves as a reference point from which broad goals are drawn and subsequent purchase behaviors are molded. They observed that low-literate consumers manage anxiety and shame, which results in the avoidance of better economic choices in favor of maintaining self-esteem by avoiding troublesome situations. This suggests that self-esteem maintenance, rather than the pursuit of an optimal outcome, is the driving force in low-literate retail decisions.

Minimum requirements

Survival requirements have also been mentioned as having an important impact on decision making (Lopes & Oden, 1999; March, 1988). In particular, minimum requirements referring to the minimum amount of income (e.g., a worker's need to pay a month's rent) are discussed (Koop & Johnson, 2012).

Five other criteria within a negotiation process

For instance, Bazerman and Neale (1991) mentioned five pieces of information within negotiation processes that are likely to serve as reference points. He suggested that a union team evaluate a wage offer not only based on the last year's wage (status quo), but also via (1) the management's initial offer, (2) the union's estimate of the management's reservation point, (3) the union's reservation point, and (4) the union's publicly announced bargaining position. Table 3 summarizes the mentioned empirical studies that include endogenously and exogenously given reference point types.

Table 3: Overview of selected empirical studies

References	Reference point	Direct or indirect measurement of reference point	Type of empirical study	Subject group
Group of reference points: Status quo				
Weber & Camerer (1998)	historical and recent status quo	indirect	decision experiment	29 engineering students, 35 and 39 business and economic graduate students
Genesove & Mayer (2001)	status quo	indirect	panel-analyze	5,792 property listings of Boston condominium market
Odean (1998)	historical status quo	indirect	field study	trading records from 1987 to 1993 for 10,000 accounts
Chen & Rao (2002)	recent status quo	indirect	field study/coin game experiment	80 adults of a professional marketing research firm/130 marketing students
Heyman et al. (2004)	recent status quo	indirect	lottery experiment	75 students
Arkes et al. (2008)	recent status quo	direct	hypothetical stock trading experiment	141–137 finance students
Group of reference points: Aspiration level and goal				
Payne et al. (1980)	aspiration level	indirect	gamble experiment/ incl. 10 verbal protocols	30 and 44 undergraduate and graduate students, and 84 top manager in European firms
Sullivan & Kida (1995)	aspiration level	indirect	decision experiment	72 investment managers
Lant (1992)	aspiration level	indirect	Marakstrat (marketing strategy game)	50 managers in an executive education program and 50 MBA students
Greve (2002)	aspiration level	direct	field data	14.468 market observation from radio stations
Camerer et al. (1997)	aspiration level	indirect	field data	New York Cab drivers, three samples from 1723 to 750 trip sheets
Park (2007)	aspiration level	Indirect	panel analyses	315 public firms in the US food industry, during the period 1985–2000
Heat et al. (1999)	goals	Indirect	decision experiment	45–60 students

References	Reference point	Direct or indirect measurement of reference point	Type of empirical study	Subject group
Group of reference points: Expectation				
Ordóñez (1998)	expectations	Indirect	decision experiments	psychology students
Winer (1986)	expectations	Indirect	panel analyses	coffee UPC scanner panel data of 1318 households in a large Midwestern cities
Bartol & Martin (1998)	expectations	Indirect	field data	152 part-time workers of a large retail organization
Abeler et al. (2011)	expectations	indirect	real-effort experiment	60 economic students
Post et al. (2008)	expectations	indirect	panel analyze	panel data from the game show Deal or No Deal of 53 episodes from shows in Australia and Netherlands from 2002–2005
Crawford & Meng (2011)	expectations	indirect	field data	21 New York Taxi drivers and 584 trip sheets, from 2000–2001
Mellers et al (1999)	expectations	indirect	lottery experiment	67 students
Medvec et al. (1995)	expectations	indirect	field data	National Broadcasting Company (NBC) videotapes of the 1992 Summer Olympic games in Barcelona, and NBC's sportscasters interviews of numerous medal winners immediately following their events
Chapman (2000)	expectations	indirect	hypothetical health plan experiments	100 community member recruited at a large airport; 79 community members recruited at two airport and one public library, 115 students
Hack & Lammers (2011)	expectations	direct	lottery experiment/ hypothetical stock price experiment	121/471 economic students

References	Reference point	Direct or indirect measurement of reference point	Type of empirical study	Subject group
Group of reference points: Others				
Fiegenbaum & Thomas (1988)/ Fiegenbaum (1990)	social comparison	indirect	field data	ROE of 2322 firms in 47 industries from 1960–1979/ ROA of 3300 firms in 85 industries from 1977–1984
Lehner (2000)	social comparison	indirect	field data	ROE of 879 US' firms from 14 industries from 1972–1991
Gneezy (2005)	historical peaks	indirect	lottery experiment	120 students
Annaert et al. (2008)	historical peaks	indirect	field data	data set of mutual fund transactions, over the period 2002–2007
Baker et al. (2009)	historical peaks	indirect	field data	23,350 unique deals from 1984–2007
Gómez-Mejía et al. (2007)	norms & ideals	indirect	field data	1,237 family-owned olive oil miles in Southern Spain who faced the choice during a 54-year period
Gau & Viswanathan (2008)	self-esteem	indirect	qualitative data	14 in-depth interviews with students and 21 in-depth interviews with adult education students

Research gaps

Kind of information

Besides the several kinds of information that might serve as salient reference points, further information also seems valuable to consider. An interesting factor might be risk. Risk is a closely connected factor within decision making, as individuals deal with risk by calculating their choices among alternative risk–return combinations. The anticipation and calculation of decision choices cause cognitive efforts. This suggests that individuals draw special attention to decision situations under risk. Moreover, studies of risk or uncertainty aversion have provided evidence that risk has important behavioral implications (Sitkin & Pablo, 1992; Wiseman & Gómez-Mejía, 1998; Epstein, 1999; Blais & Weber, 2001), as individuals show diverse decision behavior in situations under risk compared with in situations without risk. Hence, risk might be an important factor that affects decision making.

Direct measurement of reference points

The review above illustrates that most studies have taken reference points as exogenously given. Recently, a few studies have started to test the reference point directly (e.g., Arkes et al., 2008). Hack and Lammers (2011) were the first to test directly whether expectation serves as a reference point in the domain of gains. Expectations have long been considered to play a role in reference point formation, and several studies have pointed in this direction. However, clear-cut evidence on whether and how expectations affect the reference point is still lacking. For instance, Arkes et al. (2008) found different magnitudes of shifting reference points from the historical to the recent status quo between the domains of gains and losses. This suggests that such an asymmetric relationship between gains and losses can also be expected for expectations. Moreover, several pieces of information (e.g., social preferences) determining reference income have not been tested empirically to date, neither exogenously nor directly.

Subject groups

Furthermore, Table 3 shows that most experiments have been carried out with students. Only a few experiments have been conducted with managers, employees, and customers, while field data and panel analysis have considered broad subject groups.

Methods

Additional findings might be gained by using divergent experimental settings. An interesting investigation might be to explore different monetary (e.g., changes in salary) or non-monetary consequences (e.g., organizational change). In addition, a setting with different manager types (e.g., family managers, non-family managers, or entrepreneurs) might obtain further insights, as the interests of executive managers often differentiate from those of stakeholders and other groups (Lehner, 2000). This leads to the assumption that other information can serve as reference points depending on the types of managers.

3.1.2 Formation of reference points

This chapter reviews the prior research on the cognitive processes of reference point formation. The main question is how are reference points formed?

Cognitive processes

Cognitive processes emphasize the fact that everything we think, say, or do is influenced by mental processes – the cognitive mechanism through which we gather, transform, process, evaluate, and use information to accomplish decision tasks (Baron, 2004). Reference point formation is a cognitive process (Thaler, 1985). Further, the cognitive processes of reference point formation are accompanied by several heuristics and bias. Decision makers do not have the cognitive capacity to remember and process all information stimuli that arise from complex tasks (Keh et al., 2002). Thus, many day-to-day problems are so complex that decision makers tend towards cognitive simplifications.

Simon (1976) laid the groundwork with his assumption of bounded rationality, which suggests that decision makers must construct simplified mental models when dealing with complex decision tasks. To minimize cognitive efforts, individuals use heuristics (mental shortcuts). For instance, judgments of the likelihood of an event are based on the availability of past occurrences in the memory and frequently occurring events are easier to recall than infrequently occurring events (Schwenk, 1988). Marketing studies have pointed out that individuals use simple "heuristics such as "pick a product with probability equal to its market share" (Smallwood & Conlisk, 1979), or "identify the average payoff or utility of a product with its value in a small sample" (Ellison & Fudenberg, 1995)" (Joyce, 2007, p. 41). Menon and Raghubir (2003) demonstrated that distant information in the memory is unexpectedly recalled and that consumers may use the remembered information to make evaluations.

In turn, heuristic processing results in a number of cognitive biases. "Likely candidates include the optimistic bias – an inflated tendency to expect things to turn out well (Shepperd et al., 1996); the planning fallacy – the tendency to believe that we can complete more in a given period of time than we actually can (Buehler et al., 1994), and the affect infusion – the tendency for affective states to strongly influence (and often to distort) our perceptions and decisions (e.g., Forgas, 1995)" (Baron, 2004, p. 224). Further candidates might be overconfidence – the failure to know the limits of one's knowledge (Simon et al., 2000) – or the illusion of control – overemphasizing one's ability and skills to control events and people (Kahneman & Lovallo, 1993).

Multiple reference points

As shown in chapter 3.1.1, individuals have a number of potential reference points from which to choose. Initially, authors have focused on single reference points, although Lopes (1987) argued that situation factors may cause multiple relevant reference points and a shift in one's focus of attention, resulting in a shift in reference points. Weber and Camerer (1998) emphasized the need to know more about how reference points adapt and how multiple reference points are balanced.

As mentioned above, Neale and Bazerman (1991) suggested five reference points that might affect how a union team evaluates a wage offer. Some theories suggest that individuals combine multiple reference points into a single composite point (e.g., Ordóñez, 1998). Investigations into fairness have shown that people simultaneously consider multiple reference points in judgments (see Ordóñez et al., 2000). Using a field survey of the stock market, Lin et al. (2006) provided strong evidence for investors using multiple "what might have been" points in judging their regrets. This important comparison process of reference point formation includes investors' outcomes when they decide not to invest, their expectations, and the best-performing not chosen stocks.

Appling norm theory, Boles and Messick (1995) examined the influence of multiple reference points by evaluating an outcome when two reference points, the status quo and an evoked alternative, provide conflicting information. They found that an alternative outcome is more likely to be evoked as a reference point when: (1) it is certain that another choice would have led to the alternative outcome; (2) a social comparison received the alternative outcome; and (3) the alternative outcome is in a different evaluative domain than the outcome received, i.e., is negative when the outcome received is positive.

Sullivan and Kida (1995) were the first to suggest that two explicit reference points are important for a given decision task (i.e., the aspiration level and status quo of managerial performance). They empirically indicated that the presence of multiple relevant reference points results in a complex pattern of risky behavior, where managers are affected by the relative positions of risky alternatives with respect to two reference points (target and current level of job performance). Therefore, they hypothesized that when multiple reference points are important for assessment, each of these influence decision making.

More recently, some authors have described choosing data by including multiple reference points within the value function (Koop & Johnson, 2012). For instance, Wang and Johnson (2009) defined a tri-reference point theory that considers the effect of three reference points: status quo, goal, and minimum requirements. They assumed that decision makers simultaneously aim to exceed a goal, while staying above a minimum requirement and improving from their status quo. Koop and Johnson (2012) were the first to show empirically that these three reference points indeed affect decision making. They found that students seem to be systematically sensitive to all three reference points when making decisions within the same context. Moreover, they provided evidence that if reference points become uncertain, their behavioral impact decreases relative to unambiguous reference points.[19]

Baucells et al. (2011) investigated five potential reference point candidates: purchase price (historical status quo), current price (recent status quo), average price, highest/lowest price, and dashed hope/false alarm pattern. They presented students with a multiple period stock price scenario and told them to image that they had purchased a stock for the first price (which was shown on a price development graph) and that since this purchase, the price had changed. Then, participants were requested to indicate the price that would produce zero utility (i.e., the reference point) for selling the stock again. Hence, they could directly estimate the reference point of each individual. They showed that the individual reference point is best described as a combination of the historical and recent status quo of a time series. Their paper was the first step in investigating directly how multiple reference points compete and combine.

---

19 In certain conditions, the reference point status quo, goals, and minimum requirements were well defined and showed to the subjects. In uncertain conditions, the status quo was fixed but minimum requirements and goals were expressed in terms of symmetric probability distributions.

Integration and segregation of prior reference points

In settings in which multiple reference points are available, there is the question of how people cognitively deal with simultaneously given reference points.

The theory of mental accounting[20] (Thaler, 1985) provides some ideas and results. Mental accounting (e.g., Linville & Fischer, 1991; Mazumdar & Jun, 1993; Thaler & Johnson, 1990; Heath et al., 1999) distinguishes between two classes of model of the decision situation by which reference points are incorporated. Following the hedonic maximizer hypothesis (Thaler & Johnson, 1990), on one hand, this suggests an integrated model. Therefore, individuals value multiple reference points jointly into a single one. On the other hand, the hypothesis suggests a separation of reference points. Individuals compare each reference point to their outcomes before making their decisions. Thaler (1985) demonstrated that individuals typically segregate multiple gains. These individuals would be happier than individuals whose multiple gains were integrated. Moreover, he argued that individuals whose multiple losses were segregated would be unhappier than individuals whose multiple losses were integrated.

Arkes et al. (2008) assumed that their observed faster adaptation to gains than to losses is related also to hedonic maximization, especially by the tendency to segregate intertemporal gains and integrate intertemporal losses. Hack and Lammers (2011) found that decision makers employ expected value when forming a reference point (integrated mechanism) as opposed to single possible outcomes (segregated mechanism). Kahneman and Tversky (1979) presumed that individuals who have recently experienced losses and who have not yet shifted their reference points tend to behave riskier than those who have not experienced losses or who have already shifted their reference points. In addition, Tversky and Kahneman (1981) argued that decision makers include only the direct consequences of a given act when making decisions. In particular, Thaler and Johnson (1990) suggested that previously experienced gains and losses affect present choice making. They empirically confirmed that individuals tend to be more risk willing in the presence of prior gains, which they labeled the "house money" effect. They also found that individuals tend to be more risk avoiding in the pres-

20 Mental accounting refers to the cognitive process of coding, categorizing, and evaluating outcomes within mental accounts.

ence of prior losses, leading in more risk-willing behavior (get-evenitis effect).[21] Therefore, the integration of prior gains results in risk-seeking, while integration of prior losses results in risk aversion.

Following the frequency model (Diener et al., 1990), Kahneman (1992) discussed separating references when individuals determine satisfaction by comparing outcomes to several comparison points. This means that reference points are not combined but rather that one single reference point is selected because of its relative frequency.[22] Satisfaction increases when the ratio of the number of positive to negative experiences is greater than one (Ordóñez et al., 2000).

Ordóñez et al. (2000) examined the effects of references on the ratings of salary satisfaction and fairness. They argued that it seems unlikely that an individual has the cognitive capacity to use segregated models if large numbers of potential reference points were salient. Based on these experimental results, they pointed out that reference points are more likely to be integrated when referents are easily comparable and that segregation is more likely to occur when referents are not readily comparable (Baucells et al., 2011).

Adaptation of references

All the explanations above suggest that reference points are not static. Research has almost always been applied to investigations on single-period decision making, although an important question is how reference points are updated over time as a function of the outcomes of past decisions (Arkes et al., 2008). Several models (e.g., Bateman et al., 1997) have considered shifting reference points, while Shefrin and Statman (2000) emphasized the lack of multiple period models to investigate risky decision making.

Recently, the adaptation of reference points has replaced the consideration of fixed reference points (e.g., Lant, 1992; Lehner, 2000; Heyman et al., 2004; Baucells et al., 2011; Bleichrodt, 2007) and acknowledged the concept of variable and adaptive references supported by empirical evidence (Chen & Rao, 2002; Gneezy, 2005; Arkes et al., 2008, 2010; Hack & Lammers, 2011).

21 Linville and Fischer (1991), Sullivan and Kida (1995), and Arkes et al. (2008) found no empirical support for segregation in the domain of losses.

22 The frequency model was confirmed by Highhouse et al. (2003) on salary expectations.

By testing the disposition effect, financial researchers have considered how investors behave in the presence of gains and losses and how investors form and adapt their reference points over time. Therefore, most studies have presumed the reference point to be a function of past purchase price or weighted average price (Shefrin & Statman, 1985; Grinblatt & Keloharju, 2001, Barberis & Xiong, 2009). For instance, Grinblatt and Han (2005) assumed that a reference price is updated as shares are exchanged between investors. New reference prices are thus weighted averages of old reference prices and the prices at which new shares trade. In an organizational study, Lehner (2000) investigated if executives shift from the median industry return to an individual reference point. He found a shifting of reference points only for a minority of firms. In a marketing study, Bateman et al. (1997) showed how the adaptation of reference points may explain the difference between willingness-to-pay and willingness-to-accept valuations. As mentioned above, Heyman et al. (2004) evaluated the pleasure that subjects derive from a sequence of outcomes. By investigating if the historical status quo or recent status quo is more dominant to feel pleasure, they found that immediate events are more dominant.

Schmidt (2003) was the first to present a model to analyze shifts in the reference point. However, a more realistic approach is the consideration of incomplete reference dependent preferences over alternatives, which he did not consider. Therefore, Bleichrodt (2007) was the first to develop a model of preference foundation for reference-dependent utility in the case of varying reference points across decisions with incomplete reference-dependent preferences.

Models and empirical studies have rarely been concerned with labile reference points or with how reference points are updated over time. Further, few experimental studies have considered directly the dynamics of reference points, especially their adaptation.

> “To illustrate the importance of reference point adaptation, consider a prospect-theory investor who purchases a stock at \$30 per share, observes it drop to \$20, and expects that the stock price will either go up or down by \$5 with equal probability. If her reference point remains at the purchase price \$30, she will hold on to the stock because people are risk-seeking in the loss domain. In contrast, if her reference point has adapted to the new price \$20, she will sell the stock at \$20 since, owing to loss-aversion, a zero-expected-value gamble is not attractive. On the upside, if the stock were to rise from \$30 to \$40, the extent of upward migration of the reference point

> would also affect the propensity to sell the stock. These simple examples illustrate that reference point adaptation affects risk-taking decisions" (Arkes et al., 2008, p. 67).

Gneezy (2005) assumed reference point adaptation from an individual's decisions to sell their stocks when stock prices followed a random walk. Following prospect theory, he empirically reported that individuals sell their stocks when the current price equals the historical peak. This means a shift in reference point from the asset's initial price to the highest historical price.

Chen and Rao (2002) investigated adaptive references regarding individual wealth changes and found a partial reference point adaptation from the status quo to a recent level of wealth. They suggested that an individual's reference point shifts to a new state of wealth after a stimulus is presented. In addition, they observed that two events of equal magnitudes, but different valences, make individuals happier when the first event is negatively valenced and the second event is positively valenced, and so on. Their hypotheses were supported empirically.

To my knowledge, Arkes et al. (2008) were the first to evaluate the location of reference points and the magnitude of reference point adaptation. They ascertained the extent of reference point adaptation in the domains of gains and losses. They asked students what stock price today would generate the same utility as a previous change in stock price. The observed extent of reference point adaptation was significantly greater for gains than for losses. Moreover, they found a faster adaptation of reference points to gains than to losses. They showed this asymmetric adaptation in experiments with and without monetary incentives. In a further study, Arkes et al. (2010) examined reference point adaptation in securities trading using subjects from China, Korea, and the US. They found a larger adaptation for Asians than for Americans. Moreover, they found additional support for higher adapted reference points more after a gain than after an equal sized loss. Hack and Lammers (2011) extended the experimental stock price scenario game of Arkes et al. (2008) to measure the adaptation of reference points for expectations in the domain of gains. Their experiment showed that reference point adaptation is lower (higher) compared with the reported mean reference adaptation when expectations are higher (lower) in the domain of gains.

Research gaps

Direct measurement of multiple reference points and their adaptation

In sum, models and empirical studies are rare and strongly disagree on how reference points are set up. Authors have acknowledged the concept of variable and adaptive reference points and thus examined the formation of reference points over time (Gneezy, 2005; Chen & Rao, 2002; Georgellis et al., 2008; Arkes et al., 2010; Baucells & Sarin, 2010; Abeler et al., 2011). However, only a few studies have focused directly on multiple reference points and their adaptation. There exist multiple relevant reference point combinations that have not been investigated yet. For instance, Baucells et al.'s (2011) seminal experimental investigation of multiple reference points offers just one possible combination. The consideration of other factors in their experiment, such as aspiration level or expectations, might lead to other results.

Asymmetric adaptation

In addition, studies of the impact of the adaptation processing of gains and losses are also rare. Numerous findings on the integration and segregation of dynamic reference points suggest that a separate investigation of multiple reference points and their shifting in the domains of gains and losses would gain fruitful insights. To my knowledge, only Arkes et al. (2008) have systematically calculated the magnitude of reference point adaptation and have examined differences in the domain of gains compared with losses. Although Hack and Lammers (2011) also examined directly the role of expectations in the adaptation of reference points over time, they did not investigate the role of expectations in the domain of losses. However, research provides evidence for asymmetric information processing concerning probability and utilities for gains and for losses (e.g., Kahneman & Tversky, 1979; Tversky & Kahneman, 1992; Weber, 1994).

Relations to other theories

Moreover, it might be interesting to examine the theories and concepts that explain asymmetric information processing, besides mental accounting and framing effects. Concepts such as the disappointment effect, hot hand, or cognitive dissonance have not been discussed yet.

3.1.3 Determinants of reference points

Imagine the example of feeling warmth presented above. The perception of a neutral experience may differentiate by context. Imagine the following context (Wakker, 2010). There exist two pails of warm water, one objectively warmer than the other. However, an individual that who immerses one hand in one pail and the other hand in the other pail will report that both water pails are neither hot nor cold. Therefore, this chapter reviews the discussions and empirical results of factors that might influence the cognitive process of reference point formation.

Framing

The most theoretically discussed and empirically investigated factor that determines the formation of reference points is framing (Tversky & Kahneman, 1981, 1991; Kahneman & Tversky, 1984; Loewenstein & Prelec, 1993; Bateman et al., 1997). Tversky and Kahneman (1981, p. 453) defined a frame as referring "to the decision maker's conception of acts, outcomes, and contingencies associated with a particular choice." Framing has been replicated in many studies and different disciplines (for a review, see Camerer, 1995). For instance, framing effects in bargaining and negotiation have been shown to result in different outcomes (Bazerman et al., 1985; Neale & Bazerman, 1985; Neale et al., 1986).

Levin et al. (1998) demonstrated in a literature review on framing effects that there are three types of framing effects: (1) risky choice framing, (2) attribute framing, (3) and goal framing. These types differentiate in underlying mechanisms and consequences and they are critical variables involved in cognitive representing, processing, and responding to choices.

In **risky choice framing**, the outcomes of a potential choice involving options differ by level of risk and the occurrence of the gain/loss domain. A well-known example of this framing effect is the Asian disease[23] experiment by Tversky and Kahneman (1981). Subjects were asked to "imagine that the U.S. is preparing for

[23] The Asian disease is a standard experiment design in which subjects choose between two options – a sure and a risk option. Frames are manipulated by varying the salience of the reference points, so that subjects perceive the same outcomes either as gains or as losses (Kühberger, 1998). Others are gambling design (e.g., Kahneman & Tversky, 1979), tax evasion design (e.g., Chang & Nichols, 1987), bargaining design (e.g., Neale & Bazerman, 1985), and game-theory design (e.g., Brewer & Kramer, 1986) (for more details, see Kühberger, 1998).

the outbreak of an unusual Asian disease, which is expected to kill 600 people. Two alternative programs to combat the disease have been proposed" (Tversky & Kahneman, 1981, p. 453), which differ by the level of risk regarding one gain and one loss framing. The actual choices depend on whether the choice is framed as a gain or as a loss. This means that individuals are sensitive to the manipulation of reference points. Kühberger (1998) suggested that in situations in which the salience of outcomes is manipulated, applying the threat-rigidity hypothesis is relevant. This hypothesis refers to the presence of threats that may result in conservative processing strategies such as reliance upon prior expectations, attention to dominant cues, or a tendency to emit well-learned responses.

However, framing effects are not isolated to situations involving risky choice. In **attribute framing**, the characteristics of an object or event serve as the focus of manipulation, which is useful for gaining a basic understanding of how descriptive valence influences information processing (Levin et al., 1998). One illustrating study by Levin and Gaeth (1988) demonstrated that perceptions of the quality of ground beef depend on whether the beef is labeled "75 percent lean" or "25 percent fat." They showed that a sample of ground beef was rated better when it was labeled in a positive light (75 percent lean) rather than in a negative light (25 percent fat). Further, they found that the positive labeling of an attribute leads to an encoding of the information that tends to evoke favorable associations in the memory.

A well-known example of a **goal framing** effect was presented by Meyerowitz and Chaiken (1987). They showed that women were more apt to carry out breast self-examination when presented with information emphasizing the negative consequences of not doing so than when presented with information stressing the positive consequences. They suggested that there is a negativity bias in processing information, wherein negative information has a systematically stronger impact on judgment than objectively equivalent positive information, as already discussed by prospect theory with the loss aversion effect: "losses loom larger than gains."

Based on 136 empirical studies, Kühberger (1998) reviewed overall framing effects. He defined the most important characteristics as whether:

- Framing is manipulated by changing reference points or by manipulating outcome salience (see Asian disease),
- Response mode is based on choice vs. rating/judgment,
- Options differentiate qualitatively or quantitatively in risk,
- There is one or multiple risky events,
- Framing is manipulated by gain/loss or by task responsive wording,
- Dependent variables are measured between- or within-subjects and problem domains.

Moreover, framing effects differ from individual to group decisions. The question is whether prior group discussions lead groups to choose more extreme reference points. Neale et al. (1986) found within the standard gain/loss framing a reduced framing effect for group decisions. They argued that groups focus their attention on more relevant issues than individuals would do and tend to disregard irrelevant information. Kühberger (1998) assumed that this universal view is unlikely, as decisions depend on group dynamics, on the number of group members, and on the rate of positively and negatively framed group members. For more details, see Milch et al. (2009).

In addition, Kühberger (1998) argued that one has to bear in mind that the framing effect may interact with individual dimensions such as age, sex, culture, or language as well as with cognitive dimensions such as motivation, emotion, knowledge, perception, and memory. Following this view, some theoretical and empirical results that suggest or show such an effect on reference point formation are reviewed below.

Individual differences

Tversky and Kahneman (1981) mentioned that the frame adopted by an individual is moderated partly by norms, habits, and personal characteristics. However, only a few papers have investigated the influence of individual differences on reference point formation.

Some authors have theoretically pointed out that the effects coming from changes in reference points are feelings (Mercer, 2005; Heyman et al., 2004; Read, 2002). These studies have argued that individuals are not indifferent to net assets, but rather that the emotion that influences individuals most is the direction of the change, whether it is a gain or a loss relative to some reference. The risk-as-feelings hypothesis (Loewenstein et al., 2001) suggests that feelings play a prominent role in risky decision making. Emotional reactions guide responses not only at their first occurrences, but also through conditioning and memory at later points in time, serving as somatic markers. They assume feelings to be necessary and, to a large degree, mediate the connection between the cognitive evaluations of risk and risk-related behavior.

Within empirically settings, Kume and Suzuki (2010) investigated age and generational differences. They found that the elderly update their reference points after gains and tend to derive their utility from gains and losses rather than from levels of wealth. Arkes et al. (2010) explored empirically nationality effects on reference point adaptation. When they introduced a forced sale intervention that highlighted prior price changes, Americans showed greater reference point shifting towards the new price, whereas Asians showed less shifting.

Furthermore, some authors have empirically explored the influence of personality traits on reference point formation. In their work on self-esteem, Kasimatis and Wells (1995) found that individuals with high self-esteem select downward counterfactuals, while individuals with low self-esteem select upward counterfactuals. Hack and Lammers (2008) showed that entrepreneurs set significantly higher reference points compared with non-entrepreneurs. This behavior can be explained by a subsequent willingness to take on more risk.

Context/Environment

In the marketing literature, the influence of contextual and environmental factors on reference point formation has been widely acknowledged. Winer (1985) discussed how a product category moderator influences the reference point setting, such as price trends, current or anticipated economic conditions, and household demographics. Thaler (1985) showed that reference points for identical products change because of differences in shopping contexts. Further, Bucklin and Lattin (1991) found empirical evidence that consumers' reference price processing of in-store promotional activities differs depending on whether a shopping trip was planned or unplanned. In addition, frequent deals and deep price cuts have been empirically demonstrated to increase customer's reference prices (Alba et al., 1999). Other studies have investigated a changing reference point for brand choices depending on the level of service provided, assortment offered, or store styles (for an overview, see Mazumdar & Sinha, 2005).

Research gaps

Individual and contextual differences

A broad field of studies has investigated framing effects. Unfortunately, individual differences and context factors are challenging to consider in formal models, and therefore they have been ignored in most models and experimental studies. So far, individual differences and contexts represent two important understudied areas in decision making under risk (for a discussion, see Lopes, 1987; Mellers et al., 1997; Weber & Milliman, 1997). The following aspects might be interesting factors that influence reference point formation.

Personality differences

For instance, until today the influences of personality differences on reference point formation have not been considered in studies. Even though Baucells et al. (2007, p. 31) raised this issue: "personality traits (…) could enhance our understanding of individual formation and updating rules." Only the risk-taking literature aims to couple personality concepts with risk-taking (Slovic et al., 1988; Byrnes, 1998). Risk-taking can be measured by risk propensity, risk perception, and reference point adaptation. Studies have already investigated the impact of personality traits on risk propensity and perception, but no study has considered the influence on reference point adaptation.

Affectual differences

Moreover, similar to the discussion concerning the effects of emotion on decision making, the affect-cognitive theory (e.g., Mitchell et al., 2003; Pennings et al., 2003; Baron, 2008; Morris et al., 2010) emphasizes that affective expressions (emotions and feelings) influence the evaluation of the relevance of information, such as what kind of information is more salient than others. The influence of affects on the cognitive process is based on priming and heuristic cues (Schwarz & Clore, 1983; Chaiken et al., 1989; Thaler, 1985; Forgas, 1992). This suggests that affects also influence the cognitive process of reference point formation. In addition, the affect-cognitive theory approach suggests that different cognitive interpretations and evaluations towards information are influenced by affective expressions to contextual situations.

3.2 Research gaps and research questions

The investigation of reference dependency is empirically prevailing (Wakker, 2010), as the reference point is volatile and therefore hard to model theoretically (Kühberger et al., 1999; Wakker, 2010). Despite broad empirical investigations, only a few research fields have obtained meaningful and universally valid findings. Some research topics require only a deeper understanding, whereas others need to be investigated for the first time, or even be defined initially as a research field.

This dissertation sheds light on all three parts of the presented framework. In three experimental settings, it contributes to a deeper theoretical understanding, empirically investigates first ideas, and defines as well as provides empirical evidence for new research questions.

The **first experiment** with students focuses on asymmetrical reference point formation and on the derivation of theoretical explanations. In particular, the central purpose is to explore the role of expectations in the magnitude of reference point adaptation in the domain of gains compared with losses over time. The findings of Arkes et al. (2008) and Hack and Lammers (2011) assume that there is a significant difference between the extent of reference point adaptation following attractive events (gains) and painful events (losses) in consideration of expectations. Moreover, the disappointment effect as an additional explanation for the asymmetric adaptation process is presented and discussed. In sum, the aim of this experiment is to gain deeper insights into reference point formation for expectations in the domains of gains and losses and to theoretically explain my research results.

The **second experimental** study focuses on the influence of personality traits on reference point formation in the domains of gains and losses. Hence, the central purpose of this experiment with students is to investigate for the first time the impact of personality traits as potential determinants of reference point formation. Individual differences are defined as one of the most unreached topics within reference-dependent preferences. Therefore, the main aim of this article is to examine whether or not differences in personality influence reference points. The experiment considers personality traits such as the need for achievement, optimism, self-esteem, and openness to experiences. In addition, it also considers if the effects of personality traits differ for attractive and painful events. Thus, this experiment aims to gather new findings for the "reference point formation" and "determinants of reference point formation" part.

The **third experimental** study with different manager types explores four research fields. First, it defines and investigates a new determinant of reference point formation – the influence of affects. Second, it examines for the first time whether risk is a further factor besides "usual suspects" such as status quo constituting a reference point. Third, based on affect theory I investigate if different manager types have divergent cognitive outcomes based on the context-related affective expressions of managers. For instance, this experiment considers if the context factor "managerial ownership" influences the reference point formation of managers. Fourth, by using the experimental setting of Baucells et al. (2011), it investigates if risk is considered to be among other information (historical and recent status quo) within a multiple time series. In sum, this experiment provides new insights for all three parts of the framework.

Table 4 illustrates that this doctoral project focuses on reference point formation and the factors that might determine it. This is because researchers have only recently begun to investigate these research fields. New findings for these unreached topics seem to be important for the further definition of a comprehensive reference dependence theory.

Table 4: Research topics of this dissertation

	1 Constitution of reference points	2 Reference point formation	3 Determinants of reference points
Review prior research	Question: What serves as reference points? • status quo • aspiration level / goals • expectations • others	Question: How the reference point is formed? • cognitive processing • multiple reference points • integration / segregation • adaptation of reference points	Question: What influences the forming of reference points? • framing • individual differences • context / environment
Research topics of this thesis	• risk	• reference point adaptations in the domain of gains and losses considering expectations • reference point adaptation in the domain of gains and losses based on personality differences • multiple reference point settings	• personality traits • affects (feelings and emotions) • context factor managerial ownership

Part 2:
Empirical investigations

4 Research approach

The subject of investigation in this dissertation is the reference-dependent preferences of individuals and their cognitive processes. To test the relationships as hypothesized in this dissertation, I was not able to rely on secondary data, so I had to carry out my own experimental surveys. The two following sections describe the purpose, benefits, and limitations of these experiments and the statistical methods used to test the research questions of this dissertation.

4.1 Experimental design

Since 2002, all leading economics journals have frequently published articles on experimental economics. The development was predictable considering Kahneman and Smith were awarded their Nobel Prizes in 2002 (Falk & Fehr, 2003). Researchers create experiments as a methodical procedure to verify and falsify hypotheses. Hence, experiments are a tool to test theoretical ideas or observed phenomena that aims to provide predictions and the expected outcomes of decisions. There are two forms of experiments: field experiments and laboratory experiments. While field experiments have the benefit that outcomes are observed in a real setting, laboratory experiments are controlled under conditions with more precision and certainty. Recently, some research efforts have also applied web experiments (Krantz et al., 1997), enabling scholars to gain easier access to a broader subject pool.

All experiments in this dissertation are quasi-laboratory experiments, as the individual reference point is not observable using economic field data. The first two experiments were conducted with students in lesson settings. Regarding the survey with managers, a web experiment was carried out to ensure high participation.

Benefits and Limitations

Experiments allow researchers to focus on individual behavior and decision making. Several advantages have led to an increasing use of laboratory experiments. First, they enable researchers to prove reference processing in a controlled and systematical setting, combined with knowing about exogenous/endogenous variables and the theoretical equilibrium. “Control is the most important asset behind running experiments; no other empirical method allows a similarly tight control as do experiments” (Falk & Fehr, 2003, p. 399). Second, individuals have an incentive to act as they would in a realistic setting, as their behavior mostly has monetary consequences (Gläser et al., 2000). Third, the simplicity of experiments is valuable, as it increases the understanding of the interaction of the relevant variables. Fourth, experiments produce replicable evidence (Falk & Fehr, 2003). Therefore, the results of laboratory studies can serve as a rigorous empirical pre-test of economic theory, prior to the use of field studies (Falk & Fehr, 2003).

Carpenter (2002) provided three reasons why experiments complement more traditional methods of empirical analysis. Based on behavioral questions, surveys (1) suffer from hypothetical bias. This bias refers to the tendency that subjects respond to situations differently when they are hypothetical than when they are real. Carpenter (2002) also described (2) the idealized persona bias and surveyor effect. The idealized persona bias refers to the way in which a subject responds as if he/she was a special person rather than the person he/she really is. The surveyor effect means that participants often aim to understand what the research would like to hear and respond in this way. Thus, (3) incentive compatibility helps, which in this context means that subjects have an incentive to truthfully respond because of the monetary consequences (Smith, 1982). Moreover, Barr (2003) pointed out that experiments generate data that can be analyzed more directly and lead to clearer conclusions, as the controlled design helps identify and limit the relationships that are the focus of the investigation.

While this dissertation encourages economic experiments, some limitations exist, too. For instance, control can never be perfect. Just slight adjustments in protocol, frames, lab location, or experimenter sex, race, or personality can affect behavior (Cardenas & Carpenter, 2005). Running experiments is time consuming and costly, as subjects are usually paid. Moreover, it has been criticized that there is a subject pool bias because participants are often students (Falk & Fehr, 2003). Students, unlike professionals, have typically no experience with the research problem. In addition, researchers have found that participants sometimes do not take their decisions seriously, as the stakes in the experiments are too low (Holt & Laury, 2002; Falk & Fehr, 2003). Some empirical results are questioned because of the small number of participants relative to field data (Falk & Fehr, 2003). However, Bellmare & Kröger (2003) provided evidence that the survey outcomes of non-participants (target population) do not differ systematically from what the outcomes of participants (actual study subjects) would have been without the program (selection bias) (Heckman et al., 1999). Moreover, all these shortcomings can be avoided by careful experimentation (Falk & Fehr, 2003).

The experiments of this dissertation are based on hypothetical choice tasks, and therefore do not refer to incentive compatibility. Although there is broad agreement in the research community that incentives should be used whenever possible, in some experimental patterns there is no alternative to hypothetical choices (Wakker, 2010). The direct measurement of reference points does not offer the opportunity to pay monetary incentives based on choices, as occurs in gambling or real effort tasks (see, for instance, Abeler et al., 2011). However, Cameron (1999) found that participants of experiments who received monetary payments based on their choices gave the same responses as subjects who received no monetary payments; he also showed no differences in reliability and similar decision times. As Tversky and Kahneman (1992) concluded, this doctoral project also draws upon the assumption that the differences between monetary and non-monetary choices were not large enough to change any significant qualitative conclusions.

4.2 Methodology of analysis

Once hypotheses are built and the experiment has been carried out, the data can be analyzed in order to confirm or refute the hypotheses. Several different analyses to test the hypotheses were carried out. This part briefly presents the tests used.

Statistical guidelines

Statistical significance

In general, all analyses tested the significance of the results. All tests were based on the statistical inferences of a population's relationship among variables from a drawn sample of that population (Bakan, 1966; Hair et al., 2010). Interpreting statistical inferences is addressed by the letter "p" (probability). The p-value identifies the level of significance: a level p = .01 determines that there is a 99 in 100 probability that the discrepancy in scores is a valid finding. There is broad agreement among researchers that a significance level between .05 and .10 represents marginal significance, one between .05 and .01 represents neutral significance, and one far below .05 implies that the results are reliable (George & Mallery, 2007).

In particular, within group comparison, depending on the hypothesis, groups may be assessed using either one-tailed or two-tailed tests of significance. The one-tailed test is used for testing a specific difference or relationship (e.g., women do not score higher than men on an IQ test), whereas the two-tailed test measures whether the mean differs significantly from the mean of the other and depends not on the positive or negative direction of differences (e.g., there are no differences in IQ scores among subject groups) (Bakan, 1966). In the case of a two-tailed test, the p-level is twice as much as the p-level of a one-tailed test, as the latter examines a particular direction.

Reliability analyses – Cronbach's Alpha test

A test of reliability addresses the problem of whether an analysis produces the same results each time with the same person in the same setting. More reliable measures show greater consistency than less reliable measures (Hair et al., 2010). The Cronbach's Alpha test estimates internal consistency, namely whether all analyses measure the same things (Cronbach, 1951). The scale varies between zero and one, where an alpha closer to one shows greater internal consistency.

Test of associations between metric variables

Correlation

Correlation identifies whether two or more variables are significantly related to each other. It refers to the independence technique, in which variables are not divided into dependent and independent sets (Hair et al., 2010).[24] The correlation index "r" measures whether a perfect positive correlation ($r = 1$), a positive correlation ($0<r<1$), no correlation ($r = 0$), a negative correlation ($-1<r<0$), or a perfect negative correlation ($r = -1$) exists. "Perfect" means that one variable is exactly predictable from the other. "Positive" indicates that if one variable rises in value, the other variable rises as well. A negative correlation means that if one variable declines in value, the other declines as well. No correlation indicates no relation between the two variables.

Multiple regressions

A linear multiple regression (ordinary least squares (OLS) regression) is an appropriate analysis when the research problem includes one dependent metrically scaled variable that is presumed related to two or more metric independent variables (for more details see: Hair et al., 2006). Whereas in the classical linear model, the number of observations is fixed, in OLS the number of observations is allowed to grow to infinity.

The third experiment of this dissertation used a special form of the OLS regression – a multivariate pooled OLS regression. A pooled OLS regression[25] (Beck & Katz, 1995; Pennings et al., 1999) is appropriate for cross-sectional data (e.g., Baucells et al., 2011). That means that the dependent variable is based on several observations of different fixed unit groups at one point in time. These kinds of data sets may have group effects or within-subject effects (White, 1980). Therefore, the pooled OLS regression clusters standard errors by subject (Baucells et al., 2011), as errors are correlated at individual levels.

So far, regression analysis has been the most widely used dependence technique, as it is applicable in several domains of business decision making (Hair et al., 2010). Regressions are designed to come to exact inferences. More specifically, regressions are able to measure the probability that an inference is solid, and it can predict (independent variables = predictor, relative explanatory power of the dependent variable) changes in the dependent variable in response to changes in several independent variables. It is also able to define a regression

24 Independent variable: Presumed causes of any changes in the dependent variable (Hair et al., 2010).

25 For more explanation on when a pooled linear regression model is appropriate, see Park (2009).

equation, which follows the model of the general equation design to identify unknown parameters and values. The goal is to minimize the sum of squared vertical distances among the observed values within the predicted value. The formula is:

$$Y = \beta_0 + \beta_1 * X_1 + \beta_2 * X_2 + \ldots + e$$

where Y is the metrically scaled dependent variable that will be predicted by the set of independent variables, while X_1, X_2, … X_n are the independent predictor variables, and β_1, β_2, … β_n are coefficients that multiply the predictor variables. β_0 is a constant and e is the error term. The inclusion of the error term has to be considered, as predicted values are never exact, and thus this term adjusts the gap between the predicted score and the actual score.

The strength of the relationship is also measured with the letter "r" (multiple correlations). R^2 refers to the proportions of the variance of the dependent variable about its mean that is explained by the independent variables (Hair et al., 2010). The adjusted R^2 considers a better population, as it takes into account the number of independent variables included in the regression equation and the sample size. This is useful when comparing R^2 values among models with different numbers of independent variables or samples.

Next, we run a multiple regression based on several assumptions. Assumption (1), the homoscedasticity of variance, means that the variance within each observation is equal. A violation of this would result in an inefficient estimator of the OLS estimates. If this is the case, heteroscedasticity is given (Hair et al., 2010). Another central issue in regression analysis exists if (2) multicollinearity occurs. If this is the case, two or more independent variables in the regression model are highly correlated (Hair et al., 2010). This can negatively influence the significance of valid results regarding any individual independent variable. Multicollinearity may be omitted by two methods: formal detection tolerance or variance inflation factor (VIF). A common method is to estimate the VIF index, which determines how much variance of the estimated regression coefficient has been enlarged because of collinearity. High VIF values indicate multicollinearity, whereas values up to two are acceptable (Schneider, 2009).

Within a regression model, it is possible to consider a moderator effect. A moderator is a third variable that changes the strength of a causal relationship between the independent and dependent variables; it can amplify or even reverse that effect (for more details, see Frazier et al., 2004; Marsh et al., 2011). This is also known as an interactive effect (Hair et al., 2010). Moderator effects are identified through interactions of X and M in explaining Y, while it is operationalized by the product term $X*M$.

$$Y = \beta_0+\beta_1*X_1*\mathrm{M}+\beta_2*X_2*\mathrm{M}+\ldots+e$$

The effect size of a moderator is measurable by f^2 (Aiken & West, 1991), which equals the variance described by the interaction term divided by sum of the error and interaction variances.

Tests to assess the statistical significance of differences

Nominal scales

Chi-square test of independence: The chi-square analysis (Pearson, 1990) as a measurement of differences is used to compare whether observed values differ significantly from estimated values and whether two variables are dependent on each other (Hair et al., 2010). Therefore, it determines whether the observed model of a sample perfectly fits a corresponding theoretically estimated or anticipated model. The chi-square test is not based on the assumption that the sample is normally or close to normally distributed. It is a non-parametric test that deals with samples if the assumption of normality is violated.[26] A sufficiently large sample size is assumed. In the case of smaller sample sizes, the test yields an inaccurate inference. An alternative for small sample sizes, for instance, is the binomial test.

Binomial test: This non-parametric test measures whether the elements of a single dichotomous group differ from a binominal distribution (Siegel, 1956; George & Mallery, 2007). This one-sample test assumes that two values are equally likely to occur (such as a coin toss or female vs. male) ($p = .5$).

---

26 Non-parametric tests can be applied to ordinal or even nominal data (for more conditions for application, see Sprent & Smeeton, 2000), while parametric tests can be measured at least on an interval scale.

Ordinal scales

Mann-Whitney rank-sum test: This non-parametric test estimates whether two groups differ from each other based on ranked scores (Wilcoxon, 1945; Mann & Whitney, 1947). Actually, this test is comparable to a t-test (for a comparison of the t-test and Mann–Whitney test, see Siegel, 1956), but it can be used for two samples that are not normally distributed and for data that are coded at least ordinally. Accordingly, it defines the rank of each participant in the sample and then calculates the average rank for the two groups.

Kolmogorov-Smirnov test: The Kolmogorov–Smirnov test is also a non-parametric test for one-sample and two-sample analysis (Kolmogorov, 1941). The one-sample test estimates whether a particular sample differs significantly from a standard normal distribution (Kolmogorov, 1941), while the two-sample test compares the distribution of the values in two data sets (two samples). A large significance indicates that the distribution does not differ significantly.

Metric measurement scales

Independent sample t-test: A t-test identifies whether the mean of one group differs significantly from the mean of another group or groups (Gosset, known by his pseudonym Student, 1908). Within this test, the dependent variable must always be continuous, while the independent variables may be categorical. The t-test always compares two different means, by comparing one sample mean with the means of the corresponding distribution. There are three different t-tests. In this dissertation, only the independent-sample t-test is run. This compares the means of two groups and is one of the most used and best-known analyses for group comparisons.

One-way analysis of variance (ANOVA): Whereas the t-test compares only two distributions, the one-way ANOVA (Fisher, 1918) is used for analyzing group differences for two or more groups. It measures whether there are significant differences within any of the comparisons of groups in the sample (George & Mallery, 2007). The dependent variable must also be continuous, while the independent variables can be categorical.

5 First experimental study: A second look at expectations as reference points – the domain of losses

5.1 Introduction

Reference dependency has a long tradition in psychology (Lewin et al., 1944, Siegel, 1957) and it has been applied in behavioral economics with Kahneman and Tversky's prospect theory. Following Kahneman and Tversky (1979), whether a decision outcome is perceived as a gain or as a loss compared with a subjective reference point has a strong influence on risk attitudes (Hack & Lammers, 2008). In principle, individuals show risk aversion in the gain domain and risk-seeking behavior in the loss domain, as well as a significantly greater aversion to losses than an appreciation of gains. The literature that examines the individual reference point is relatively poorly conceived, although it is vital to define what constitutes a reference point.

Most studies have assumed some kind of reference point, such as for status quo (Samuelson & Zeckhauser, 1988; Thaler, 1999; Kühberger, 1998; Hoeffler et al., 2006) or for expectations and goals (Köszegi & Rabin, 2006; Heidhues & Köszegi, 2008; Heath et al., 1999). However, based on the specification of a reference point, the research may result in inconsistent predictions. Imagine the following scenario (Hack & Lammers, 2011) in which an investor decides to sell stocks from his portfolio. When he bought those shares at the initial purchase price, he might have formed expectations about the stock's subsequent performance. Furthermore, he might observe the current stock price. In this case, the reference point could be the initial purchase price, his expected price, or the current stock price. This example shows that different reference points might exist. The decision outcome and its final perception as a gain or a loss depends on the different reference points, as the initial purchase price differs from the expected price or from the current stock price. Following Köszegi and Rabin (2006, 2007), different predictions on risk-taking behavior occur from the application of different reference points. Therefore, the question of what exactly constitutes a reference point is of essential importance (Hack & Lammers, 2011).

Based on a model theory approach, Köszegi and Rabin (2006, 2007, 2009) brought different predictions on risk attitudes in line, drawing on the assumptions that a decision maker's reference point is his/her recent expectations about outcomes. They argued that the assumption that the status quo serves as the reference point only comes from situations in which decision makers plausibly show status quo bias. For instance, different results on the willingness-to-pay, willingness-to-accept gap (see Plott & Zeiler, 2005) or on explanations for the working hours of New York cab drivers (Camerer et al., 1997) can be reconciled in this way. Recently, for example, Crawford and Meng (2011), Card and Dahl (2010), and Pope and Schweitzer (2011) all provided empirical support for the findings of Köszegi and Rabin in a controlled experimental environment. They verified the assumption of expectations-based reference points and subsequent applications of their model. Moreover, Hack and Lammers (2011) also showed in an empirical setting that when expectations are present, they have a significant impact on reference point formation.

Although there are theoretical and empirical findings suggesting that expectations serve as reference points, up to now no study has considered the extent of reference point adaptation because of expectation levels (adaptation means a shift in reference point in the direction of a realized outcome, see Arkes et al., 2008, p. 67). This is even more surprising in light of a number of papers that have tested for the impact of expected outcomes on satisfaction with the actual outcome and indicated a change in the reference point because of expectations (Medvec et al., 1995; Mellers et al., 1999; Breiter et al., 2001; Heyman et al., 2004; Brown et al., 2008). In addition, Abeler et al. (2011) and Post et al. (2008) found that previous expectations influence the final reference point.

Furthermore, researchers have recently comprehended the concept of variable and adaptive reference points to theoretically and empirically examine the formation of reference points over time (Chen & Rao, 2002; Gneezy, 2005; Georgellis et al., 2008; Arkes et al., 2010; Abeler et al., 2011). Following Arkes et al. (2008, 2010), if prospect theory applies to more realistic dynamic settings such as stock trading, repeated bargaining and negotiation, and work efforts, it is important to understand how reference points are updated after an individual experiences outcomes over time. Depending on how individuals adapt their reference points, different evaluations of a person's outcome of choice will occur. As the literature shows, reference points are an important factor in explaining risk behavior and thus play an important role in predicting economic phenomena. Any advances to the understanding of the evolution of reference points are of particular importance for further economic modeling. Hence, it is important to gain a better understanding of how individuals adapt their reference points.

In this spirit, some authors have shown that dynamic reference point adaptation concerning different status quo levels exists. Hoeffler et al. (2006) predicted in their examination of the path dependency of preferences a key role of the historical status quo in shaping preferences. Arkes et al. (2008) considered the historical and the recent status quo to examine shifts in reference points following gains and losses. They showed that adaptation is significantly greater following gains than following losses. However, none of these papers investigating expectations as reference points has considered dynamic reference points. More specifically, different from this study, they did not calculate the magnitude of reference point shifts because of new information such as different levels of expectations.

To my knowledge, the paper by Hack and Lammers (2011) is the first to directly examine the role of expectations on the adaptation of reference points. Their experiment showed that reference point adaptation is higher compared with the reported mean reference adaptation when expectations are higher and vice versa. However, they did not investigate the role of expectations in the domain of losses and only concentrated on adaptation in the domain of gains. Following prior research providing evidence for asymmetric information processing concerning probability and utilities for gains and losses, this suggests that the results of Hack and Lammers cannot directly be applied to the domain of losses (e.g., Kahneman & Tversky, 1979; Tversky & Kahneman, 1992; Weber, 1994). Therefore, I complete the study of Hack and Lammers (2011) by examining the role of expectations in the adaptation of reference points in the domain of losses as well as addressing the differences between adaptation in the domains of gains and losses. In addition, I examine theories and concepts that explain my results such as mental accounting and framing effects. Furthermore, I allude to a further effect to explain my results – the disappointment effect.

The remainder of this study is organized into seven chapters. Chapter 5.2 illustrates the impact of expectations on risk preferences. Chapter 5.3 explains the method for measuring reference point adaptation. The derivation of the predictions is presented in chapter 5.4. Chapter 5.5 presents the sample, setting, and empirical study with the results. Chapters 5.6 and 5.7 provide concluding comments.

5.2 Potential impact of expectations given prospect theory preferences

Before the experimental design is presented, based on explanations by Hack and Lammers (2011) for the domain of gains, I illustrate how reference point adaptation may be affected by expectations[27] in the domain of losses and how this adaptation may affect subsequent risky choices in more detail.

Imagine the scenario that only the current status quo plays a role in reference point adaptation over time. At some initial date $t = 0$, the initial reference point R_0 will be formed. For instance, this could be the purchase price of a stock for 30 € (historical status quo). This reference point defines the origin of the value function (see solid line in Figure 3).

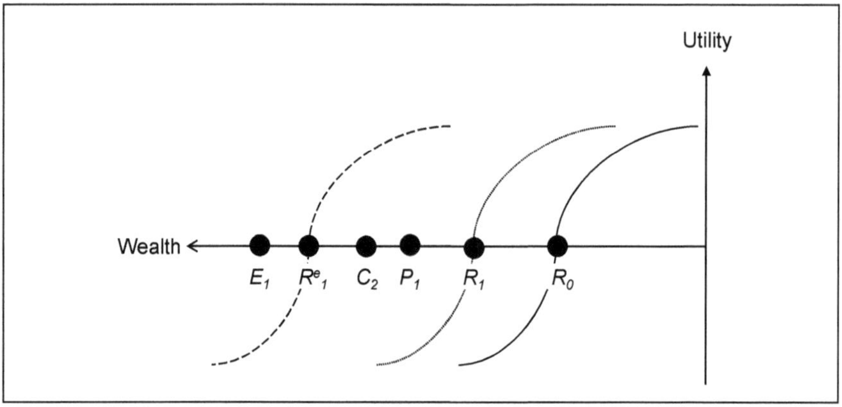

Figure 3: Potential role of expectations in the domain of losses

27 Expectations are defined as recently formed expectations on prospective outcomes in the subsequent time period.

At $t = 1$, the decision maker receives new information, for instance regarding the current stock price of 24 € (current status quo). In a comparable setting, Arkes et al. (2008) and other related studies have shown a partial reference point adaptation towards the current status quo P_1, resulting in a new reference point R_1. Figure 3 illustrates this adaptation based on the assumption that the shape of the value function remains unchanged (dotted line). At $t = 2$, the decision maker evaluates the current outcome C_2. For example, if C_2 lies further below the reference point R_1, the outcome will be perceived as a loss. Given prospect theory preferences, a decision maker in this situation will generally show risk-seeking behavior.

The question is how expectations may affect behavior. Imagine again the scenario at $t = 1$. Now, the decision maker not only learns the current status quo, but also forms expectations regarding the possible outcome at $t = 2$.[28] The decision maker should have the same reference point adaptation towards R_1 as before if expectations have no influence on the later assessment of the outcome. If expectations do play a role in the adaptation of the new reference point at $t = 1$, there would be the situation presented in Figure 3 (dashed line). In this scenario, expectations E_1 exceed the current status quo and I thus see a greater adaptation of the reference point towards a point $R^e_1 > R_1$. The actual outcome C_2 would then be perceived as a gain relative to this new reference point R^e_1. A decision maker would show risk-averse behavior in this kind of situation. In contrast to the loss scenario, decision makers with higher reference points in the domain of gains will find themselves more often in the domain of losses.

[28] Based on Hack and Lammers (2011), I follow Köszegi and Rabin (2006, 2007) and consider those expectations held in the "recent" past (t = 1) about recent outcomes ($t = 2$). As Köszegi and Rabin (2006) argued: "When somebody finds out five minutes ahead of time that she will for sure not receive a long-expected \$100, she would presumably immediately adjust her expectations to the new situation, but she will still five minutes later assess not getting the money as a loss" footnote 9).

5.3 Measuring reference point adaptation due to expectations

Lately, reference dependence theory has found its way into economic modeling (e.g., Chen & Rao, 2002; Sugden, 2003; Masatlioglu & Ok, 2005; Köszegi & Rabin, 2006; Arkes et al., 2008; Kume & Suzuki, 2010; Baucells et al., 2011). Few models provide an algorithm to translate any existing reference-independent model into the corresponding reference-dependent one (e.g., Arkes et al., 2008; Baucells et al., 2011). Hence, up to now, there has been no standard practice for the examination of reference points. One reason for this might be that reference points are not directly observable and therefore hard to analyze.

This study is built on the approach by Arkes et al. (2008), where subjects answer questions about a hypothetical stock trading scenario. To my knowledge, this approach is the only one to calculate the magnitude of reference point adaptation. The impact of expectations on reference point formation is tested by extending the approach of Arkes et al. (2008) to incorporate expectations, and then translated into German. Specifically, subjects receive different information regarding the expected price movement. Subjects' responses are then used to calculate the newly formed reference point. It was found that price expectations have a significant impact on reference point adaptation.

Following Hack and Lammers (2011), participants read the following scenarios, where expectations and status quo are salient:

"Two months ago, you bought a stock for 30 € per share. One month ago, you were disappointed to learn the stock was trading lower – at 24 € per share. *[Only in experimental treatments: "One month ago you also learned that this month's stock price is expected to range between x € and y €, with each price within this interval being equally likely."]* This month, you decide to check the stock's price again. At what price would the stock need to trade today to make you just as sad with the stock's price this month as you were when you learned the stock had dropped from 30 € to 24 € last month?"

The question of what stock price today would cause the same utility for subjects as a recent stock price that decreased from the historical purchase price allows me to evaluate the magnitude of reference point adaptation under the assumptions that the purchase price serves as the historical reference point ($P_0 = R_0$) and that the value function remains stable over time (Hack & Lammers, 2011). This assumption is based on that fact the recent price change is calculated by the historical reference point R_0, leading to utility $U_{R0}(P_1)$ at $t = 1$. Subjects are asked what stock price P^* at $t = 2$ would cause the same utility. For instance, without a reference point adaptation, subjects would still state P_1 (Hack & Lammers, 2011). I am interested in the updated reference point R^* with $U_{R^*}(P^*) = U_{R0}(P_1)$. Under the assumption that the shape of the value function remains unchanged, the following equation holds:

$$P^* - R^* = P_1 - R_0 \rightarrow \Delta R = R^* - R_0 = P^* - P_1$$

Given this equality, this study is able to derive the reference point adaptation (ΔR).

5.4 Formulation of predictions

Arkes et al. (2008) ascertained to what extent the reference point shifts following gains or losses in the status quo. As mentioned, in this experimental study the method of Arkes et al. (2008) is extended to incorporate expectations.

Table 5: The four treatments: loss control, loss base, loss high, and loss low[29]

		Gain scenario		Loss scenario	
Treatment	Description	Expectations	Resulting expected value	Expectations	Resulting expected value
Control treatment	As Arkes et al. (2008)	None given	–	None given	–
Base treatment	Base expectations	30 € to 50 €	40 €	10 € to 30 €	20 €
High treatment	High expectations	35 € to 45 €	45 €	15 € to 35 €	25 €
Low treatment	Low expectations	25 € to 45 €	35 €	5 € to 25 €	15 €

29 The results of the gain scenario are published in Hack and Lammers (2011).

A between-subjects design is used with four treatments: one loss control treatment and three experimental treatments. The treatments vary in the information concerning expected price movements (Table 5). The *loss control treatment* is equal to the loss scenario of Arkes et al. (2008) to test the comparability of the samples. I expect that the results are consistent with the results from Arkes et al. for painful events.

> Replication 1 (post-hoc):
> The results of the loss control treatment are consistent with the results of the loss scenario in Arkes et al. (2008; experiment 1, p. 70).

The *loss base treatment* incorporates explicit expectations ranging from 10 € to 30 € into the scenario. The given expected value of the future stock price of 20 € roughly fits the mean reported stock price (21.49 €) in the *loss control treatment* of Arkes et al.'s (2008) loss scenario where individuals' responses were only based on the current status quo. The given expectations in the *loss base treatment* therefore hold no new information for the adaptation of the reference point. The *loss control* and *loss base treatments* are designed to test the feasibility of my extended experimental design. Therefore, I predict no significant differences for the two mean reported stock prices.

> Prediction 2 (post-hoc):
> There are no differences in the magnitude of reference point adaptation between participants in the loss control treatment compared with their counterparts in the corresponding loss base treatment.

As proposed in the model of Köszegi and Rabin (2006), it is assumed that any reference point changes might occur because of information contained in the expected values. Hack and Lammers (2011) found a significant impact of expectations on reference point adaptation in the domain of gains. Therefore, I also expect to find a significant impact in the domain of losses. The role of expectations in reference point adaptation conducting a *low* and a *high treatment* is examined. In the *loss high treatment,* I offered a price range from 15 € to 35 € with an expected price of 25 € and in the *loss low treatment* from 5 € to 25 € with an expected price of 15 €. Following Hack and Lammers (2011), the ranges were constructed in a way that each should encompass the recent status quo (24 €) as well as the mean reported price in the control treatment of Arkes et al. (2008). If expectations indeed play a role in reference point adaptation, one must expect lower (higher) reported mean stock prices compared with the *loss control and loss base treatments* when expectations are lower (higher) (Hack & Lammers, 2011).

> Prediction 3a:
> The differences in the magnitude of reference point adaptation are significantly lower among participants in the loss high treatment compared with their counterparts in the corresponding loss control and loss base treatments.
>
> Prediction 3b:
> The differences in the magnitude of reference point adaptation are significantly higher among participants in the loss low treatment compared with their counterparts in the corresponding loss control and loss base treatments.

Comparing reference point adaptation in the domains of gains and losses, the curvature of the value function allowed Arkes et al. (2008) to derive some predictions. In their study, Arkes et al. (2008) found that the size of reference point adaptation after gains tends to be greater than after losses. They assumed that the faster adaptation to gains than to losses is related to hedonic maximization (Tversky & Kahneman, 1981; Thaler, 1985, 1989), which explained the tendency to segregate intertemporal gains and integrate intertemporal losses. Following a gain, a hedonic maximizer (Thaler, 1999) might adapt the reference point closer to the new level of wealth, because in this way the gain will be enjoyed most. This is because of the concave shape of the value function. By contrast, after a loss, if the hedonic consideration were the only factor underlying reference point adaptation, one would never adapt to losses. The migration of reference points towards the first loss would be more painful than if the status quo reference point were to be maintained. Arkes et al. assumed that the partial integration of losses in their study was because of the sense of reality. This may force individuals to take into account the current price to some extent, which increases the degree of reference point adaptation. However, Thaler and Johnson (1990) proposed that when subjects are faced with a two-stage gamble involving a prior loss, subjects do not integrate subsequent losses with the initial loss. They called this the quasi-hedonic editing hypothesis, as it follows hedonic editing rules only partly (both the gain and the loss are segregated from the prior loss). Thus, Thaler and Johnson (1990) assumed that owing to quasi-hedonic maximization the framing of prior losses might increase risk aversion, which would also lead to minor adaptation in the domain of losses, particularly when there is no opportunity to break even. In addition to these assumptions, I suppose that the sense of reality to losses is determined by the avoidance of disappointment. Disappointment theory (Bell, 1985; Loomes & Sugden, 1986) deals with the notion that people consider risks to be a disappointment when the outcome is not evaluated as positively as expected (Delquié & Cillo, 2006). Therefore, individuals make decisions that are less likely to lead to a feeling of disappointment, which might affect reference adaptation in the domain of losses. To conclude, overall I also expect asymmetric adaptation in the domains of gains and losses, when expectations are salient.

> Prediction 4:
> The magnitudes of reference point adaptation are significantly higher among participants in all four treatments after gains compared with their counterparts in the four treatments after losses.

Moreover, I assume that the impact of expectations on the magnitude of reference point adaptation in the *loss base* to *loss high treatments* is greater compared with that in the *loss base* to *loss low treatments.* This is because the information on expected outcomes is different. In the *loss high treatment* (35 – 15 €), there exists a possibility of a gain, while in the *loss low treatment* (25 € – 5 €), a loss is definitely expected (historical status quo was 30 €). This prediction is related to the assumption that adaptation after gains is greater than after losses (Arkes et al., 2008; Tversky & Kahneman, 1981; Thaler, 1989). Therefore, it is expected to find support for a greater magnitude of reference point adaptation for the *loss base* to *loss high treatments*.

> Prediction 5:
> The magnitudes of reference point adaptation are significantly greater among participants in the loss base to loss high treatments compared with their counterparts in the loss base to loss low treatments.

5.5 Study

5.5.1 Sample and setting

In a classroom setting in 2010, at a large German university, the Technische University Dortmund, 369 business undergraduates answered a questionnaire. Subjects had the chance to win 40 cinema vouchers as an incentive for their participation. No variable payment could be used because of the pure psychological nature of reference points. Thus, the questionnaires were filled out voluntarily. The total number of respondents for each scenario is denoted by *n*. In the (1) *loss control treatment* 93 students, in the (2) *loss base treatment* 90 students, in the (3) *loss high treatment* 93 students, and in the (4) *loss low treatment* 90 students participated. The mean age of the subjects was 21.2 and 42 percent of them were women.

As described above, the experiment used a between-subjects design with four treatments (Table 5). The subjects were randomly assigned to one treatment. After that, they were given task instructions and asked to fill out a paper-based questionnaire (Hack & Lammers, 2011) with the adjusted scenario from Arkes et al. (2008). Subjects were then instructed to make a decision according to their spontaneous judgments without making any mental calculations.

5.5.2 Analysis and results

The *loss control treatment* aimed to test whether there are any significant differences in the way of conducting this study or in the subject pool in comparison with Arkes et al. (2008). I predicted that there would be no such differences. In the *loss control treatment*, a downward movement in the stock price to 20.11 € would on average cause the same sadness as the previous month's price decrease to 24 €. Given equation (1) and an unchanged prospect value function (Hack & Lammers, 2011), the adaptation of reference point is –3.89 € ($P^* - P_1$ = 20.11 € – 24 €) and the new reference point is 26.11 €.

Comparing these results with those of Arkes et al. (2008), the mean reported price was 21.49 $ with 18.44 percent indicating a price equal to or below 18 $, 7.80 percent between 18 $ and 20 $, 26.95 percent equal to 20 $, and 46.8 percent above 20 $. Using the Kolmogorov-Smirnov test, a comparison of the differences in both the location and the shape of the distribution of the two samples shows that the two data sets are not significantly different ($Z = 0.483$, $p = .49$). Hence, the results are consistent with those of Arkes et al. (2008) for painful events. Any differences in the experimental treatments should therefore stem from the differences in expectations given and not from differences in my way of conducting the study or differences in the subject pool.

As in the gain scenario, the *loss base treatment* incorporates explicit expectations into the loss control scenario. These treatments are designed to test the feasibility of the extended experimental design. Table 6 contains the distributions and means by subject of the *loss control* and *loss base treatments*. The hypothesized value of future stock prices in the *loss control treatment* (20.11 €) shows no significant differences from the mean reported stock prices in the *loss base treatment* (19.82 €) (Mann-Whitney U-test (MWUt) = 4169.50; $p = .965$). This study indicates that with 4.18 €, adaptation in the *loss base treatment* exceeds that in the *loss control treatment* slightly by 0.32 €.

Table 6: Distribution of the reported prices for the loss control and loss base treatments

	Loss scenario *Loss control treatment*	Loss scenario *Loss base treatment*
Price	Frequency	Frequency
P < 18 €	12	14
P = 18 €	16	14
18 € < p < 20 €	16	11
P = 20 €	15	13
20 € < p < 24 €	9	16
P = 24 €	22	19
24 € < p < 30 €	3	3
Total	93	90

Table 7: Distribution of the reported prices for the loss high and loss low treatments

	Loss scenario *Loss high treatment*	Loss scenario *Loss low treatment*
Price	**Frequency**	**Frequency**
P < 18 €	8	22
P = 18 €	12	22
18 € < p < 20 €	11	13
P = 20 €	18	15
20 € < p < 24 €	13	9
P = 24 €	19	8
24 € < p < 30 €	12	1
Total	93	90

The role of expectations in reference point adaptation was then examined by conducting a *low* and a *high treatment*. I expected to find that expectations had a significant impact on reference point adaptation in the *loss high* and *loss low treatments*. In the *loss high treatment,* a price range from 15 € to 35 € with an expected price of 25 € and in the *loss low treatment* from 5 € to 25 € with an expected price of 15 € was offered. If expectations play a role in the adaptation of reference points, then reference point adaptation for the *loss high treatment* should be lower compared with the *loss control* and *loss base treatments* when expectations are higher (prediction 3a). In the opposite case, when expectations are lower, the adaptation of reference points for the *loss low treatment* should be greater compared with the *loss control* and *loss base treatments* (prediction 3b). Table 7 contains the distributions and means by subject for the *loss high* and *loss low treatments*.

The average answer to the *loss high treatment* was 21.65 €, which indicates a reference point adaptation of 2.35 €. The average answer to the *loss low treatment* was 18.10 €, which indicates a reference point adaptation of 5.9 €. As predicted, participants on average reported higher prices if the expected value is higher than the adaptation information contained in the current status quo. Participants on average reported lower prices if the expected value is lower than the adaptation information contained in the current status quo. According to Hack and Lammers (2011), the statistical comparisons of means show significant differences both between the *loss control* and *loss high treatments* (MWUt = 3622.20; $p = .012$) as well as between the *loss control* and *loss low treatments* (MWUt = 3055.50; $p < .0001$). Comparisons between the *loss base* and *loss high treatments* (MWUt = 3537.00; $p = .015$) as well as the *loss base* and *loss low treatments* (MWUt = 2988.00; $p < .0001$) are equally significant. Therefore, predictions 3a and 3b were confirmed. To consider all four treatments simultaneously, a one-way ANOVA was conducted. The results confirm the predicted role of expectations on reference point adaptation at a significant level ($F = 8.660$, $p < .0001$). The investigated treatments in the domain of gains from Hack and Lammers (2011) also correspond to these results. Further, the statistical comparisons of the means reported similarly high significance levels between the different treatments for attractive events.

Furthermore, I predicted that the magnitude of reference point adaptation after gains is significantly greater than after losses in all scenarios. Table 8 shows the mean adaptation for each of the four scenarios in the domains of gains and losses (Hack & Lammers, 2011). The results of each scenario in the domains of gains and losses were compared with the t-test for independent samples and with a level of significance of $p < .0001$ for each scenario. To consider all four treatments in the domains of gains and losses, an ANOVA was conducted. The results confirm the predicted difference on the adaptation of reference points at a significant level ($F = 6015.89$, $p < .0001$).

Moreover, I assumed in prediction 5 that the impact of expectations on the magnitude of reference point adaptation in the *loss base* to *loss high treatments* is smaller compared with that in the *loss base* to *loss low treatments.* Table 8 shows the differences in the magnitude of reference point adaptation. When comparing the *loss base treatment* with the *loss high treatment*, information on the higher expected outcomes yields a deemphasized adaptation of 1.83 (2.35 € – 4.18 €). By contrast, information on the lower expected outcomes (*loss low treatment*) provokes a higher adaptation of 1.72 € (5.9 € – 4.18 €) (Table 8). An ANOVA on the squared differences in reference point adaptation confirms the

Table 8: Mean reported prices and reference point adaptation

	Gain scenario			Loss scenario		
Treatment	N	Mean reported price (€)	Reference point adaptation (€)	n	Mean reported price (€)	Reference point adaptation (€)
Control treatment	64	41.12	5.12	93	20.11	3.89
Base treatment	68	41.69	5.69	90	19.82	4.18
High treatment	70	43.88	7.89	93	21.65	2.35
Low treatment	64	40.09	4.09	90	18.10	5.90

differences at a significant level ($F = 16.1667$; $p = .0002$). The influence of expectations on the adaptation of reference points is consequently stronger for expected gains than for expected losses. Hence, I also found support for prediction 5. Moreover, this finding is also consistent with the results of Arkes et al. (2008) regarding changes in the recent status quo (recent stock price). In addition, it is comparable with the results of Hack and Lammers (2011) for attractive events. Both found that adaptation after gains is greater than after losses.

5.6 Discussion

In summary, the experimental results of this study confirm all initial predictions. In the following, I discuss the findings. Similar to Arkes et al. (2008), an asymmetric magnitude of reference point adaptation to gains and losses was found. However, the present study is the first to explore the role of expectations in the adaptation of reference points in the domain of losses and found significant differences between the extent of reference point adaptation in the domains of gains and losses. Interestingly, by comparing all investigated scenarios it can be shown that individuals adapt their reference points less strongly in the domain of losses than that of gains. The magnitude of mean reference point adaptation after gains is not only significantly higher than after losses, but it also results in lower outcomes compared with the domain of losses. For instance, Hack and Lammers

(2011) indicated a slightly exceeded adaptation in the *gain control* to *gain base treatments* of 0.57 €. I detect an adaptation only by 0.29 € in the domain of losses. To conclude, the adaptation after gains is greater than after losses even though expectations are present.

The question remains why this study finds an adaptation in the domain of losses. Drawing upon the theory of the hedonic maximizer (1980, 1985), no adaptation in the domain of losses should occur. Given the convex shape of the value function and the principles of hedonic framing, individuals should integrate losses (Thaler, 1999). However, in contrast to the hedonic editing hypothesis, Thaler and Johnson (1990), Linville and Fischer (1991) and Arkes et al. (2008) did not find a full integration of losses. However, the literature discusses a quasi-hedonic editing hypothesis for framings, which considers prior losses as in my scenario in this study. Initial losses might increase risk aversion (Thaler & Johnson, 1990), which leads to minor reference point adaptation. Moreover, Thaler (1999) described that individuals experience losses one by one, making them more sensitive to the next. These effects should be supported by disappointment theory,[30] which also helps explain the different rates of adaptation between gains and losses.

The anticipated role of disappointment in decision making was first formalized independently by Bell (1985) and Loomes and Sugden (1986).[31] In these theories, decisions are partly based on the tendency to make choices that minimize future disappointment (disappointment aversion). Consequently, an individual compares the outcomes within a given prospect, giving rise to the possibility of disappointment (elation) when the outcome compares unfavorably (favorably) with what it might have been. Therefore, individuals make decisions that are less likely to lead to a feeling of disappointment. If individuals partly adapt to the first loss, then they might assess the outcome more often as a gain, because they will have more often higher (negative) reference points compared with the actual outcome. The lower (negative) outcome is then perceived as a gain (see explanation for R^e_1 in chapter 5.2). Thus, according to disappointment

30 Schimmack and Diener (1997) showed that disappointment is the most negative emotion. In addition, Weiner and Lerman (1979) found that disappointment is one of the most frequently experienced emotions.

31 There is a lot of empirical evidence that supports this assumption in the psychological literature (Van Dijk & Van der Pligt, 1996; Zeelenberg et al., 2002; Van Dijk et al., 2003).

aversion, individuals adapt to the first loss in the domain of losses to find themselves more often in the domain of gains. The disappointment effect is especially expected in the *loss high treatment*, as based on the expected outcomes in this treatment a gain is more likely to occur. Following prospect theory, individuals in the gain domain behave in a more risk-averse manner. This is also observable in the magnitude of reference point adaptation. Reference point adaptation in the *loss high treatment* was 1.83 €, while it was 1.7 2 € in the *loss low treatment*. The greater adaptation in the *loss high treatment* proves the more risk-averse behavior of participants. This new additional substantiation of only partly integrated losses also completes the argumentation of Arkes et al. (2008). The authors deemed that the tug of reality may increase the degree of reference point adaptation in the domain of losses. This sense of reality is allegeable through disappointment aversion, so that individuals take into account the current price to some extent.

These findings are also explainable by the "hot hand effect" (Croson & Sundali, 2005). Experimental studies have shown that individuals who won/lost a higher amount of money in a first lottery believe in a run of good luck/bad luck. Hence, individuals might believe that losing money in the first period might predict a continuation of bad luck, even if facing random sequences (Gilovich et al., 1985). This cold hand is often described as a belief in the negative serial autocorrelation of a non-autocorrelated series (Croson & Sundali, 2005), which results in risk-averse behavior. Following the explanation above, individuals show risk-averse behavior when the decision outcome is perceived as a gain. In this case, individuals partly adapt to the first loss to find themselves more often in the domain of gains. The cold hand effect is also expected to occur more likely in the *loss high treatment*, as based on the expected outcomes in the *loss low treatment* a gain is less likely to occur.

Besides the abovementioned effects on decision making, other biases support the integration and segregation of losses. For instance, the (1) sunk cost effect (Arkes & Blumer, 1985), (2) disposition effect (Shefrin & Statman, 1985), or (3) escalation of commitment (Staw, 1981) may explain the inability of people to segregate losses from the consideration of future prospects. Prelec and Loewenstein (1998) showed that closing an account in the "red" produces immediate misery. Following the disposition effect, the consequence of this is keeping the prior account open, which is consistent with the integration of losses. Moreover, some framings support the integration of losses. In the case of prior gains, and losses that are smaller than the original gain, these gains can be integrated with the prior loss, thus mitigating the influence of loss aversion (house money effect; Thaler & Johnson, 1990).

Framings that offer the opportunity to return to the original reference of break-even (Kahneman & Tversky, 1979) have a positive impact on integration as well. The third treatment of this study with expected expectations from 15 € to 35 € offers the opportunity to break even, because the initial stock price is 30 €. I found that subjects significantly shift reference points upward if expected values exceed the information on adaptation contained in the recent status quo, and vice versa, namely that they adapt more strongly if expected values are lower. Therefore, besides the present expectations, the break-even effect could additionally support the smaller adaptation seen in the third treatment compared with the fourth.

Otherwise, as already discussed, framings may explain segregation in the domain of losses. Individuals will assess outcomes contingent on hedonic framing. If prior losses are present (loss framing), this initial loss seems to increase risk aversion (Thaler & Johnson, 1990). Therefore, loss aversion is even more important than prospect theory's value function suggests (Thaler, 1999).

5.7 General conclusion

The aim of the present study was to investigate the impact of expectations on reference point adaptation over time. First, this study provides additional evidence that expectations influence the adaptation of reference points for the domain of losses. Therefore, I support the results of other studies (e.g., Heath et al., 1999; Köszegi & Rabin, 2006; Post et al., 2008; Abeler et al., 2011), namely when expectations are present it is not sufficient to equate the reference point, for instance, with the current status quo (Hack & Lammers, 2011). Second, I was able to show significant differences between the extent of reference point adaptation following attractive events (gains) and painful events (losses) in the consideration of expectations. Similar to the gain scenario (Hack & Lammers, 2011), the expected price ranges have a significant impact on the degree of reference point adaptation. However, the degree of the adaptation of reference points caused by expectations has not yet been explored in the reference-dependent preferences literature.

To sum up, this study has not only shown what constitutes a reference point and that reference points are adapted over time, but it has also indicated – for the first time – the magnitude of reference point adaptation because of expectations in the domain of losses. The extent of adaptation in the domains of gains and losses has also been discussed. This explicit consideration of differences through the asymmetric information process in the domains of gains and losses is lacking in many previous studies of reference dependency. Moreover, I present disappointment effects as an additional explanation of the segregation of losses besides the quasi-hedonic editing hypothesis of mental accounting.

The results complement the insights provided by previous studies. For instance, the assumption that expectations serve as reference points has already been applied by studies in other fields of research such as behavioral operation management. Ho et al. (2010) incorporated reference dependence into the newsvendor framework by assuming that psychological aversion to leftovers is greater than the disutility for stock outs. Expected demand serves as a reference point by which the manager evaluates the effectiveness of his or her order decisions. Hence, the findings of this study help improve order decisions by estimating the degree of reference point adaptation and evaluating accordingly a person's outcome of choice.

Nevertheless, there are some limitations to this study. For instance, the advantage of the applied method is its direct measurement of reference point adaptation. However, the hypothetical questionnaire study suggests that student's choices have no monetary consequences, which may lead to unrealistic answers being provided. Furthermore, the explanations of risk behavior (setting higher reference points leads to more risk-averse behavior) are based on prospect theory and not on the directly tested risk propensity of individuals. In addition, this study assumes the given equation and an unchanged value function. The observed results would not be validated if these assumptions were incorrect. Moreover, the results were not obtained under a variety of circumstances. However, Arkes et al. (2008) considered whether their results would hold in different settings. Similar results were observed including several questionnaire studies, investigations using financial incentives, and scenarios that included portfolios as well as individual stocks.

Besides dealing with the limitations of this study, the reference dependence literature in general needs further research. Below are just some of the unanswered questions on the reference point adaptation process. Since reference point updating is still an under-researched field in behavioral economics, there are important future research directions worth considering. This study can be seen as the first step in the investigation of the impact of expectations in the adaptation process of reference points. For further studies, it would be interesting to apply this study's approach in the field. Moreover, the results should be considered to be applicable not only in situations of monetary comparisons but also in situations such as advancements in key workplace attributes (Georgellis et al., 2008) or general life quality.

A further open field of research is the impact of interactions between several mental accounts. Only recently, Baucells et al. (2011) provided a model of reference point adaptation where multiple references are visible during the process. However, Kahneman (1992) called for attention to the multiplicity of relevant reference points and the gap in behavioral decision research. Because situations involving multiple reference points are abundant (e.g., Baucells et al., 2011), there is a strong need for further research into the impact of multiple reference points on the magnitude of adaptation.

6 Second experimental study: Personality traits and their influence on reference point formation in the domains of gains and losses

6.1 Introduction

A reference point is an essential element of prospect theory, and there is a great deal of evidence that it plays an important role in a person's evaluation of the outcome of choice (Hack & Lammers, 2011).[32] In different research fields, reference dependency has been employed to describe risk attitudes that are inconsistent with expected utility theory, such as the framing effect[33] (Tversky & Kahneman, 1981), endowment effect (Thaler, 1980), status quo bias (Samuelson & Zeckhauser, 1988), default preferences (Johnson et al., 1993), and disposition effect (Shefrin & Statman, 1985; Odean, 1998; Weber & Camerer, 1998; Genesove & Mayer, 2001; Grinblatt & Keloharju, 2001; Dhar & Zhu, 2006).

In spite of the important role of prospect theory in economics, the literature examining the reference point is relatively new. This literature has encompassed the following aspects: factors that constitute the reference point (Heath et al., 1999; Bolton & Ockenfels, 2000; Hoeffler et al., 2006; Köszegi & Rabin, 2007), how individuals adapt their reference points dynamically (Chen & Rao, 2002; Gneezy, 2005; Hoeffler et al., 2006; Arkes et al., 2008, Abeler, 2011), and the conditions that influence adaptation. For instance, research has examined intergenerational and emotional differences in the formation and adaptation of reference points. Kume and Suzuki (2010) investigated age and generational differences and found that older subjects tend to update their reference points after gains, whereas younger subjects tend to keep the initial reference points through-

---

32 For summaries, see Harless and Camerer (1994), Luce and von Winterfeldt (1994), and Starmer (2000).

33 For the framing effect, see also Kahneman and Tversky (1984), Tversky and Kahneman (1991), Loewenstein and Prelec (1993), and Bateman et al. (1997).

out repeated experiments. Further, Arkes et al. (2010) pointed out cross-cultural differences in reference point adaptation from individuals in China, Korea, and the US. Moreover, some authors have highlighted the importance of emotions in the formation of reference points (Read, 2002; Heyman et al., 2004; Mercer, 2005).

The central purpose of this research study is to provide a deeper understanding of individual factors that might determine reference point formation. In particular, the aim is to examine whether differences in personality influence reference point adaptation. Moreover, this study considers differentiations that might occur in the domains of gains and losses.

To my knowledge, the influence of personality differences on reference point adaptation has not yet been examined in the literature. So far, only the risk-taking literature have aimed to link personality concepts to risk-taking. Risk-taking is an important form of human behavior that has been the subject of numerous investigations and scholarly analyses (Slovic et al., 1988; Byrnes, 1998). It can be measured by risk propensity, risk perception, or reference point adaptation. Studies have already investigated the impact of personality traits on risk propensity and perception, but no study has considered their influence on reference point adaptation. Baucells et al. (2007, p. 31) raised this issue: "personality traits (…) could enhance our understanding of individual formation and updating rules."

It should be noted that while no studies have directly measured the influence of personality traits on reference point adaptation, some have measured the influence of framing or loss aversion. For instance, McElroy et al. (2007) investigated how individual aspects influence the imposition and subsequent processing of negatively or positively framed decision tasks. Levin et al. (2002) ascertained that personality influences risky-choice framing, while Pope and Schweitzer (2011) found that overconfidence and nervousness do not determine loss aversion.

This study examines the effects of personality traits on reference point formation and asks whether differences in the domains of gains and losses occur. The research provides evidence for asymmetric information processing in the probability and utilities for gains and losses (Kahneman & Tversky, 1979; Tversky & Kahneman, 1992; Weber, 1994). Furthermore, Tversky and Kahneman (1981, p. 453) pointed out that "The frame that a decision-maker adopts is controlled partially by the formation of the problem and partly by the norms, habits, and personal characteristics of the decision-maker." Within the scope of this study, these effects are of special interest. The location of the reference point affects the coding of outcomes as gains and losses. This coding, in turn, affects preferences because of individual differences in the evaluation of positive and negative outcomes.

The aim of this study is thus to examine the influence of personality traits on reference point adaptation. As a first step in this direction, I discuss and test selected personality traits that might affect the formation of reference points by considering the traits need for achievement, optimism, and self-esteem as well as three of the Big-Five model (e.g., Digman, 1990; Costa & McCrae, 1992): neuroticism, openness to experiences, and conscientiousness. I take need for achievement and optimism into account because prior research has shown that these traits are related to goals and expectations. It has been argued that goals and expectations play an important role in the formation of reference points (Camerer et al., 1997; Heath et al., 1999; Köszegi & Rabin, 2006). Moreover, these factors are related to traits that refer to target-oriented actions. Furthermore, in the self-concepts part of personality psychology, the trait of self-esteem is one of the most popular intrapersonal psychological aspects of self-justified interest (Crocker & Wolfe, 2001). I assume that individuals aim to cause or avoid outcomes or upcoming events that would have, respectively, a positive or negative impact on their evaluations of their own worth. Therefore, I presume an influence on reference point-dependent preferences. I also take the traits of neuroticism, openness to experiences, and conscientiousness into account. Studies have shown that the Big-Five model is related to decision making across a variety of contexts, attitudes, behaviors, and phenomena (Barrick & Mount, 1991; Saulsman & Page, 2004; Deck et al., 2008; Malouff et al., 2006). With respect to the Big-Five traits, agreeableness and extraversion are not considered in this study. The trait of agreeableness[34] describes interpersonal behavior with respect to relationships with and the manner of other individuals (Costa & McCrae, 1992). However, this study aims to investigate the intrapersonal way of reference

[34] The trait of agreeableness is characterized by altruism, nurture, trust, straightforwardness, tolerance, forgivingness, compliance, and generosity (Goldberg, 1981; Hogan, 1983; McCrae & Costa, 1985).

point adaptation. Moreover, extraversion[35] describes the behavior of extraverted people in connection with optimism (Marshall et al., 1992). This behavior could cause the setting of higher reference points. However, on the opposite side of the spectrum, introverted subjects are not unhappy or pessimistic (Marshall et al., 1992; Mroczek et al., 1993). Therefore, no influence on the formation of reference points is assumed.

The questionnaire study shows that individuals who have a high need for achievement set significantly higher reference points in the domain of gains compared with individuals with a lower need for achievement. Additionally, it is demonstrated that in the domain of gains, optimists set higher reference points, whereas in the domain of losses, they adapt their reference points to a lower extent. Moreover, it is shown that in the domain of losses, low self-esteem individuals adapt their reference points to a lower extent than high self-esteem individuals. Finally, it is shown that individuals with a strong openness to experiences adapt their reference points in the domain of losses significantly stronger than individuals with a lower openness to experiences.

The remainder of this article is organized into six chapters. Chapter 6.2 discusses the methods for measuring reference point adaptation. Chapter 6.3 examines selected personality traits and formulates the hypotheses for the domains of gains and losses. Chapter 6.4 describes the sample and setting and explains how the variables have been operationalized. It also presents the results. Chapters 6.5 and 6.6 provide concluding comments.

6.2 Measuring reference point adaptation

To study the effect of personality traits on reference point adaptation, I need to be able to measure how reference points adapt over time. This study draws upon a recent approach developed by Arkes et al. (2008), in which subjects answered questions about a hypothetical stock trading scenario. This approach allows for the examination of the magnitude of reference point adaptation after a gain and a loss, and it is thus the focal point of this study.

---

[35] Extraversion (Eysenck, 1973) underlies traits such as sociability, activity, a tendency to experience positive emotions such as joy and pleasure (Barrick & Mount, 1991, Costa & McCrae, 1992), and a linkage to sensation seeking (Zuckerman, 1971).

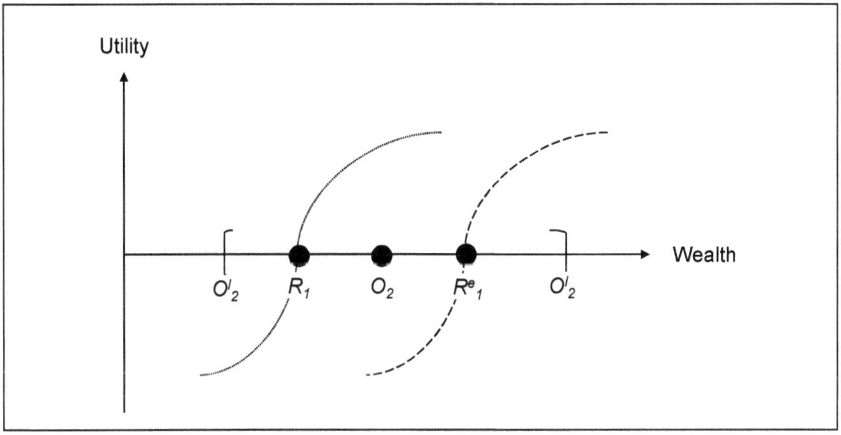

Figure 4: S-shaped value function with different reference points and impacts on the gain/loss region

In the approach by Arkes et al. (2008), subjects read the following scenario for the gain (loss) domain: "Two months ago, you bought a stock for 30 € per share. One month ago, you were delighted (disappointed) to learn the stock was trading higher (lower) – at 36 € (24 €) per share. This month, you decide to check the stock's price again. At what price would the stock need to trade today to make you just as happy (sad) with the stock's price this month as you were when you learned that the stock had risen (dropped) from 30 € to 36 € (24 €) last month?" After reading the scenario, subjects were asked to indicate the stock price that would generate the same utility as the previous price increase (decrease).

In the context of prospect theory, the value function remains unchanged; the distance between the indicated stock price and the new reference point must be equal to the distance between the prior stock price and the old reference point. Therefore, this model provides a measurement to ascertain reference point adaptation in the domains of losses and gains. Figure 4 illustrates this relationship.

At $t = 1$, one person has a lower reference point (Ra_1) compared with another person (Rb_1). At $t = 2$, an outcome will occur with a distribution between O^l_2 and O^h_2. Furthermore, there exist some actual outcomes O_2 that are perceived by the first individual (Ra_1) as a gain and by the second individual as a loss (Rb_1). Hence, individuals who set higher reference points (Rb_1) find themselves more often in the domain of losses and so will behave in a manner that is more risk-seeking. This behavior has been observed in experimental settings (Heath et al., 1999). However, in contrast to the gain scenario, the location of reference points would create the effect that people with higher reference points in the domain of losses find themselves more often in the domain of gains. In this example, the outcome O_2 is perceived as a loss by the first individual (now Rb_1) and as a gain by the second individual (now Ra_1).

Comparing reference point adaptation in the domains of gains and losses, the curvature of the value function allowed Arkes et al. (2008) to formulate some predictions. Following a gain, a hedonic maximizer (Thaler, 1999) might adapt the reference point closer to the new level of wealth. More specifically, in this way the gain will be enjoyed most. This result is because of the concave shape of the value function in the domain of gains. By contrast, after a loss, a hedonic maximizer does not adapt its reference point to the first loss. Thus, the migration of reference points towards the first loss will be more painful than would be the case if the status quo reference point were maintained.

In this setting, Arkes et al. (2008) found that the size of reference point adaptation after gains tends to be greater than after losses. As mentioned above, they hypothesized that the greater adaptation to gains than to losses is related to hedonic maximization (Tversky & Kahneman, 1981; Thaler, 1985, 1989), which explains the tendency to segregate intertemporal gains and integrate intertemporal losses. If the hedonic consideration were the only factor underlying reference point adaptation, individuals would never adapt to losses, but only to gains. Thus, Arkes et al. (2008) argued that in the domain of gains, adaptation is also impacted by the maximization of the likelihood that future prospects are in the gain domain. In addition, a sense of reality may force individuals to take into account the current price, to some extent, which would increase the degree of reference point adaptation.

I assume that the personality of an individual defines the maximization of the likelihood in the domain of gains as well as the perception of the sense of reality in the domain of losses. Moreover, it is hypothesized that the sense of reality to losses is determined by the avoidance of disappointment. Disappointment theory (Bell, 1985; Loomes & Sugden, 1986) deals with the notion that people consider risks to be a disappointment when the outcome is not evaluated as positively as expected (Delquié & Cillo, 2006). Therefore, individuals tend to make decisions that are less likely to lead to a feeling of disappointment. This suggests that individuals set reference points that are then compared with the actual outcome of a decision situation perceived as a gain. In the domain of losses, this would lead to setting higher reference points, as an individual in this case would more often face an outcome below his/her reference point. The actual outcome would then be perceived as a gain and no disappointment would occur. Hence, it is assumed that disappointment aversion affects reference adaptation. The disappointment aversion effect is mainly expected to occur in the domain of losses, as in the domain of gains other effects (e.g., the segregation of gains) might overlay the disappointment aversion effect. This is because individuals do not directly face the probability of a loss as they do in the domain of losses.

6.3 Formulation of hypotheses

6.3.1 Need for achievement

Need for achievement is a motive that refers to an individual's wish to take responsibility for finding solutions to problems, mastering complex tasks, and setting ambitious goals (McClelland, 1961). Individuals with a high need for achievement scores have been described as "maintaining high standards" and "aspiring to accomplish difficult tasks" (Jackson, 1974, p. 6). Need for achievement is related to the difficulty of tasks people choose to undertake. High need achievers who are allowed to participate in the goal-setting process set more difficult goals than do low need achievers (Locke et al., 1981). Those individuals with a low need for achievement choose easy tasks, as they have a relatively stronger motive to minimize the risk of failure (McClelland & Liberman, 1949; Atkinson et al., 1960). By contrast, subjects high in need for achievement set challenging but achievable goals for themselves (Luthans, 2002).

As has been argued previously, goals can serve as reference points (Camerer et al., 1997; Heath et al., 1999). Therefore, I hypothesize that high need achievers set themselves more demanding goals and therefore evaluate the likelihood of future prospects more positively, while low need achievers set themselves lower goals to reduce the risk of failure. This predilection leads individuals with a high need for achievement to set higher reference points compared with their counterparts in the domain of gains. In the domain of losses, it is assumed that high need achievers adapt their reference points to a greater extent than individuals with a lower need for achievement because of their approach to setting challenging goals. It is also presumed that the possible effects of losses have a more pleasant impact on high need achievers, as they search for challenging tasks to master, while low need achievers perceive small losses as already too challenging.

> Hypothesis 1a:
> In the domain of gains, people with a higher need for achievement set higher reference points than people with a lower need for achievement.
>
> Hypothesis 1b:
> In the domain of losses, people with a higher need for achievement adapt reference points to a greater extent than people with a lower need for achievement.

6.3.2 Optimism

Optimism describes a person's individual expectations. Dispositional optimism is defined as a bias towards holding positive expectations across time and situations (Wrosch & Scheier, 2003). People who are dispositionally optimistic believe that, in general, their life goals will be met (Chang, 2001) and that bad things are scarce (Scheier & Carver, 1992). By contrast, dispositional pessimism refers to the tendency to expect negative outcomes in the future and the belief that bad events are caused by stable, global, and internal factors (Peterson et al., 1988). Moreover, over-optimism limits the search for information (Kaish & Gilad, 1991) and motivates a rosy forecast of the future (Kahneman & Lovallo, 1993). In summary, optimism is directly related to positive expectations (which could serve as reference points). It also has an indirect effect on goal setting because it is geared towards meeting challenging goals (Hack & Lammers, 2008).

Therefore, I hypothesize that optimistic subjects adapt their reference points to a higher level than pessimistic ones. This response is because of their tendency to overestimate the likelihood of positive outcomes, whether as a consequence of rosy forecasting or of setting more challenging goals. In the domain of losses, I hypothesize that pessimists adapt their reference points more than optimists (because the latter believe that their positive expectations will be met). As pessimists ascribe negative outcomes to internal factors, they are more anxious to avoid disappointments. This reaction, in turn, leads to stronger reference point adaptation.

Hypothesis 2a:
In the domain of gains, optimistic individuals set higher reference points than pessimistic individuals.

Hypothesis 2b:
In the domain of losses, optimistic individuals adapt their reference points to a smaller extent compared with pessimistic individuals.

6.3.3 Self-esteem

Self-esteem is one of the most important concepts for the study of personality (Crocker & Wolfe, 2001). High self-esteem individuals show, for instance, more life satisfaction (Diener, 1984; Myers & Diener, 1995) and less anxiety (Brockner, 1984; Pyszczynski & Greenberg, 1987) than low self-esteem individuals. Furthermore, high self-esteem individuals who consistently evaluate themselves positively and report optimism (Pilegge & Holtz, 1997) seem to suggest that their self-set goals should place more demands on their ability and thus be more difficult to achieve than goals set by low self-esteem individuals (Locke et al., 1981). In addition, individuals with low self-esteem are willing to accept negative feedback and reject favorable feedback (Schlenker et al., 1979; McFarlin & Blascovich, 1981). Some studies have examined how self-esteem influences decision making. For instance, McElroy et al. (2007) found significant differences between low and high self-esteem individuals in a typical loss-framing task (see the Asian disease in Tversky & Kahneman, 1981). They ascertained that low self-esteem individuals interpret ambiguous information more negatively and are risk-seeking when decisions are framed as a loss.

In consideration of the lower anxiety, higher optimism, and more demanding goals set by high self-esteem individuals, we assume that in the domain of gains the evaluation of likelihood results in significantly greater reference point adaptation compared with low self-esteem individuals. Owing to this relation in the domain of losses, we suppose that low self-esteem individuals adapt their reference points less often than their counterparts. The acceptance of negative feedback and the risk-seeking behavior of individuals who score low on self-esteem in the domain of losses may have no effect on the desire to avoid disappointment.

> Hypothesis 3a:
> In the domain of gains, high self-esteem individuals set higher reference points than low self-esteem individuals.
>
> Hypothesis 3b:
> In the domain of losses, low self-esteem individuals adapt their reference points to a smaller extent than high self-esteem individuals.

6.3.4 The constructs of the Big-Five

As mentioned, the Big-Five model[36] is one of the most commonly used personality taxonomies in the management and psychology literature. There is evidence that it subsumes the competing trait models of personality (e.g., Costa & McCrae, 1992; Gill & Hodgkinson, 2007). I consider three of the Big-Five (neuroticism, conscientiousness, and openness to experiences) to assess their influence on the formation of reference points.

Neuroticism[37] is associated with being anxious, depressed, angry, embarrassed, emotional, worried, and insecure (Barrick & Mount, 1991). The core of this scale is described by the manner in which people deal with negative emotions (Costa & McCrae, 1992). Individuals who score high on this dimension have a strong tendency towards negative emotions, particularly in the form of being worried a lot, feeling down, and frequently being tense. They are more likely to interpret ordinary situations as a threat and minor frustrations as hopelessly difficult.

I anticipate that subjects with a high score on neuroticism set lower reference points in the domain of gains than their counterparts because of their anxiety and negative emotions. In this spirit, a greater adaptation of reference points in the

---

36 Some psychologists gauge these personality constructs as higher-level traits (Lauriola & Levin, 2001), as these dimensions can be measured with high reliability and impressive validity (Digman, 1990).

37 Extraversion and neuroticism are two of the Big-Five identified by Eysenck (1947) that have existed for over 50 years.

domain of losses is expected, because they are afraid of emotions and thus more disappointment-averse.

Hypothesis 4a:
In the domain of gains, individuals who score high on neuroticism set lower reference points than individuals who score low on neuroticism.

Hypothesis 4b:
In the domain of losses, individuals who score high on neuroticism adapt their reference points to a greater extent than individuals who score low on neuroticism.

The dimension of openness to experiences is associated with being imaginative, cultured, curious, original, broad-minded, intelligent, and artistically sensitive (Barrick & Mount, 1991). This trait refers to a propensity to adjust beliefs and behaviors when exposed to new types of information or ideas (John, 1990). High openness to experiences individuals are non-dogmatic in their attitudes and values (Costa & McCrae, 1992) and flexible in their thoughts (Digman, 1990). Individuals who score high on this trait perceive accentuated negative and positive feelings. Individuals scoring low on this trait tend to be less inclined to consider alternative opinions and are more steadfast in their own beliefs (John, 1990), which makes them more likely to rely upon information that is familiar and conventional (McCrae & Costa, 1997).

In the domain of gains, I assume that individuals who score high on openness to experiences set higher reference points compared with individuals who score low on this personality dimension. Their tolerance of uncertainty and propensity to adjust beliefs and behaviors may cause a stronger belief that future prospects are in the gain domain compared with their counterparts. In the domain of losses, I presume that because of the accentuated negative or positive feelings of high-score individuals, the avoidance of disappointment leads to a significant difference in the adaptation of reference points.

Hypothesis 5a:
In the domain of gains, people with a higher openness to experiences set higher reference points than people with a lower openness to experiences.

Hypothesis 5b:
In the domain of losses, people with a higher openness to experiences adapt their references to a greater extent than people with a lower openness to experiences.

Subjects with high values of conscientiousness describe themselves as neat, accurate, organized, careful, accountable, reliable, deliberate, and conscientious (Costa & McCrae, 1992). This personality trait influences the way in which subjects regulate their impulses to achieve high levels of success through purposeful planning and persistence (Costa & McCrae, 1992; Hogan & Ones, 1997). It can be presumed that conscientious individuals are careful and deliberate and evaluate decisions based on their experiences, which reflects dependability (Hogan, 1983; Botwin & Buss, 1989; John, 1990; Barrick & Mount, 1991).

In light of these statements, it is assumed that subjects with high values of conscientiousness act consciously to achieve a high level of success. Owing to their careful acting, we presume that they set lower reference points than their counterparts with low values of conscientiousness in the domain of gains. In the domain of losses, I assume that subjects with high scores on conscientiousness adapt their reference points more than others in order to protect themselves from perceived disappointment.

Hypothesis 6a:
In the domain of gains, people who score high on conscientiousness set lower reference points than people who score low on conscientiousness.

Hypothesis 6b:
In the domain of losses, people who score high on conscientiousness adapt their reference points to a greater extent than people who score low on conscientiousness.

6.4 Study

6.4.1 Sample and setting

A total of 501 undergraduates at a large German University, who were studying economics or business administration, were asked to fill out a paper-based questionnaire, which took 15 minutes to complete. All participants filled out the questionnaire voluntarily. The mean age of students was 21. Thirty-eight percent of participants were women. Subjects were divided into two groups (subjects of the winner problem and subjects of the loser problem). The total number of respondents for each scenario is denoted by n. Each group included approximately the same number of women and men, and members of each were of the same mean age. All participants were offered the chance to win 40 movie theatre tickets.

6.4.2 Operationalization of variables

A questionnaire was constructed to measure each of the following independent factors (personality traits): need for achievement, optimism, self-esteem, neuroticism, openness to experiences, and conscientiousness. The dependent variable was reference point adaptation. There were two control variables: general risk propensity and gender. In the following discussion, each variable is described in the order in which they occurred in the questionnaire (Figure 5).

Control variables

As mentioned previously, risk-taking is a behavioral pattern conditioned by cognitive perceptions, risk propensities, and situational factors (Eysenck & Eysenck, 1977; Sitkin & Pablo, 1992). Different risk perceptions are not part of this study. To incorporate situational factors, reference point adaptation was measured. As a control variable, I focus on risk propensity in terms of a trait and as a determining factor of risk-taking behavior. Risk propensity was measured by asking about the general willingness to take risk on the harm- avoidance scale of the Jackson Personality Inventory (Jackson, 1976, 1994; Stumpf et al., 1985). This inventory is widely considered to be one of the most psychometrically sound measures of personality and is based on Murray's (1938) personality system, which has received considerable attention. The harm-avoidance scale comprises 16 true/false statements. The number of "true" answers results in a high score on harm-avoidance behavior. Reviews have shown good measurement properties for this instrument (Johnson, 1990). This scale was reliable, with α = .77. Additionally, risk propensities were measured over lotteries with known probability distributions (Schneider & Lopes, 1986). Moreover, demographic information was included in the questionnaire. Owing to low variances in the age, race, and education variables of the sample, only gender as a potential influencing factor was used in the analysis (Weber et al., 2002).

Dependent variable: Reference point adaptation

To estimate reference point adaptation, this study also employed the scenario from Arkes et al. (2008). Subjects were asked what stock price today would generate the same utility for them as a previous stock price that increased from the initial purchase price. This question allows us to calculate the magnitude of reference point adaptation under the assumptions that the purchase price serves as the initial reference point ($P_0 = R_0$) and that the value function remains stable over time. The reasoning is based on the R results. The previous change in price is based on the initial reference point R_0, resulting in utility UR_0 (P_1) at t = 1. Subjects were asked what stock price P^* at $t = 2$ would generate the same utility. For example, without a shift in the reference point, subjects would still state P_1. I am interested in the new reference point R^* with $UR^*(P^*) = UR_0(P_1)$. Under the assumption that the shape of the value function remains unchanged, the following equation holds:

$$P^* - R^* = P_1 - R_0 \rightarrow \Delta R = R^* - R_0 = P^* - P_1$$

Given this equality, we are able to derive the reference point adaptation (ΔR).

Independent variables

To assess the independent variables, self-reported measures were used to ask direct questions about behaviors and personality traits in order to easily gain

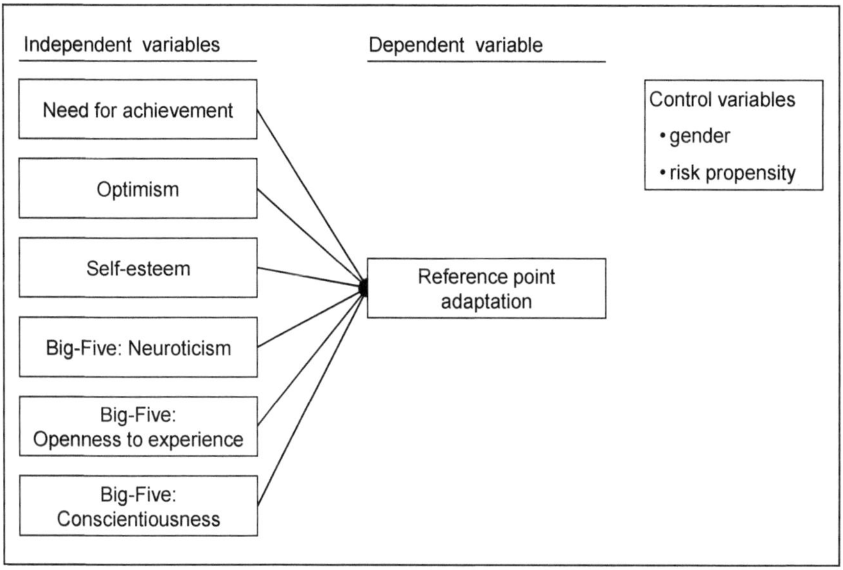

Figure 5: Study design for the domains of gains and losses

insight into a subject's personality.[38] Self-reports are generally a suitable method for studying human characteristics (Howard, 1994). Additionally, Paulhus and Vazire (2007) emphasized the practicality and efficiency of self-reported measures in obtaining data from a large number of participants at one time, as was the case in the university setting. A large number of cases in this study were desirable to improve the statistical strength of the results. Beyond that, the applicability of testing social desirability is generally debatable. Therefore, this

---

38 Many potential problems and errors could occur on the part of the respondent. Moskowitz (1986) recognized that self-reports leave a lot of room for response biases, which, according to Paulhus (1991, p. 17), involve "a systematic tendency to respond to a range of questionnaire items on some basis other than the specific item content (i.e., what the items were designed to measure)." Moreover, respondents often reply in a way that presents them in a more favorable light, even if these responses do not reflect how they actually think or behave. This socially desirable responding (Paulhus, 1991) describes the tendency of respondents to reply in a manner that will be appear to be socially suitable and acceptable by others. Despite this and other criticisms, we used – as have most others – self-reported questionnaires. More than 95 percent of the studies reported in the *Journal of Personality* in 2006 used self-report questionnaires (Kagan, 2007). In addition, studies comparing self-reports with observer ratings support the conclusion that self-image is generally accurate (McCrae & Costa, 1989, concerning the NEO Five Factor Personality Inventory).

study did not consider social desirability. However, subjects were instructed to make a decision according to their spontaneous judgments without making any mental calculations.

Big-Five model (neuroticism, openness to experiences, and conscientiousness)

To capture the Big-Five model's behavioral patterns, we reverted to the German version (Borkenaus & Ostendorf, 2008) of the NEO Five Factor Personality Inventory (Costa & McCrae, 1992). This is a 36-item questionnaire (short version) comprising 12 items representing three of the facets encompassed by the Big-Five model of personality. Respondents are required to answer each statement on a five-point Likert scale (strongly disagree to strongly agree). Higher scores on the sub-scales of the NEO represent higher levels of the named trait. The alpha reliability for testing the neuroticism scale was $\alpha = .82$, for openness to experiences it was $\alpha = .66$, and for conscientiousness it was $\alpha = .79$.

Need for achievement

The literature has extensively discussed the distinct differences between projective and self-reported measures of achievement motivation. McClelland (1972) stated that projective measures (such as the TAT) constitute the only method to accurately assess achievement motivation because it is a subconscious trait. Spangler (1992) reported the psychometric deficiencies of the TAT. For practical reasons, the German version of the need for achievement scale of the Jackson Personality Inventory (Jackson, 1976, 1994), namely the Deutsche Personality Research Form (Stumpf et al., 1985), was used. The need for achievement scale comprised 16 true/false statements. Sixteen true answers described the maximum need for achievement, and 16 false answers corresponded to a minimal need for achievement. This scale was reliable, with $\alpha = .67$.

Optimism

To deduce the optimism of participants, the German version of the Life Orientation Test (Scheier & Carver, 1985) was chosen. This test consists of eight five-point Likert-type items plus four filler items ranging from "strongly disagree" to "strongly agree." The test provides a single summary score, with high scores indicating a more optimistic orientation and low scores indicating a more pessimistic orientation. The alpha reliability for testing optimism using this scale was $\alpha = .81$.

Self-esteem

After a review of the literature, the German version (Ferring & Filipp, 1996) of Rosenberg's (1965) self-esteem scale was chosen to assess subjects' self-esteem levels. This scale[39] consists of 10 items. In a four-point Likert format, the scale for each item was presented from strongly agree to strongly disagree. The scores for the scale are obtained by adding participants' responses to the items, with higher scores indicating higher levels of self-esteem. Within the study, the scale was reliable, with $\alpha = .83$.

6.4.3 Analysis and results

Descriptive statistics for the dependent variable show that reference point adaptation following gains is greater than that following losses, as was the case in the study by Arkes et al. (2008). For the winner scenario, subjects, on average, believed that a gain of 41.71 € would give them the same pleasure as the previous month's price increase from 30 € to 36 €. Hence, I have a reference point adaptation amount of $R^* - R_0 = 5.71$ €. By contrast, the subjects regarded a loss down to 20.76 € on average to be as painful as the previous month's price decrease from 30 € to 24 €. Consequently, the reference points were adapted downward to 3.24 €. Hence, the difference between gains and losses is 2.47 € (5.71 – 3.24). Thus, my data could qualify as an adequate sample in comparison with Arkes et al. (2008).

I find that personality traits have different effects on reference point shifting depending on whether the event is represented as a gain or a loss. Personality traits are soft variables and therefore are statistically different only in the ex-

[39] Whereas some studies have shown that the scale is a valid and reliable unidimensional measure of self-esteem, others have demonstrated that Rosenberg's (1965) self-esteem scale comprises two factors: self-confidence and self-depreciation. However, investigations that used high school or college students supported the scale's unidimensionality (Crandall, 1973; McCarthy & Hoge, 1982), or obtained factors that were interdependent and had similar patterns of correlates (Rosenberg, 1979; Hagborg, 1993). Overall, enough research has accumulated to indicate that it is a powerful predictor of self-esteem in adolescents (Nunnally, 1967).

treme values of a measurable trait. I assume that the consideration of marginal areas and not the whole sample has a higher explication power.

Hence, the extreme value of a trait was examined to identity statistical differences within a group. In contrast to a median split (MacCallum et al., 2002; Dimitruk et al., 2007), merely the upper and lower thirds of the sample was used. Obviously, I lost a third of the sample and thus suffered a loss of power (Aiken & West, 1991), but this result is because of dispersions about the arithmetical average that blurred the differences.

The German version of the Personality Research Form, which is used to measure subjects' achievement motivations, is a standard nine-scale methodology (Stumpf et al., 1985). It utilizes a normalized standard score, ranging in value from 1 (very low) to 9 (very high). Its distribution has a mean of 5 and a standard deviation of 2. It places absolute values in relation to standard values according to gender and age. Using this scale, I can compare subjects who score high and well above average with those who score low or well below. For all other traits, the extreme values (e.g., very high-score and very low-score individuals in self-esteem) were used to identify statistical differences. Then, a Mann–Whitney U-test was performed, with reference point adaptation as the dependent variable and the extreme parameter values of personality traits (ordinal scaled) as independent variables. Therefore, this study was able to compare the two extreme groups of sampled data. This analysis shows that the traits of need for achievement, optimism, self-esteem, and openness to experiences differed at a significant level in the separately considered domains (Table 9).

In the domain of gains, I was able to demonstrate that individuals who score well above the average on need for achievement differ significantly in the adaptation of reference points from individuals who score well below. Individuals with a high need for achievement shift their reference points to a greater degree than others (median of individuals who score low on need for achievement: 40.37 €; median of individuals who score high in need for achievement: 41.38 €; MWUt = 774,500; p = .048). Moreover, the results show no significant differences concerning losses (low: 21.06 €; high: 20.63 €; MWUt = 2004,500; p = .324). Therefore, hypothesis 1a is supported, while hypothesis 1b is not.

Table 9: Results of Mann–Whitney U-tests on reference point adaptation

Independent Variables	Gain region		Loss Region	
	N	Mann–Whitney U	N	Mann–Whitney U
Need for achievement	164	652,500**	165	1156,000
Optimism	192	617,000**	180	537,500**
Self-esteem	110	1336,000	121	1458,500**
Neuroticism	106	1192,500	107	1225,500
Openness to experiences	138	1778,000	135	1369,000***
Conscientiousness	117	1542,500	109	1310,000

Note: p< .10; *p< .05; **p< .01, ***p< .001.

The results support hypothesis 2a. Subjects who score high on optimism adapt their reference points greater than do pessimists in the domain of gains. The Mann–Whitney U-test corroborates the hypothesized relationship at a highly significant level (pessimism: 40.95 €; optimism: 42.47 €; MWUt = 617,000; p = .05). In addition, the statistical test showed a significant relationship in the domain of losses, but no support for hypothesis 2b. In the domain of losses, optimists adapt their reference points more than pessimists (pessimism: 21.23 €; optimism: 19.51 €; MWUt = 537,500; *p* = .02).

For self-esteem, significant differences in the domains of gains and losses are assumed. I was able to find support for hypothesis 3b. In the domain of losses, low self-esteem individuals adapt their reference points significantly less than high self-esteem individuals (low: 21.31 €; high: 20.22 €; MWUt = 1458,500; p = .03). However, in the domain of gains, no significant differences occur (low: 41.00 €; high: 41.74 €; MWUt = 1336,000; p = .188).

Regarding the Big-Five model, significant differences are only found with regard to one trait – openness to experiences. I found no support for hypotheses 4a or 4b (neuroticism) or for 6a or 6b (conscientiousness). However, with regard to openness to experiences, individuals who score high adapt their reference points in the domain of losses to a greater level than individuals who score low (low: 20.88 €; high: 19.42 €; MWUt: 1369,000; p = .0006). For hypothesis 5a, I found no statistical differences (low: 41.55; high: 42,17; MWUt: 1778,000; p = .0218). Therefore, only hypothesis 5b is supported.

After controlling for risk propensity and gender, none of the control variables showed a significant relationship to the migration of reference points. The correlation matrix indicates no correlation between risk propensity and reference point adaptation (Kendall's rank correlation coefficient in the gain region: .676; in the loss region: .490). Risk propensity is an independent determining factor of risk-taking behavior with no influence on this model. The separation of the trait-induced risk propensity and situation-induced risk propensity into diverse parameters of risk-taking is in line with the literature (Miner & Raju, 2004). The Mann–Whitney U-test (gain region: 6,740,000; loss region: 6,519,500) for the control variable gender shows that both variables are independent of each other.

6.5 Discussion

In summary, this study has been able to confirm a generally weak direct effect of personality traits on reference point adaptation. Moreover, the results support the assumption that these effects differ in the domains of gains and losses.

In most cases, the hypotheses for the three traits of the Big-Five model were not confirmed. I presumed in the domain of losses that individuals who are open to experiences adapt their reference points to a greater extent than individuals who score low on this trait because of the element of feeling, which constitutes one element measured by the NEO. The trait of feeling is considered to be receptive to inner emotional states and emotional experience. As mentioned previously, individuals who score high on this trait might accentuate negative and positive feelings. Thus, in the domain of losses, these individuals might avoid losses to protect themselves from poignantly negative feelings. Other authors may refer to risk-seeking behavior by high openness to experiences individuals. However, such behavior would not affect the tendency to avoid disappointment. Consequently, openness to experiences is sufficiently related to feelings to lead to a higher adaptation of reference points.

Moreover, in this sample, the traits of neuroticism and conscientiousness do not influence the formation of reference points either in the domain of gains or in the domain of losses. The statistical differences between high- and low-score individuals in each of the Big-Five traits in relation to reference point adaptation is not significant because each Big-Five trait comprises several other personality traits. Because of the diverse factors that might influence the adaptation of reference points, a meta-level view seems not to be the right way to investigate determining factors. Further investigation should concentrate on single factors rather than on major components of psychological differences. Therefore, further studies of the influence of the Big-Five model on reference point adaptation are necessary.

Furthermore, although the results support hypothesis 1a, no support was found for hypothesis 1b. It was hypothesized that individuals high in need for achievement adapt their reference points more than individuals low in need for achievement. However, no significant difference in the magnitude of reference point adaptation in the domain of losses was observed. On one hand, owing to the tendency to minimize the risk of failure, individuals with a low need for achievement might adapt their reference points to the same extent as individuals with a high need for achievement. This tendency might be supported through the disappointment aversion effect. On the other hand, Wicker et al. (2004) found that individuals high in need for achievement reduce their goal levels when their expectations decline. To conclude, these reasons might have led to a slight adjustment in the new level of wealth for both types of individuals.

In addition, I discuss the unsupported hypothesis 2b. It was assumed that in the domain of losses, optimistic individuals adapt their reference points to a lower level than pessimistic individuals. Accordingly, this study's results show that optimistic individuals adapt their reference points to a greater extent than pessimistic individuals. Owing to the previously mentioned relationship between self-esteem and optimism (Pilegge & Holtz, 1997), I assume that the trait of self-esteem dominates the trait of optimism. Pearson's chi-square $\chi 2 = 27{,}314$ (***$p \leq 0.001$) shows a strong relationship between high- and low-score self-esteem individuals and optimistic and pessimistic individuals. Therefore, one explanation for the unconfirmed hypothesis could be that the magnitude of low-score self-esteem individuals dominates the optimism of low-score individuals.

Moreover, I point out that the hypothesis regarding self-esteem for the domain of losses is in line with the study of McElroy et al. (2007). These authors also found significant differences between low and high self-esteem individuals in a typical loss-framing task. They ascertained that low self-esteem individuals interpret ambiguous information more negatively and are risk-seeking when decisions are framed as losses. However, in the domain of gains it was assumed that high self-esteem individuals set higher reference points than low self-esteem individuals, based on their suggested higher goal setting (Locke et al., 1981). The findings of this study show that high self-esteem individuals shift their reference points to a slightly greater degree than their counterparts, but not by a significant level. This is in line with studies that have observed that high and low self-esteem individuals set equivalent goals (Korman, 1970; Hollenbeck & Brief, 1987; Tang & Sarsfield-Baldwin, 1991).

6.6 General discussion and conclusion

Despite decades of research into prospect theory, the reference point as one main determinant of this theory is still not well understood. One important field of research is the discovery of the factors that determine the location and adaptation of reference points. However, so far, there has been no empirical evidence for personality traits and their influence on reference point adaptation.

To my knowledge, this study is the first to investigate how personality traits affect the adaptation of reference points. In particular, differences in the formation of reference points are examined in the domains of gains and losses. This study shows that personality traits can influence the magnitude of reference point adaptation through their influence on maximizing the likelihood of these points in the domain of gains as well as the perception of the sense of reality in the domain of losses. Moreover, I conclude that the sense of reality to losses is determined by the avoidance of disappointment. Individuals in the loss region make decisions that are less likely to lead to a feeling of disappointment.

In the domain of gains, it has been shown that people who score high on need for achievement set significantly higher reference points. In addition, in the domain of gains optimists set higher reference points than low self-esteem individuals. Furthermore, in the domain of losses optimists adapt their reference points to a lesser extent than low self-esteem individuals. Moreover, it has been demonstrated that in the domain of losses low self-esteem individuals adapt their reference points to a lesser extent than do high self-esteem individuals. Significant evidence has thus been provided on how those who score high on openness to experiences adapt their reference points to a greater level in the domain of losses.

By contrast, I found no significant impact for the Big-Five traits of conscientiousness and neuroticism. To conclude, the relationship between global personality dimensions such as the Big-Five personality factors and reference point formation is small or negligible, whereas very specific traits such as need for achievement and optimism are determinants of reference point adaptation. Therefore, other personality traits, such as anxiousness and perceived self-efficacy, are more likely to explain the adaptation differences in reference point formation. Bandura (1997) defined self-efficacy as a cognitive dimension that reflects one's belief in one's ability to succeed in specific situations. It is a judgment of one's ability to execute given types of performances. One's sense of self-efficacy might play a major role in how one approaches goals, tasks, and challenges.

Personality traits in general seem to have a weak influence on reference point adaptation. This result could be because of the different variables that simultaneously influence reference point adaptation, such as emotions, social comparisons, cognitive efforts, different contexts and situations, age, and national origin. This result leads to further implications for reference dependence theory. Additional factors of reference point adaptation should thus be identified, weighted, and placed in a specific order of precedence to ascertain a comprehensive overview.

One limitation of this study is that subjects' decisions had no monetary consequences in a stock scenario. The advantage of this method is that it allows for the direct measurement of reference point adaptation. A method for future research could be to measure the adaptation of personality traits not in relation to a stock price change, but rather to changes in salary, advancement opportunities, or organizational change. In addition, recruiting participants outside of the university environment or from the population of undergraduates could also increase the validity of the findings. Furthermore, this sample was composed of students in Germany, who may have important cultural and/or personality differences from students in the US or other nations. Even though globalization might have led to more comparable students, more research is needed to generalize the findings.

7 Third experimental study: Managerial reference point formation: risk, affects, and ownership

7.1 Introduction

There is broad agreement that reference points play an important role in evaluation situations and in making decisions (e.g., Kahneman & Tversky, 1979; Lant, 1992; Camerer, 1998). Reference points are formed within cognitive processes (Thaler, 1999). In spite of the important role of reference points, prospect theory does not specify how information is used to form the reference point (Loewenstein, 1988). Meanwhile, theoretical/empirical studies have shown that information such as status quo (Odean, 1998; Genesove & Mayer, 2001), aspirations or goals (Kahneman & Tversky, 1979; Heath et al., 1999), and expectations (Chen & Rao, 2002; Köszegi & Rabin, 2007) determine reference points. However, several potential pieces of information such as risk have still not been considered sufficiently.

In particular, few theoretical/experimental studies have investigated the effects of the multiplicity of relevant information (Kahneman, 1992). Although situations involving visible multiple information are abundant (Baucells et al., 2011), the recent paper by Baucells et al. (2011) was the first to address this gap by experimentally estimating reference points using a student sample. They demonstrated that reference points were best estimated by a combination of the first price (historical status quo) and the last price (status quo) of a time series.

Moreover, preliminary findings suggest that information used within the reference point formation process depends on the context and relevance of information. Some papers have shown that personality traits (McElroy et al., 2007), social comparisons (Linde & Sonnemans, 2009), or cultural contexts (Arkes et al., 2010) play a role in reference point formation. Early thoughts also suggested that the characteristics of information affect reference point formation (Kahneman & Tversky, 1982; Thaler, 1999) depending on how often information arises, how easy information stages are to process, and how salient the information is.

This further suggests that information used within the reference point formation process depends on the context and relevance of information.

Affect-cognitive theory (e.g., Mitchell et al., 2003; Pennings et al., 2003; Baron, 2008; Morris et al., 2010) emphasizes that affective expressions influence the evaluation of the relevance of information. In addition to prospect theory (Kahneman & Tversky, 1982; Thaler, 1999), affect-cognition research (e.g., Mitchell et al., 2003; Pennings et al., 2003; Baron, 2008; Morris et al., 2010) has suggested that reference point formation is affected by priming and heuristic cues (Schwarz & Clore, 1983; Thaler, 1985; Chaiken et al., 1989; Forgas, 1992). However, previous studies have not yet considered how the multiplicity of information and cognitive priming affect reference point formation, neither theoretically nor empirically.

I develop my hypotheses by applying prospect theory and affect-cognition research and by using experimental survey data from family and non-family top managers in Germany. Following affect-cognition research (e.g., Forgas, 1999; Mitchell et al., 2003; Pennings et al., 2003; Baron, 2008), I assume that different cognitive interpretations and evaluations are influenced by underlying contextual situations. Specifically, this study tests two information conditions to examine context-related differences in information: the conditions in which risk is strongly influenced by affects and the conditions in which status quo is weakly influenced by affects. Therefore, I choose different groups of managers that might differ regarding their affect towards risk, but which might be similar regarding their affect towards status quo. I expect that family manager-owners (FMs) prefer to avoid risk, whereas non-family managers in family firms (NFMs) and non-family managers in public firms (PMs)[40] prefer to seek risk. Indeed, previous research has suggested, but never empirically shown, that family firms avoid risky investments and act more conservatively in order to protect family wealth (Schulze et al., 2002; Stanley, 2010).

This study makes three main contributions to the literature. First, it contributes by extending the reference dependence literature. To my knowledge, for the first time it is argued that affects may determine reference point formation. This

40 FMs are top management members of a firm that is owned and operated by a family. NFMs in family firms have been hired as professional executives. PMs are classified as professional managers who run a cooperation owned by non-related investors (Combs, 2008).

is an important conceptual contribution to obtain a more comprehensive view of reference dependence theory, as the results emphasize that even the same information and situations lead to different cognitive outcomes based on the context-related affective expressions of decision makers. Second, by contributing to answering the question on which kind of information plays a role in reference point formation, this study is the first to show empirically that risk perceptions add to the explained variance above and beyond the normal predictors of reference points. Third, it contributes to the family business literature by providing experimental evidence that FMs have lower risk preferences compared with professional executives and that these perceptions are tied to ownership.

The remainder of this study is organized as follows. Chapter 7.2 discusses the influence of affects on reference point formation and formulates hypotheses. Chapter 7.3 explains the quasi-experimental model, setting, sample, and measures, and presents the results including post-hoc tests. Chapter 7.4 concludes with a discussion and implications for research and practice. The translations of the experimental instructions can be found in the Appendix.

7.2 Theory and hypotheses

The main feature that distinguishes prospect theory from expected utility and rank-dependent utility theory is that choices are based on gains and losses compared with a reference point (Benartzi & Thaler, 1995). "The major prediction of this approach is that organizations are both risk-averse and risk-seeking, depending upon whether decision-makers perceive themselves to be in the domain of gains or losses, respectively" (Fiegenbaum et al., 1996, p. 211). This phenomenon has been confirmed in many empirical and theoretical studies (e.g., Thaler, 1980; Levin et al., 1985; Loewenstein & Kahneman, 1991), and some have included managers as subjects (e.g., Fishburn & Kochenberger, 1979; Crum et al., 1980). However, few papers have addressed how a reference point is formed (Fershtman, 1996; Köszegi & Rabin, 2006).

Individuals use a variety of heuristic procedures in order to simplify the evaluation of choices, which are likely to vary depending on the formulation of the problem as well as individuals' norms and habits (Kahneman & Tversky, 1979; Tversky & Kahneman, 1981). Specifically, some decision choices might be evaluated differently depending on the context in which the decision is made

(Tversky & Kahneman, 1986, 1992). Indeed, Loewenstein (1988, p. 213) pointed out "the influence of framing and context effects on intertemporal choices merits further investigation."

For the purpose of this study, I consider how the affect primes decision making and serves as a heuristic cue (Baron, 2008). Research stresses that affects (feelings and emotions) have a strong impact on cognition (e.g., Forgas, 1995, 2000; Isen, 2002; Baron, 2008) and that the interface is both continuous and pervasive (Baron, 2008). Theoretical concepts such as the somatic marker (Damasio, 1994), affect-as-information (Clore et al., 1994), and affect heuristic theories (Slovic et al., 1991) support the notion that individuals examine their emotional reactions within cognitive interpretations of decision problems and respond accordingly (Loewenstein et al., 2001; Baron, 2008). This effect has been proven in several studies and different settings (e.g., George & Brief, 1992; Isen, 1993; Staw & Barsade, 1993; Weiss et al., 1999; Cropanzano & Wright, 1999).

Moreover, the involvement of memory is important in this context. Each memory with the thousands of instances is weighted differently depending on its relative importance, resulting in more or less attention and reaction to an event (Morris et al., 2010). Research evidence suggests that events involving high risk and uncertainty have a powerful effect on affects and cognition and a faint effect on more certain and predictable events (Loewenstein et al., 2001; Forgas et al., 2005; Baron, 2008). Furthermore, research suggests that individuals who experience a positive affect rather tend towards a positive approach, while those who experience a negative affect rather tend towards a more negative approach of events (Bower, 1991; Baron, 2008). Accordingly, I argue that differences in positive and negative affects play an important role in reference point formation via affects.

In light of these findings, it seems crucial to include affects as a determinant in research efforts investigating reference-dependent preferences. In the following, I develop hypotheses that suggest an influence of affects on the cognitive process of reference point formation. These hypotheses are tested in the next chapter.

7.2.1 *The information: purchase price, current price, and average price*

Before I expand on the current state of the literature, I briefly review the work of Baucells et al. (2011) and restate their hypotheses. I do so to establish the validity of their findings, as their hypotheses were tested with a sample of students, whereas I utilize a sample of real-life managers. Within a multiple-period price path setting, they tested factors previously shown to influence the formation of reference points. Specifically, the purchase price, recent status quo (e.g., Chen & Rao, 2002; Arkes et al., 2008), and weighted average purchase price have also been identified as predictors (e.g., Odean, 1998; Grinblatt & Keloharju, 2001). I expect the results of this study to be consistent with the results of Baucells et al. (2011, pp. 510–511) on reference point formation. Therefore, I hypothesize:

> Replication Hypothesis 1a:
> Purchase price has a significant effect on the reference point.
>
> Replication Hypothesis 1b:
> Current price has a significant effect on the reference point.
>
> Replication Hypothesis 1c:
> Average price has a significant effect on the reference point.

7.2.2. *The information: risk*

In addition, I also argue that risk is an essential aspect of reference point formation. March and Shapira (1987, p. 1404) defined risk as "most commonly conceived as reflecting variation in the distribution of possible outcomes, their likelihoods, and their subjective values. Risk is measured by (…) the variance of the probability distribution of possible gains and losses associated with a particular alternative. (…), a risky alternative is one for which the variance is large (…). The idea of risk is embedded, of course, in the larger idea of choice as affected by the expected return of an alternative." Hence, risk is a tied factor within decision making as decision makers deal with risk by calculating their choices among alternative risk–return combinations. The anticipation and calculation of decision choices thus represents a cognitive process (Loewenstein et al., 2001).

Research provides evidence that risk has important behavioral implications (Sitkin & Pablo, 1992; Wiseman & Gómez-Mejía, 1998), as individuals show diverse decision behavior in situations under risk compared with situations without risk. The attractiveness of choice alternatives is assumed to be more negative under risk (Arrow, 1965; March & Shapira, 1987), as individuals show the tendency to ignore the probability of losses within risky decision situations, which is related to loss aversion (Kahneman & Tversky, 1982) and to regret aversion (Bell, 1983). In risky alternatives whose possible outcomes are generally poor, individuals tend to be risk-seeking, while in alternatives whose outcomes are generally rich, individuals tend to be risk-averse (Kahneman & Tversky, 1979). In addition, experimental studies have shown that different individuals see the same risk situation in different ways (Kahneman & Tversky, 1982; Wiseman et al., 2000). Furthermore, attitudes towards risk are usually guided by aspects of personality and culture (Douglas & Wildavsky, 1982), mood (Hastorf & Isen, 1982), and feelings and emotions such as anxiety, fear, and joy (Johnson & Tversky, 1983; March & Shapira, 1987). All these important facts for understanding choices in risky situations are irrelevant under certainty.

Accordingly, I argue that risk should be an influencing factor on decision making (Allais, 1953; Crouch & Wilson, 1982; March & Shapira, 1987). This leads to the assumption that risk influences the decision making process of reference price settings. Therefore, I hypothesize:

Hypothesis 2: Risk has a significant effect on reference point formation.

7.2.3 Managerial reference point formation based on affects

After hypothesizing the general factors that influence reference point formation, I now focus on the contextual moderators of the aforementioned relationships (see also Weiss & Cropanzano, 1996; Morris et al., 2010). Experiences are related to prior knowledge, beliefs, and appraisals about an event's causes and consequences (Morris et al., 2010). In a study of start-ups, Morris et al. (2010) showed that in similar contexts, assessments vary significantly for family founders and non-family founders.

Similarly, I assume that the unique characteristics of family and non-family firms differentiate FMs from NFMs as well as from PMs. Among these distinguishing factors are governance structures, stakeholders, planning time horizons, capital structures, the motives of family owners, risk proclivity, compensation systems, and intergenerational succession (Aronoff & Ward, 2000; Sirmon & Hitt, 2003). Indeed, cognitive differences between family and non-family managers have been suggested (Mitchell et al., 2003). This suggests that the cognitive interpretations of FMs, NFMs, and PMs of similar events are likely to diverge.

Studies have shown that affective expressions can be described in terms of two dimensions: a positive/negative valence dimension and an arousal dimension (Watson & Tellegen, 1985; Mano & Oliver, 1993; Morris et al., 2010). Arousal is a reflection of a person's relative emotional intensity or excitement and regulates consciousness, attention, and information processing (Morris et al., 2010). The valence dimension describes if a context is agreeable or not (Morris et al., 2010). Morris et al. (2010) showed that family and non-family managers differ in perceiving events with high states of arousal, with neutral states or a lack of arousal, and with negative, positive, and neutral valence.

While I do not expect differences in purchase price, current price, or average price, as these are likely to be similarly valenced and affected by similar states of arousal across groups, I expect differences for risk preferences by type of manager. Wiseman et al. (2000) argued that differing levels of gained experiences in firms may affect expectations regarding the magnitude and probability of loss associated with taking a particular risk. Similarly, Stanley (2010) argued that divergent managerial affective expressions lead to different risk-taking preferences.

Following Stanley's (2010) argument suggesting that divergent experience may explain differences in risk-taking behavior among family and non-family firms, this study presumes that FMs' affects towards risky events are more negative than they are for NFMs and PMs. The literature broadly agrees that family firms tend to be more risk-averse in their business decisions than non-family firms (e.g., Galve-Górriz & Sala-Fumás, 1996; McConaughy et al., 2001; Eddleston & Kellermanns, 2007). The long-term and sustainability focus of business policy (Zellweger, 2007) is a typical characteristic of family firms (Chua et al., 1999; Sirmon & Hitt, 2003; Le Breton-Miller & Miller, 2006), and is more important than growth rates or high returns on investment decisions (Tagiuri & Davis, 1992; Galve-Górriz & Sala-Fumás, 1996). Therefore, family firms are less likely to take risks because of the desire to preserve family wealth.

By contrast, investors in public firms typically accept greater risk in the hope of greater (usually short-term) returns (Garrod & Valentincic, 2004). This, in turn, leads to underinvestment in long-term projects (Hill & Snell, 1988) and to seeking capital for large-scale and high-risk projects (Harvey, 1999). Indeed, PMs have immense control over corporate resources and use their influence to direct resources towards projects that maximize managers' power, compensation, and stakeholder returns (Walsh & Seward, 1990). Accordingly, the cognitive differences between FMs and PMs should be observable regarding their reference point formation.

NFMs should also differ from FMs and PMs. NFMs are aware that family owners place a much higher importance on survival and family employment opportunities than trying to maximize profit or market returns (Athanassiou et al., 2002). NFMs tend to adopt the culture, norms, and cognitive styles of family members in order to be accepted (Mitchell et al., 2003; Morris et al., 2010), which may result in lower risk preferences of NFMs compared with PMs. However, they still evaluate risk more positively than FMs. NFMs are attracted to family firms, because of the greater degree of entrepreneurial tolerance than in public firms (Aronoff & Ward, 2000; Morris et al., 2010). Stanley (2010) argued that NFMs provide alternate perspectives about the competitive environment. This encourages more thoughtful and informed decision making with respect to risk and leads to higher risk-taking behavior than in family firms without an external professional executive. Therefore, I assume that FMs interpret risk more negatively and deal with risk more conservatively and more circumspectly than their non-family counterparts. In turn, I assume that NFMs interpret risk more positively than FMs. Accordingly, I hypothesize:

Hypothesis 3a:
PMs show higher levels of risk preferences in uncertain decision situations than NFMs. This results in higher reference point settings of PMs than of NFMs.

Hypothesis 3b:
NFMs show higher levels of risk preferences in uncertain decision situations than FMs. This results in higher reference point settings of NFMs than of FMs.

7.3 Study

7.3.1 Framework

Reference dependence theory has found its way into economic modeling (e.g., Chen & Rao, 2002; Sugden, 2003; Sagi, 2006; Köszegi & Rabin, 2006; Arkes et al., 2008; Baucells et al., 2011). However, there is no standard practice for the examination of reference points. In this study, I draw upon on the recent approach developed by Baucells et al. (2011), where a student sample answered questions about a hypothetical stock trading scenario. They estimated the reference point directly by asking subjects which selling price would make them neither happy nor unhappy after they observed a multi-period stock price path. To my knowledge, this approach is the only one that measures how the situational factors of multiple relevant information influence reference point formation.

I tested the managerial reference point formation of different types of top managers as well as the impact of risk and ownership on reference point formation by adjusting and extending the approach of Baucells et al. (2011). Participants read the following scenario:

Instruction for individual choice task (translated from German):

> "A few days ago, on day 0, you made an important investment decision for your company (e.g., acquisition of a firm or joint venture), which is essential to the survival of your firm. However, on the same day you took some time off. During you time away, you were able to monitor the development of the investment but you could neither manage it nor make decisions. Today, the day before your return to work, you once again look at the investment development since your purchase on day 0. Because you can make a decision again the next day back work, you ask yourself how you would feel if you were going to sell the investment the next day. You ask yourself at what selling price you would feel neutral about the sale of the investment, i.e., be neither happy nor unhappy.
>
> On the following screens, you will be confronted with several decision situations of this kind. You will be shown a price development chart starting from the purchase on day 0 until the day before your return. The return on investment price one day before your return is today still unknown. After the price sequence has been plotted, you will be asked to indicate at which selling price you would just feel neutral regarding the sale. Hence, I want you to indicate the selling price at which you would have neither

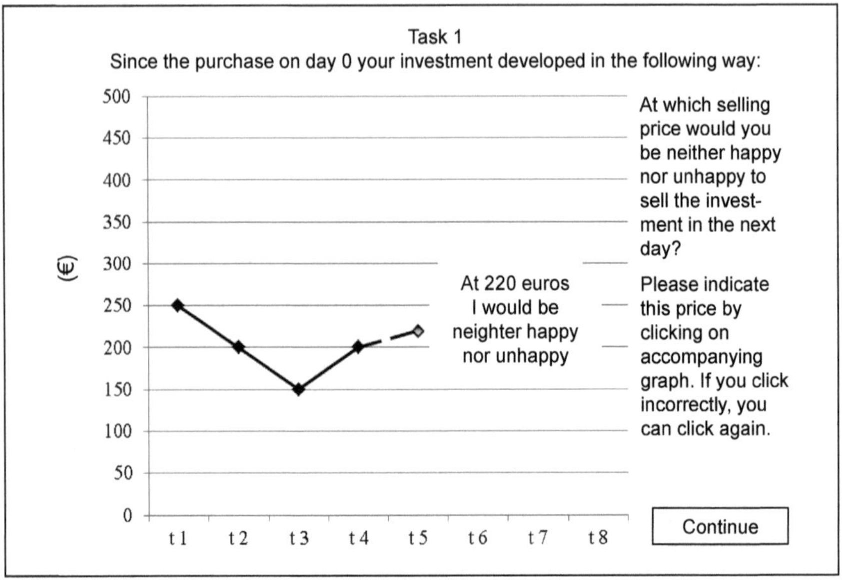

Figure 6: Translation of the price sequences on the computer screen

positive nor negative emotions about the sale of the investment. You can choose the price at which you would feel exactly neutral by clicking on the corresponding price on the graph (see Figure 6 for a translation of the price sequences on a computer screen). This task is not about your mathematical skills and there are no right or wrong answers. Instead, I ask you to estimate intuitively at which selling price you would be neither happy nor unhappy about the sale of the investment."

In my hypothetical scenario, a top manager purchases a substantial investment for his/her company in period one at price y_1. In the following periods $i = 1, 2, 3, \ldots$, the manager observes the performance of the investment and experiences feelings of gains and losses. These feelings result from a comparison of the current return on investment price, y_{n+1}, to some reference price. The reference price is the return on investment price that would produce zero experience utility ($\hat{y}_{n+1}$) at period $n + 1$. Hence, the single reference price, $r + 1$, is a function of the information observed in the past. The prospect value function with $v(0) = 0$ denoting the emotional neutrality (Kahneman et al., 1997) in period $n + 1$ is given by:

$$v\,(y_{n+1} - r_{n+1}), \quad \text{where} \quad r_{n+1} = f(y_1, y_2, \ldots, y_n).$$

Instead of a stock price scenario as in the study of Baucells et al. (2011), I chose an investment scenario, as I wanted to examine the reference prices of managers in different governance structures, which make decisions for the company and not private property decisions. Therefore, I developed a framing in which business decisions have to be taken.

I expect that these managerial reference points are price levels as I present to participants price paths. Besides the purchase price (y_1), current price (y_n), and average price ($\sum i - 1, \ldots, n\ y_{i/n}$), risk is a further factor that influences the reference price formation of managers. Risk can be measured in experimental studies by lotteries (Kahneman et al., 1982; Schneider & Lopes, 1986) or by volatility patterns (Coles et al., 2006; Fellnera & Maciejovsky, 2007). In this study, volatility refers to the standard deviation of the expected returns on an asset over a period of time. Risky assets are characterized by extreme observations and distributions of price sequences. The used multiple-period price path experiment enables authors to consider the presence of the extended factor risk. Therefore, I tested the influence of risk by comparing highly volatile price sequences with flat price sequences.

As the investigated factors are potentially highly correlated and their effects difficult to isolate, Baucells et al. (2011, p. 509) originally designed 60 price sequences in order to create 33 paired comparisons. The respective pairs for the investigated factors are identical except for one higher value for one investigated factor in one sequence. To take into account that my participants are members of top management teams in organizations, I chose only those factors and sequences that showed a significant effect and which described the reference price formation best in order to reduce the average processing time of the experiment. This results in 14 pairs that test the purchase price, current price, average price, and extended factor risk. Table 10 contains the sequences of all the price paths presented to the managers. The length varies between three and eight periods. In order to experience the feelings of gains and losses one by one, there is a three-second delay before each new price is added to the sequences, from the purchase price (left) to the current price (right). I randomized the order in which each manager saw the price sequences.

Table 10: The 22 price sequences used in the experiment

Sequences *k*	*y 1 = 1*	*y 2 = 2*	*y 3 = 3*	*y 4 = 4*	*y 5 = 5*	*y 6 = 6*	*y 7 = 7*	*y 8 = 8*	Avg. Rk			
									All	FM	NFM	PM
1	250	200	150	200					243.94	237.12	252.61	251.33
2	150	200	250	200					200.63	193.27	211.30	203.89
3	200	150	200						208.94	204.23	214.35	213.74
4	150	200	200						189.33	185.96	191.30	193.74
5	250	200	200						238.69	233.46	246.96	243.15
6	200	250	200						220.39	215.38	223.91	225.93
7	250	200	150	210	190	210	200		236.94	229.04	253.04	239.44
8	150	200	250	210	190	210	200		200.29	195.58	201.30	206.67
9	200	150	200	250					228.19	225.19	226.09	235.74
10	200	250	200	150					203.50	199.04	213.04	204.07
11	200	200	150						196.70	193.46	205.65	195.19
12	200	200	250						229.08	226.73	228.70	235.00
13	200	150	170	200	250	230			226.46	219.81	237.83	231.67
14	200	250	230	200	150	170			210.97	204.42	223.04	211.85
15	250	250	200						243.01	238.46	250.43	245.19
16	150	150	200						185.24	183.27	186.52	187.41
17	200	150	200	250	250	250	250	200	227.96	220.00	244.35	228.52
18	200	250	200	150	150	150	150	200	216.50	209.23	228.70	218.89
19	200	250	250	250	250	200	150	200	224.76	218.46	236.09	226.30
20	200	150	150	150	150	200	250	200	215.83	211.73	223.48	217.78
21	200	400	50	400	50	400	50	200	265.69	248.08	271.30	289.85
22	200	10	430	50	550	10	300	200	283.88	260.96	280.00	325.56

Notes: Columns y_i contain the ith prices of sequences. The last four columns contain the elicited reference prices (average across participants and groups). Price units are in Euros. N = 108; *FMs* n = 57; *NFMs* n = 23; *PMs* n = 28.

7.3.2 Sample and setting

I gathered all data from different mailing lists provided by a family business center affiliated with a German university, social community groups from the German equivalent to the business network community *linkedIn,* and the alumni associations of two German universities. The experiment was conducted using an online questionnaire. The questionnaire was sent to 2100 managers in May 2011. To ensure that participants in the sample were one of the three desired types of managers, they were asked: "What kind of designation is best applicable to you: family owner-manager in a family-owned firm, external manager in a family firm, external manager in a public firm, or others." A family firm was defined as one in which the members of a family have legal control and are involved in managing the firm (Mitchell et al., 2003). This study also determined whether managers identified the firm as a family firm themselves (e.g., Westhead & Cowling, 1998), whether the firm employed family members (e.g., Eddleston & Kellermanns, 2007), which family generations were involved in corporate affairs (Zahra, 2005), and in the case of FMs to which generation the participant belonged. I ensured that only executive managers in key positions were considered in the sample by asking participants which positions they occupied: CEO, member of the management board, director/senior vice president, member of the supervisory board, or others.

The study was conducted in Germany, although questionnaire items were taken from the English literature, where available, and translated into German. To ensure consistency with the original form, an independent translator back-translated these items into English. No inconsistency occurred. This study also asked subjects to indicate whether the instructions were comprehensible on a scale from 1 (very comprehensible) to 5 (barely comprehensible). The average scale value was 2.1, so I believe that subjects understood my elicitation procedure and knew what I meant with regard to emotional neutrality. The average processing time was 29 minutes. The pretest led to comparable results.

From the mailing list, 315 questionnaires were received (response rate = 15 percent). Given the highly sensitive nature of evaluation questions and the required seniority of respondents, 108 questionnaires were completed and thus useful. This response rate and the amount of missing data are, however, comparable with similar studies of family firms (e.g., Zellweger et al., 2011) and recent studies of reference point examinations (e.g., Arkes et al., 2008; Baucells et al., 2011). Because of the psychological nature of the reference point, I was not able to use variable payments. Therefore, all participants filled out the questionnaire on a voluntary basis. Respondents' average age was 43.2, 17.8 percent of whom were female. Further, the average age of firms was 86.2 years and average sales were 259,000,000 Euros.

7.3.3 Operationalization of variables

Dependent and independent variables

Similar to Baucells et al. (2011), the dependent variable was expressed by the individual reference price (*R*) for each subject s and price sequence k. This study considers four independent variables: purchase price (PP), current price (CP), and average price of price sequences *k*(AP). The extended independent variable risk (*R*) was given by the volatility index of each sequence k. Therefore, the generalized volatility was expressed by the standard deviation (σ_{SD}) of the average reference point of each sequence k and the logarithmic time period P:

$$R = \sigma_{SD}/\sqrt{P}.$$

The regression model with the error term is expressed by $e_{s,k}$:

$$Rs,k = \beta_0 + \beta_{pp}PP_k + \beta_{CP}CP_k + \beta_{AP}AP_k + \beta_r R_k + e_{s,k}$$

Control variables

In contrast to Baucells et al. (2011), this analysis controlled for a number of variables that potentially affect the relation between the dependent and independent variables. The risk of business and strategic decision processes (Fredrickson & Iaquinto, 1989) tend to vary by firm size. For instance, larger companies do not show the tendency to encourage entrepreneurial activities (Zahra, 2005). In this study, I measured firm size by the number of full-time *employees* and *sales*, both transformed by natural logarithm.

Older firms also tend to act in a more risk-averse manner (Schwer & Yucelt, 1984) and are often unwilling to change (Sathe, 2003). To control for this through long-term association, I asked for the *organization age* by measuring the years elapsed since a firm's founding, transformed by natural logarithm.

There is potential for managers to vary widely in their risk preferences by industry (Cooper & Dunkelberg, 1981; Schwer & Yucelt, 1984). In this study, I thus classified firms by industry. Participants were able to choose from eight industries (from the automotive sector to the finance sector) including “others.” This construct was measured using eight dummy codes.

Moreover, risk-taking preferences also vary by gender (DeCarlo & Lyons, 1979; Cuba et al., 1983; Carlsson et al., 2005). Hence, *gender* as a potential influencing factor was collected in the analysis. This was measured using dummy codes (woman = 1; man = 0). This study also took into account if other active *family members* in the company affect the setting of reference points. The subjects were asked, “If you are in employment in a family business, how many family members are active employees in your company?” The responses of this survey item were logarithmized.

Furthermore, I controlled for the different top management positions in a firm. It should be noted that I focus on a two-tier corporate governance model. The one-tier board model (such as in the US) is based on only one board of directors responsible for management and supervision, whereas the two-tier board model (such as in Germany) is based on a strict separation between top management and the supervisory board (Weimer & Pape, 1999; Anderson & Reeb, 2004). I thus asked participants if they were a *CEO*, *a member of management board*, *a member of supervisory board*, *a director/senior vice president,* or *other*. This was measured using four dummy codes.

This study also controlled for the *willingness to take risks* by asking participants to rate themselves on a scale of risk attitude, either in general or for specific domains of life (financial matters, career, and health) (Dohmen et al., 2005). Managers graded themselves on an 11-point scale: “How do you see yourself: Are you in general a person who takes risks or do you try to evade risks?” The grades ran from 0: “not at all prepared to take risks” to 10: “very much prepared to take risks.” This measure is a good predictor of actual risk-taking behavior, as the general risk question predicts all behaviors, whereas the standard lottery measure does not (Dohmen et al., 2005; Hack & Lammers, 2008). This scale was reliable, with $\alpha = .762$.

7.3.4 Analysis and results

In testing hypotheses 1a, 1b, 1c, and 2, I ran a binomial test (Siegel, 1956). Table 11 shows the results of the test. To interpret the table, consider the pair of sequences 1 and 2 in Table 10. The reference price in column "All" is for sequence 1 $R1$ = 243.94 and for sequence 2 $R2$ = 200.63. These sequences only vary in their purchase prices (same current price, same average price, and same lowest

Table 11: Unit effect for the pairs of sequences and p-values for all types of managers

Factors	Pairs of sequences	All	FMs	NFMs	PMs
Purchase price	1–2	0.433***	0.438***	0.413*	0.474***
	3–4	0.391***	0.365***	0.461**	0.400***
	5–6	0.372***	0.362***	0.461*	0.344**
	7–8	0.378***	0.335***	0.517***	0.328***
Current price	9–10	0.254***	0.262***	0.131*	0.317**
	11–3	0.243***	0.215***	0.174*	0.371***
	6–12	0.179**	0.227*	0.096	0.181*
	14–13	0.265***	0.256***	0.247*	0.330**
Average price	15–5	0.090**	0.101	0.079	0.049
	16–4	0.089***	0.050*	0.103	0.138
	17–18	0.238***	0.215***	0.313**	0.193*
	19–20	0.189***	0.135**	0.252	0.170
Risk	17–21	37.731***	28.077*	26.950*	61.330**
	22–19	59.125***	42.500***	43.910**	99.260***

Notes: Each entry indicates a pair of sequences $_{j\text{-}k}$, as labeled in Table 10. The unit effect represents how the change in the row factor affects $R_j - R_k$, and the p-values of the binomial test. N = 108; FMs n = 57; NFMs n = 23; PMs n = 28; p< .10; *p< .05; **p< .01, ***p< .001.

and highest price), which is higher in sequence 1 (250 vs. 150). To measure the effect that every unit increase in purchase price has on the reference price, I divided the differences in reference price, $R1 - R2 = 43.31$ by the 100 difference in the purchase price. These unit effects for each factor and pair are the data for the binomial test. The binomial test is of goodness-of-fit type, which matches the 22 reference price pairs to check if differences are significant. The reference price pair for sequence 1 and sequence 2 is matched as follows: "subject 1 sequence 1" vs. "subject 1 sequence 2," "subject 2 sequence 1" vs. "subject 2 sequence 2," etc. In line with Baucells et al. (2011), I allocated the number 1 to each individual if the reference price for sequence 1 goes beyond that for sequence 2, the number 0 if the reference price for sequence 2 goes beyond that for sequence 1, and excise the cases where both reference prices are equal. Then, it was tested whether the hypothesis that zero and one are equal is reasonable to believe or not. The column "All" of the binomial test confirms that all four factors have a significant effect on the reference price.

Means, standard deviations, and zero-order correlations of the sample for all manager groups are shown in Table 12.

A pooled OLS regression model was used, which allows us to cluster error terms by subject in order to control for the within-subjects effect (e.g., White, 1980) to estimate the effects on reference points. As the potential for multicollinearity of the independent variables may sometimes be a problem, I ran an additional test. The VIF did not exceed 1.71 for all variables. Thus, multicollinearity did not appear to be a concern (Hair et al., 2006; Tabachnick & Fidell, 1996). Estimates of the model were obtained in the STATA 11.0 program (Stata Corporation, 2003). Table 13 provides the results of the regression analysis.

I entered the control variables in Model 1, while the independent variables were entered in Model 2. Overall, the adjusted R^2 for Model 1 is .064 and the model is significant ($p < .000$). Model 2 shows that the formation of reference prices are positively and highly significantly related to the independent variables: purchase price ($p < .001$), current price ($p < .001$), and risk ($p < .001$). The independent variable average price is not significantly related to the dependent variable reference price. In Model 2, the adjusted R^2 increases to .186. Hence, adding the independent variables to the control variables explains significantly more variance ($\Delta R^2 = .123$). Thus, hypotheses 1a, b, and 2 are supported. The regression model does not confirm hypothesis 1c.

Table 12: Correlation matrix, means, and standard deviations – main model (all types of managers)

Variables	Mean	SD	1.	2.	3.	4.	5.	6.	7.	8.	9.	10.	11.	12.	13.	14.	15.	16.	17.	18.	19.	20.	21.	22.	23.	24.	25.	26.
1. Reference Price (log))	5,37	0,22																										
2. Sales (log)	18,26	2,93	.01																									
3. Employee (log)	6,17	2,56	.01	.80***																								
4. Firm Age (log)	3,98	1,13	–.10***	.45***	.55***																							
5. Gender	0,10	0,25	–.01	–.11***	–.07**	.01																						
6. Managerial Ownership (log)	1,45	1,71	.03	–.33***	–.37***	–.17***	–.01																					
7. Family members as employees (log)	0,89	0,71	–.08**	–.18***	–.23***	–.07***	–.07**	.24***																				
8. FMs	.53	.50	–.12***	–.29***	–.35***	–.12***	.08***	.77***	.45***																			
9. NFMs	0,22	.41	.06**	.02	–.07***	–.04*	–.15***	–.46***	.19***	–.55***																		
10. Position: CEO	0.13	.27	–.04*	–.17***	–.19***	–.20***	–.07**	.43***	.03	.26***	–.30***																	
11. Position: Management Board	0,28	.47	–.06**	–.18***	.05***	.30***	.35***	–.28***	–.22***	–.55***	–.38***	–.41**																
12. Position: Director	.23	.33	.07***	.30***	.41***	.18***	–.08***	–.50***	–.09***	–.55***	.12***	–.34***	–.44***															
13. Position: Supervisory Board	.06	.20	–.05**	.01	–.03	.11***	–.04*	–.01	.10***	.11***	–.01	–.15***	–.20***	–.23***														
14. Industry: Automotive	.03	.13	–.01	.07***	.11***	.03	–.08**	–.17***	–.01	–.01	–.10***	–.09***	.10***	.07***	–.06**													
15. Industry: Metal Processing	.15	.27	–.03	.34***	.45***	.29***	–19***	–.02	–.09***	–.05**	–.14***	–.05**	–.04*	.20***	–.08***	–.10***												
16. Industry: Chemical	.03	.15	0.2	–.01	–.07***	–.04	–.09***	.18***	–.11***	.12***	–.15***	.12***	–.04*	.16***	.23***	–.04*	–.11***											
17. Industry: Electronic/Mechatronic	.03	.16	–.04**	–.02	–.04*	–.00	–.03	–.24***	–.03	–.04*	–.05*	–.06**	.16***	.30***	–.02	–.02	–.05*	–.02										
18. Industry: Energy; Oil, Gas	.03	.16	.16***	–.00	–00	.01	–.07***	–.05*	–.01	–.07***	.19***	.06**	–.06**	.00	–.05**	–.03	–.08***	–.04*	–.02									
19. Industry: Commerce & consumer goods	.06	.20	–.02	.07***	–.04	.01	–.04*	.11**	.13***	.11***	–.09***	.01	.01	–.16***	–.10***	–.06**	–.16***	–.07***	–.03*	–.05**								
20. Industry: Construction	.05	.17	–.05**	–.08***	–.09***	–.03	–.00	.11***	.10***	.10***	.05*	–.03	.10***	–.19***	.18***	–.05**	–.13***	–.06**	–.03	–.05*	–.08***							
21. Industry: Transport/Logistic	.03	.13	.04	.06**	.02	–.05**	–.08***	.01	.02	–.01	.14***	–.10***	.04*	.07***	–.06**	–.04*	–.10***	–.04*	–.02	–.03	–.06**	–.05**						
22. Industry: Banking/Insurance	.06	.19	.01	–.12***	–.19***	–.08***	–.03	–.17***	–.14***	–.19***	.17***	–.06**	.14***	.14***	–.10***	–.06**	–.15***	–.07***	–.03	–.05**	–.10***	–.08***	–.06**	–.10***	–.08***			
23. Personal Trait: Risk–taking	2,00	0,25	.10***	–.10***	–.10***	–.18***	–.18***	.10***	–.20***	.03	–.05**	.16***	–.09***	.00	.11***	–.08***	–.15***	.29***	–.15***	.02	–.12***	–.24***	.03	.13***				
24. Purchase Price	196,16	30,76	,31***	.00	.00	.00	.00	.00	.00	.00	.00	.00	.00	.00	.00	.00	.00	.00	.00	.00	.00	.00	.00	.00	.00			
25. Current Price	200,00	21,30	,12***	.00	.00	.00	.00	.00	.00	.00	.00	.00	.00	.00	.00	.00	.00	.00	.00	.00	.00	.00	.00	.00	.00	,00		
26. Average Price	200,32	17,44	,23***	.00	.00	.00	.00	.00	.00	.00	.00	.00	.00	.00	.00	.00	.00	.00	.00	.00	.00	.00	.00	.00	.00	,48***	,17***	
27. Risk	2,11	0,37	,10***	.00	.00	.00	.00	.00	.00	.00	.00	.00	.00	.00	.00	.00	.00	.00	.00	.00	.00	.00	.00	.00	.00	,04*	,00	–,01

Notes: $N = 2593$, $p < .10$; $^{*}p < .05$; $^{**}p < .01$, $^{***}p < .001$

Table 13: Results of the OLS estimation for each subject and sequence - main model (all types of managers)

Variables	Model 1		Model 2	
Constant	5.267***	(.055)	5.259***	(.051)
Sales (log)	.003	(.002)	.003	(.002)
Employee (log)	.002	(.003)	.002	(.003)
Firm age (log)	-.021***	(.005)	-.021***	(.004)
Gender	.052**	(.018)	.052**	(.016)
Managerial ownership (log)	.017***	(.004)	.017***	(.004)
Family members as employees (log)	.002	(.009)	.003	(.008)
FM	-.092***	(.019)	-.092***	(.018)
NFM	-.004	(.019)	-.004	(.019)
Position: CEO	.035	(.023)	.035	(.017)
Position: Management Board	.017	(.015)	.017	(.014)
Position: Director	.041	.024)	.041	.022)
Position: Supervisory Board	.026	(.027)	.026	(.025)
Personal Trait: Risk-taking	.052**	(.019)	.052**	(.019)
IV: Purchase Price			.064***	(.004)
IV: Current Price			.027***	(.004)
IV: Average Price			.002	(.004)
IV: Risk			.020***	(.003)
R^2	.071		.194	
Adjusted R^2	.064		.186	
ΔR^2			.123	
F	9.47***		24.67***	

Notes: N = 2593; Unstandardized coefficients shown, with robust standard errors; standard errors are clustered by subject; $p < .10$; $*p < .05$; $**p < .01$, $***p < .001$.

Table 14: Unit effects – test of differences among all types of managers – risk

Factor	Pair of sequen-ces	Unit effect for pairs			Results of the independent two-sample t-test			
		Avg. FM	Avg. NFM	Avg. PM	FM vs. NFM	FM vs. PM	NFM vs. PM	FM & NFM vs. PM
Risk	1	28.077	26.950	61.330	F = 1,430	F = .485*	F = 3.235*	F = 1.326**
	2	42.500	43.910	99.260	F = 1.633	F = 8.502**	F = 1.366**	F = 6.916**

Notes: N = 108; FMs (n = 57; NFMs n = 23; PMs n = 28; p < .10; *p < .05; **p < .01, ***p < .001.

In order to circumvent the fact that the four independent variables are highly correlated, I tested if the results differ depending on the factor average price. No statistical significance changed by excluding the variables average price or risk. The relatively low adjusted R^2 is, however, comparable to other regression models of quasi-experimental settings (e.g., Mayer & Davis, 1999; Smith et al., 1990). A comparison with the data set of Baucells et al. (2011) is impossible, as their R^2 is unknown.

In testing hypotheses 3a and 3b, I ran an independent t-test to check the statistical significance among the three groups of managers. As Table 10 shows, there exist differences among the groups of managers. For instance, the average FMs' reference prices in all sequences are lower than the average NFMs and PMs' reference prices. Table 14 contains the significant results of the t-test by group.

As expected, this study did not find significant differences among the three groups of managers for the factors purchase price, current price, and average price. I found significant results for the factor risk, however. The average answers to the factor risk were for FMs 28.08 (pair 1)/42.50 (pair 2); for NFMs 26.95/43.9; and for PMs 61.33/99.26. The unit effect of PMs for pair 1 33.25 (61.33-28.08) is higher than for FMs and 34.38 (61.33-28.08) is higher than for NFMs. For pair 2, the unit effect of PMs 56.76 is higher than for FMs and 55.36 is higher than for NFMs. This results in significant differences within the groups FM vs. PM (pair one: F = .485, p = .050; pair two: F = 8.502; p = .016), NFM vs. PM (pair one: F = 3.235; p = .050; pair two: F = 1.366; p = .022), and FM & NFM vs. PM (pair one: F = .326; p = .041; pair two: F = 6.916; p = .011). Thus, volatile price sequences lead to lower unit effects for FMs as well as NFMs. This results in setting lower reference prices compared with PMs. It also means that they will find themselves more often in the domain of gains, which results in more risk-averse behavior. Nevertheless, it is important to note that the level of the average reference point for pair 1 (sequences 17–21) and pair 2 (sequences 22–19) is always higher for NFMs than for FMs. Therefore, NFMs' reference prices are higher than FMs' reference prices. Hence, I found support for hypotheses 3a and 3b.

7.3.5 *Post-hoc tests*

I next conducted multiple post-hoc tests to consider the possibility of non-response bias. This concerns whether late respondents are more similar to non-respondents than they are early respondents (Chrisman et al., 2004; Oppenheim, 1966; Zellweger et al., 2011). Therefore, this study compared the data yielded from early and late respondents using ANOVA. No statistically significant differences were found in either sample for any of the variables analyzed in this study, which at least partially reduces non-response concerns.

I also conducted a post-hoc test to find out whether the level of *family manager-ownership* interacted with the independent variables to influence reference point formation. Emotional experience may run deep in family firms (Kellermanns & Eddleston, 2004), which is particularly true for the factor family ownership. Family ownership is related not only to financial aspects, but also to non-financial aspects such as socioemotional wealth (Gómez-Mejía et al., 2007; Zellweger et al., 2011), which only occurs in a family context. In family research, socioemotional or emotional wealth (Zellweger & Astrachan, 2008) refers to aspects that include the ability to exercise authority (Schulze et al., 2003), perpetuation of family values through the firm (Handler, 1990), preservation of the family dynasty (Casson, 1999), conversion of the family firm's social capital and status (Arregle et al., 2007; Zellweger & Astrachan, 2008), and fulfillment of family obligations based on blood ties (Athanassiou et al., 2002). Losing this socioemotional wealth would result in lost intimacy and status or a failure to meet the family's expectations (Gómez-Mejía et al., 2007). It is assumed that depending on the percentage of family ownership, there is a diverse range of distinguishing experiences for family-owners. The greater the proportion of a family firm owned by a FM, the less intense is the influence of arousal and valence dimension through family members and the less affective expressions are influenced by experiences with the family. With an increasing degree of ownership, the family owner-manager will act more like a business founder without a family (Morris et al., 2010). As a majority shareholder, he/she does not have to deal with sibling rivalry and identity conflicts among family members (Eddleston & Kellermanns, 2007). At the same time, founders act like entrepreneurs (Daily & Dollinger, 1992; Astrachan & Shanker, 2003). Hence, high ownership is an encouraging environment for entrepreneurial activities (Aldrich & Cliff, 2003; Rogoff & Heck, 2003). By contrast, the lower the percentage of a family firm owned by a FM, the more intense are the affective expressions based on gathered experiences within the family context. These differences in experiences should, following the discussion above, have important implications for their affective expressions and thus for their reference point formation.

Specifically, being an entrepreneur means making less risk-averse decisions compared with other managers (Knight, 1921; Kihlstrom & Laffont, 1979; Stewart & Roth, 2001; Cramer et al., 2002). Entrepreneurs prefer creative activities and an innovative combination of resources for profit (Carland et al., 1984). Hack and Lammers (2008) found that entrepreneurs set a higher reference point on average than other individuals. With a higher reference point and a given distribution of outcomes, outcomes are thus more likely in the loss domain compared with the reference point. Based on prospect theory (Kahneman & Tversky, 1979), people in a loss situation will show more risk-seeking behavior than others. This suggests increasing ownership heightens the risk-taking behavior of owners. Family ownership was measured by the logarithm percentage of company stocks held by the FM, consistent with prior research (Sharma et al., 1996; Zahra, 2005).

Descriptive statistics and correlations are provided in Table 15. I performed an OLS regression analysis for the potential moderator effect. As shown in Table 16, I entered the control variables in Model 1, the independent variables were entered in Model 2, the interaction variable was entered in Model 3, and in Model 4 the interaction effects were entered. Overall, the adjusted R^2 for Model 1 is .066 and the model is significant ($p < .000$). In Model 2, the adjusted R^2 increases to .216 with the inclusion of the independent variables ($p < .000$). The setting of

Table 15: Correlation matrix, means, and standard deviations – FM

Variables	Mean	SD	1.	2.	3.	4.	5.	6.	7.	8.	9.	10.	11.	12.	13.	14.	15.	16.	17.	18.	19.	20.	21.	22.	23.	24.
1. Reference Price (log)	5,34	0,20																								
2. Sales (log)	17,46	2,50	–.05*																							
3. Employee (log)	5,31	2,02	–.08**	.78***																						
4. Firm Age (log)	3,85	1,13	–.16***	.62***	.60***																					
5. Gender	0,12	0,26	–.07**	.04	.09**	.15***																				
6. Managerial Ownership (log)	2,76	1,42	.13***	–.16***	–.16***	–.10***	[illegible]																			
7. Family members as employees (log)	1,18	0,57	.00	–.04	.08**	–.06*	[illegible]	.01																		
8. Position: CEO	0.20	.311	.12***	–.05	–.03	–.08**	[illegible]	.39***	–.18***																	
9. Position: Management Board	0,39	.48	–.07*	–.18***	.05***	.30***	[illegible]	–.17***	–.22***	–.41**																
10. Position Director	.06	.20	.02	–.03	.10***	–.21***	[illegible]	–.18***	[illegible]	–.19***	–.25***															
11. Position: Supervisory Board	.09	.23	–.06*	.17***	.02	.15***	–.03	–.01	–.35***	–.23***	–.30***	–.12***														
12. Industry: Automotive	.02	.13	–.03	.08**	.24***	.09***	–.09**	–.37***	.17***	–.12***	.05	.28***	–.07**													
13. Industry: Metal Processing	.12	.26	–.06*	.19***	.26***	.27***	.27***	–.08**	–.06*	.02	..11***	–.14***	–.03	–.09**												
14. Industry: Chemical	.05	.18	–.06*	.04	–.05	.02	–.13***	.16***	–.25***	.13***	–.22***	–.09**	.32***	–.05*	–.13***											
15. Industry: Electronic/Mechatronic	.03	.16	–.04**	–.02	–.04*	–.00	–.03	–.24***	–.03	–.06**	–.11***	.30***	–.02	–.02	–.05*	–.02										
16. Industry: Energy; Oil, Gas	.02	.13	.00	–.13***	–.17***	–.13***	[illegible]	.03	–.02	.21***	–.11***	–.04	–.05	–.03	–.06*	–.04	–.02									
17. Industry: Commerce & consumer goods	.09	.23	–.02	.17***	–.04	.08**	–.03	–.01	.03	–.12***	.14***	–.12***	–.14***	–.07**	–.17***	–.10***	–.03	–.05								
18. Industry: Construction	.06	.20	.02	–.04	–.02	–.04	[illegible]	.07****	–.09**	–.06*	–.12***	–.10***	.08**	–.06*	–.14***	–.09**	–.03	–.04	–.12***							
19. Industry: Transport/Logistic	.02	.13	.14***	–.13***	.03	–.31***	[illegible]	.04	[illegible]	–.12***	.24***	.–06*	–.07**	–.04	–.09**	–.05*	–.02	–.03	–.07**	–.06*						
20. Industry: Banking/ Insurance	.03	.13	–.02	.04	–.09**	.01	[illegible]	–.06*	.13***	–.12***	.05	.28***	–.07**	–.04	–.09**	–.05*	–.03	–.03	–.07**	–.06*	–.04					
21. Personal Trait: Risk– taking	2,01	0,27	.14***	–.01	.10	–.17***	–.28***	.20***	–.16***	.34***	–.25***	–11***	.12***	.05	–.01	.31***	–.14***	–.03	–.14***	–.32***	.21***	–.01				
22. Purchase Price	196,15	30,78	.34***	.00	.00	.00	.00	.00	.00	.00	.00	.00	.00	.00	.00	.00	.00	.00	.00	.00	.00	.00	00			
23. Current Price	200,00	21,31	.14***	.00	.00	.00	.00	.00	.00	.00	.00	.00	.00	.00	.00	.00	.00	.00	.00	.00	.00	.00	.00	.00		
24. Average Price	199,98	16,56	.27***	.00	.00	.00	.00	.00	.00	.00	.00	.00	.00	.00	.00	.00	.00	.00	.00	.00	.00	.00	.00	.12**	.16**	
25. Risk	2,11	0,37	.10***	.00	.00	.00	.00	.00	.00	.00	.00	.00	.00	.00	.00	.00	.00	.00	.00	.00	.00	.00	.00	,04	.00	,00

Notes: N = 1369, p< .10; *p< .05; **p< .01, ***p< .001

Table 16: Results of the OLS estimation for each subject and sequence – FM

Variables	Model 1		Model 2		Model 3		Model 4	
Constant	5.054***	(.073)	5.047***	(.067)	.5.069***	(.066)	.5.069***	(.066)
Sales (log)	.013***	(.004)	.013***	(.003)	.013***	(.003)	.013***	(.003)
Employee (log)	–.016**	(.005)	–.016**	(.005)	–.016**	(.005)	–.016**	(.005)
Firm Age (log)	–.014	(.007)	–.014	(.007)	–.014	(.007)	–.014	(.007)
Gender	.014	(.022)	.014	(.020)	.014	(.020)	.014	(.020)
Family members as employees (log)	.007	(.011)	.007	(.010)	.007	(.010)	.007	(.010)
Position: CEO	.037	(.029)	.037	(.027)	.037	(.027)	.037	(.027)
Position: Management Board	–.016	(.018)	–.016	(.017)	–.016	(.017)	–.016	(.017)
Position: Director	.007	(.041)	.007	(.037)	.007	(.037)	.007	(.037)
Position: Supervisory Board	–.005	(.034)	–.005	(.031)	–.005	(.031)	–.005	(.031)
Personal Trait: Risk–taking	.079**	(.025)	.079**	(.023)	.079**	(.023)	.079**	(.023)
IV: Purchase Price			.068***	(.005)	.068***	(.005)	.057***	(.006)
IV: Current Price			.028***	(.004)	.028***	(.004)	.018**	(.006)
IV Average Price			–.003	(.005)	–.003	(.004)	–.002	(.007)
IV: Risk			.020***	(.005)	.020***	(.005)	.010	(.006)
Interaction: Managerial Ownership					.025***	(.007)	.024**	(.007)
Purchase price x Managerial Ownership							.015**	(.006)
Current Price x Managerial Ownership							.013**	(.005)
Risk x Managerial Ownership							.013*	(.005)
Average price x Managerial Ownership							–.001	(.006)
R^2	**.079**		**.229**		**.229**		**.239**	
Adjusted R^2	**.066**		**.216**		**.216**		**.225**	
ΔR^2			**.150**		**.000**		**.010**	
F	**6.10*** **		**17.40*** **		**17.40*** **		**15.66*** **	

Notes: N = 1369; Unstandardized coefficients shown, with robust standard errors; Standard errors are clustered by subject; p< .10; *p< .05; **p< .01, ***p< .001

reference price in this model is again highly and positively significantly related to the independent variables purchase price ($p < .001$), current price ($p < .001$), and risk ($p < .001$). Similar to the main model, no significant relations occur for the independent variable average price. Overall, in Model 2 the adjusted R^2 increases to .216. However, I again found support for hypotheses 1a, 1b, and 2. As indicated in Model 3, the interaction factor managerial family ownership is positively and significantly related to the dependent variable ($p < .000$). Model 4 shows the results for the interaction effect ($p < .001$). Indeed, purchase price ($p < .01$), current price ($p < .01$), and risk ($p < .05$) are associated with managerial family ownership. The adjusted R^2 increases again to .225.

To be better able to interpret these interactions, they were plotted (Aiken & West, 1991). Managerial family ownership and the independent variables took values of one standard deviation below ("low") and above ("high") the mean. Figure 7 suggests that above a certain degree, an increased purchase price and higher amount of managerial family ownership results in setting higher reference prices.

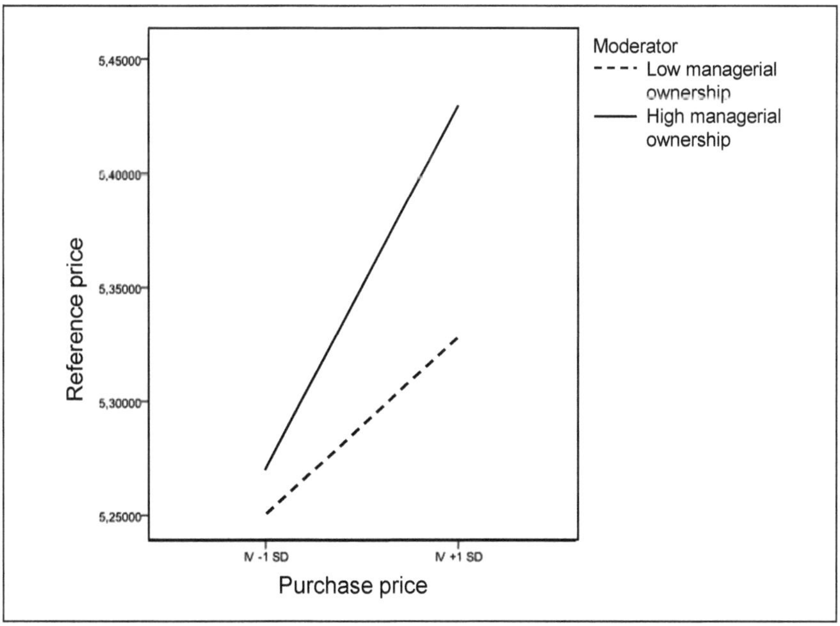

Figure 7: Interaction effect between ownership and purchase price – FM

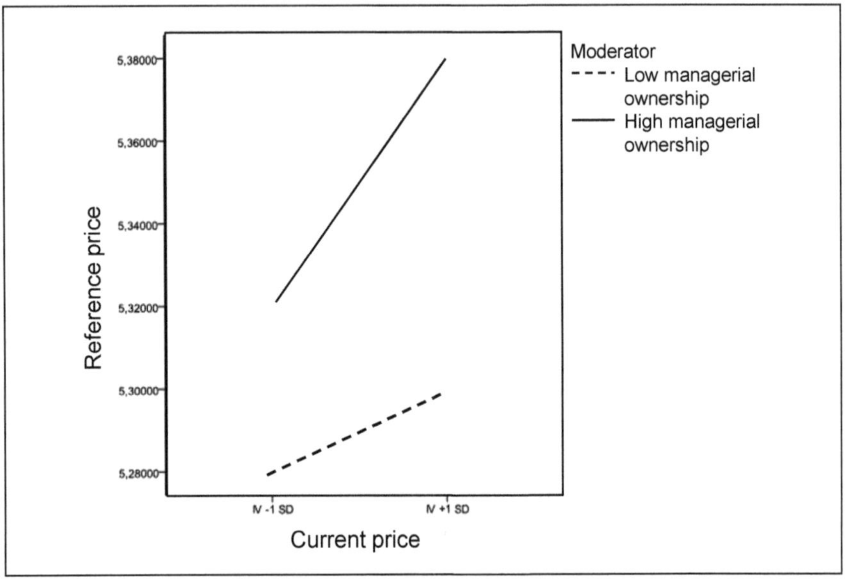

Figure 8: Interaction effect between ownership and current price – FM

Figure 8 further suggests that above a certain degree an increased current price and a higher amount of managerial family ownership results in setting higher reference prices.

Figure 9 suggests that only a higher degree of risk and a higher degree of managerial family ownership results in setting higher reference prices. These results support the notion that ownership mediates the relationship between the independent variables and dependent variable. Furthermore, these results imply that with a higher reference point, family managers are more often in the domain of losses and thus behave in a more risk-seeking manner. It is important to note that the main effect does not change with the addition of a moderator term; the apparent change is the result in a shift from the main affect test to a test of a particular simple effect in the moderator model (Irwin & McClelland, 2001).

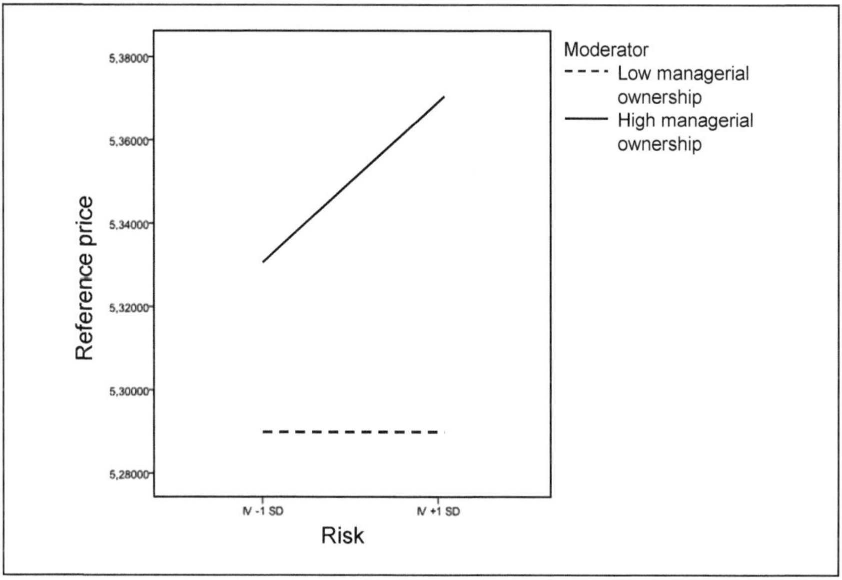

Figure 9: Interaction effect between ownership and Risk – FM

7.4 Discussion and conclusion

7.4.1 General discussion

The results of the binomial test show that purchase price, current price, average price, and risk have a significant effect on the reference point. While in the univariate analysis, the average price was significant for the whole sample, in both regression analyses this coefficient was not significant. This is not in line with the findings of Baucells et al. (2011). My findings might stem from including risk as an additional factor as well as the multiple controls used.

In addition, this study is able to confirm that FMs take lower risks than their public counterparts. The t-test supports the notion that risk is significant depending on the type of manager, while both status quo and average price are not significantly different. Volatile price developments lead to lower unit effects for pairs of sequences for FMs and NFMs, while PMs display at least twice as high unit effects. For that reason, the t-test indicates significant group differences among FMs vs. PMs, NFMs vs. PMs, and FMs and NFMs vs. PMs. The lower unit effects for pairs of sequences for FMs and NFMs result in lower reference point levels. Therefore, FMs and NFMs will find themselves more often in the domain of gains compared with PMs, leading to more risk-averse behavior.

Although the t-test does not indicate significant differences between FMs and NFMs, the average reference point of FMs for all price sequences (Table 10) is constantly below the average reference point of NFMs. These findings show that NFMs have a higher starting point and thus usually take more risks than their family counterparts. However, in the case of risky decision situations, for both groups every unit increase in volatility has almost the same effect on the reference price. Therefore, my findings are also in line with the literature assuming higher risk-taking of NFMs compared with FMs, while at the same time adopting family firm characteristics.

Moreover, as shown in the post-hoc analysis, the results provide evidence that managerial ownership for FMs moderates the relationships among purchase price, current price, and risk to FMs' reference points, leading to higher risk-taking behavior. At higher levels of managerial ownership, reference points were significantly higher for increasing levels of purchase price, current price, and risk (see Figures 7, 8, and 9 for a graphical depiction of these relationships).

The results have several implications for reference dependence theory. By testing two types of information conditions (risk and status quo), which have been discussed in prior studies to be approached differently by managers (risk strongly and status quo weakly influenced by affect), I provide an important contribution to the literature. For the first time, the theoretical and empirical results of this study suggest that context influences reference point formation. I also show that managerial ownership serves as a moderator. Although Tversky and Kahneman (1981) stated that the frame adopted by an individual is moderated partly by norms, few studies have investigated context- or individual-related impact factors. Interestingly, some authors have already pointed out that the effects of changes from reference points are feelings (Read, 2002; Heyman et al., 2004; Mercer, 2005). They have argued that individuals are not indifferent to net assets, but rather emotion's influence is predominantly in the direction of change, whether it is a gain or a loss relative to some reference. However, context factors are challenging to be considered in models, and therefore are ignored in most experimental studies. Hence, this research field represents an important understudied area in decision making (e.g., Lopes, 1987; Mellers et al., 1997; Weber & Milliman, 1997).

Furthermore, this study contributes to the literature by highlighting risk as an important factor in the reference point formation process. In addition, within reference-dependent preferences, this study offers a unique sample design, not only by measuring managerial reference point formation within multiple relevant reference point settings in multiple time series, but also by considering different manager types and offering group comparisons. The results show that varying subject groups leads to dissimilar results. They also suggest that the decision maker is an important factor in reference point investigations, as individuals display dissimilar formulae in decision making.

The findings suggest that FMs and PMs interpret some events similarly depending on their affective states based on gathered experiences. Furthermore, I found additional support for the lower risk-taking of FMs compared with PMs in an experimental setting. I provide a new approach by combining the quasi-experimental design used in behavioral economics with the family firm literature. In addition, despite the growing literature on the differences between PMs and FMs (e.g., Anderson & Reeb, 2004), the role of NFMs is under-researched (Astrachan et al., 2002; Chua et al., 2003). As this study considers NFMs, I also contribute to the literature by showing that the usual risk behavior of NFMs is higher compared with FMs.

The moderator effect of managerial ownership contributes not only to family business research but also to compensation research. The findings suggest that a higher level of managerial ownership leads to risk-seeking behavior. In spite of some conflicting evidence (e.g., Wright et al., 1996), a preponderance of economics and empirical studies has observed that management equity is positively related to risk-taking (e.g., Amihud & Lev, 1981; Hill & Snell, 1988; for family business research: Zahra, 2005; Wiseman & Gómez-Mejía, 1998). More importantly, the results suggest that ownership is probably a relevant variable to explain the risky behavior of FMs that has been observed in some studies (Gómez-Mejía et al., 2007). Gómez-Mejía et al. (2007) found that family firms are willing to accept greater performance hazard (risk) in order to protect their socioemotional wealth. However, their results are discussed by considering the loss of family control. My results assume that ownership might be another variable that explains the loss of family control, thus resulting in risk-seeking behavior. Moreover, according Becker et al. (2005), FMs expect potential NFM candidates for top management positions to show entrepreneurial engagement. Therefore, if FMs want to encourage NFMs to take risks, they might offer them company shares.

7.4.2 Limitations and future research

The main limitation of this study is that I have not directly measured the relationship of affects on cognitive reference point formation. Based on previous studies, these analyses suggest that experiential affective processing influences the cognitive processes of managerial reference point formation. Nevertheless, I call for more research efforts on affects and reference-dependent preferences.

Moreover, the potential for non-response and common method bias may exist given the low response rate and single respondents in my sample. However, I conducted tests and the results of the univariate and multivariate analysis corroborate the results of Baucells et al. (2011), which provides evidence for the reliability and validity of my findings. The results are built on a sample of German managers, which may have cultural differences compared with managers in other nations. However, business practices between Europe and the US have become more comparable (Carr, 2005), for example because of the increasing globalization of businesses.

In addition to my limitations, I would like to mention avenues for future research. One extension of my experiment would be to investigate other information conditions and combinations. For instance, researchers have found that expectation and aspiration levels also affect reference point formation. Moreover, deeper insights would be obtained by considering different framing treatments. For example, Kuvaas and Kaufmann (2004) found that congruent framing information (positive mood/positive framing) has significantly better recall and significantly less overconfidence. Furthermore, understanding the evolution of reference points has potentially important applications. However, there is still no formally accepted theory available for reference point formation. In addition, longitudinal research, a larger sample size, and obtaining data from multiple sources could be useful. Moreover, the results should be examined to hold not only in situations of monetary comparisons, but also in non-monetary situations such as advancements in key workplace attributes (Georgellis et al., 2008).

Combs (2008) discussed a fourth ownership structure – private equity and venture capital. In practice, such research is increasingly focused on firms that invest in other firms. For instance, it would be intriguing to investigate to what extent the pooling of large sums of capital, search for high returns, and extreme risk fits with the results of this study. Furthermore, within finance research, it is widely acknowledged that family firms perform better compared with non-family firms (Anderson & Reeb, 2003). Thus, it would be interesting to explore which managerial reference point results in better firm performance. Another interesting field of further research would be to consider the possible impact of sunk costs (Thaler, 1980) on a manager's reference point formation, specifically in the context of the long tenures of managers. For example, it could be investigated how ignoring past sunk costs when making present decisions affects reference point formation.

7.4.3 *Practical implications*

The presented findings also have important practical implications. Managerial reference points and risk preferences help describe behavior concerning new product introductions, capital expenditures, entry into new markets, the willingness to use non-traditional methods, and investments policies (Larraza-Kintana et al., 2007). Hence, the strategy choices of organizations can be influenced directly by a manager's reference points. Replacing managers, even if he/she has the same qualifications, may have an important effect, as it introduces a manager with a different reference point.

In finance, these results may be directly applied to predict investor sentiments. Buyers and sellers in investments as well as in negotiation processes should be aware of the different reference point levels of managers, as a lower reference point because of risk might result in an advantage in negotiation processes. It would also have an important impact on typical win–win situations. In terms of compensation structures, these findings suggest that ownership is an efficient way in which to increase risk-taking policies. Family firms for which it is optimal to implement risky strategies should refer to higher sensitive wealth such as holding onto shares in the firm. Furthermore, the cognitive evaluation of decision tasks offers the opportunity to improve the quality of decisions, as in contrast to personal traits, cognitive processes can be changed, learned, or mastered (Sulsky & Day, 1992; Palich & Bagby, 1995).

Part 3:
Summary and discussion

8 Summary, implications, and outlook

8.1 Summary

Prospect theory has done more to describe actual human decision behavior by bringing psychology concepts into the heart of economics models than any theory of decision making or even any other approach. As a result, prospect theory has gained much ground in recent years. According to Montier (2002, p. 20), "Prospect theory bears more than a passing resemblance to expected utility theory." However, the findings on reference points as one of the most pronounced empirical phenomena in decision under risk and uncertainty are lacking within this theory.

Despite research into reference-dependent preferences, the absence of a theory of reference points has been acknowledged (Wakker, 2010). For researchers, the intrasubjective formations of reference points are not easy to model. According to Wakker (2010), researchers should use the reference-dependent concept in a more pragmatic way without a well-developed theory available.

Nevertheless, this does not prevent us from shedding more light on this under-researched field. Therefore, I chose promising research questions that combine initial and new ideas, consider all research parts of reference-dependent preferences, and evaluate reference points in a direct way. As the literature review showed, most studies have indicated ideas and made suggestions regarding factors that might influence and determine reference point formation, but without investigating the actual reference point of each decision maker. Without directly measuring the reference point, researchers are unable to discuss the contributions of studies of reference-dependent preferences; they are only able to make suggestions. Therefore, all experimental studies in this area are based on the evaluation of the individual reference points of each survey subject. Hence, my results directly contribute to the reference-dependent preferences literature.

In particular, this dissertation contributes to the reference-dependent preferences literature through several findings. In the **first empirical study,** this dissertation project provided additional support that a person's outcome of choice is indeed strongly influenced by his/her reference point. An important premise of these applications of prospect theory is the consideration that reference points shift over time and thus the adaptation processes of reference points influence the risk-taking decisions of individuals. For the first time, it has been demonstrated that when expectations are prevalent, they also have a significant influence on reference point adaptation in the domain of losses. Hence, this dissertation project confirms the results of other studies (e.g., Köszegi, 2006; Post et al., 2008; Abeler et al., 2011; Hack & Lammers, 2011) that when expectations are prevalent, it is insufficient to equate the reference point, for instance, with the recent status quo.

More importantly, a major finding of this study is the significant difference between the extent of reference point adaptation following attractive events (gains) and painful events (losses) in the consideration of expectations. Similar to Arkes et al. (2008), this project also found an asymmetric magnitude of reference point adaptation to gains and losses even when expectations are present. Interestingly, within a comparison of all investigated scenarios, it could be shown that individuals adapt their reference points less strongly in the domain of losses than that of gains. Not only is the magnitude of mean reference point adaptation after gains significantly greater than after losses, but it also results in lower outcomes within the comparison of treatments in the domain of gains compared with the domain of losses.

Moreover, this dissertation contributes to the literature by discussing for the first time an additional theoretical approach besides hedonic maximization to explain the asymmetric adaptation process. According to the theory of hedonic maximization, no adaptation in the domain of losses should occur, while this experiment found a shifting of reference points. Some researchers have suggested that initial losses might increase risk aversion (Thaler & Johnson, 1990), which leads to minor reference point adaptation in the domain of losses. Moreover, Thaler (1999) described that individuals tend to experience losses one by one in order to make them more sensitive to the next. However, it has also been argued that adaptation in the domain of losses might be supported by disappointment aversion (Bell, 1985; Loomes & Sugden, 1986). It has long been discussed that subjects might try to minimize future disappointment, as they compare the outcomes within given prospects, giving rise to the possibility of disappointment when the outcome compares unfavorably with what it might have been. Therefore, individuals make decisions that are less likely to lead to a feeling of disappointment.

The **second empirical study** mainly contributes by focusing on factors that might determine the reference point formation process. For the first time, the determinants of reference point formation were empirically investigated by measuring individual reference points at the same time. More precisely, this study explored the influence of personality traits on reference point formation and adaptation. Despite the observed marginal significant effects of personality traits on reference point formation, the results suggest a generally weak direct effect of personality traits on reference point adaptation. Moreover, the results support the assumption that these effects are different for the domains of gains and losses.

In particular, the experimental tests showed that the personality traits need for achievement, optimism, self-esteem, and openness to experiences affect reference point adaptation, although no significant impact for the Big-Five traits of conscientiousness and neuroticism could be found. In the domain of gains, this experiment showed that people who score high on need for achievement set significantly higher reference points. In addition, it ascertained that in the domain of gains, optimists set higher reference points than low self-esteem individuals. Furthermore, in the domain of losses, optimists adapt their reference points to a lesser extent than low self-esteem individuals. Moreover, it was shown that in the domain of losses, low self-esteem individuals adapt their reference points to a lesser extent than high self-esteem individuals. Significant evidence was also shown for how those who score high on openness to experiences adapt their reference points in the domain of losses to a greater level. To conclude, this study provides the first support that personality differences might affect reference point formation.

The **third experimental study** provides theoretical and empirical contributions concerning all research parts of reference-dependent references. First, it contributes by extending the reference dependence literature on the determinants of reference point formation. To my knowledge, for the first time it was discussed that affects determine reference point formation. By showing that even the same information and situation lead to different cognitive outcomes based on the context-related affective expression of decision makers, we also provide an important conceptual contribution on how contextual factors influence the formation of reference points. This experiment also observed that managerial ownership moderates reference point formation. Further, this study also showed for the first time that risk is a further piece of information besides the "usual suspects" of status quo, aspiration level, or expectations. In particular, it evidenced that risk is salient information within multiple relevant reference point settings. Within these settings, which includes historical status quo, recent status quo, average price, and risk, this study also found that a subject's reference point can be best described by the historical status quo, the recent status quo and risk. This partly confirms the first investigation into multiple reference points by Baucells et al. (2011) and extends it by including risk as a factor. Third, we contribute to the literature by providing a first experimental study of manager types and their reference points. The results evidenced that different subject groups differ in their reference point formation. This experiment was able to show that family managers have lower risk preferences compared with professional executives.

8.2 Limitations

Besides the limitations already discussed in each experimental chapter, this chapter highlights the limitations of experimental investigations in general. Following behavioral economists such as Arkes et al. (2008) and Baucells et al. (2011), this dissertation used data that usually lie outside the traditional scope of economics. I performed experiments using questionnaires and questioning hypothetical choices. In particular, I used mental states such as "At what price would the stock need to trade today to make you just as happy/sad…" and "At what selling price you would be neither happy nor unhappy…" to gather neural imaging data on the physiological processes inside the brain. Although these methods of hypothetical choices are the simplest way to collect intrapersonal data, they violate the actual advantage of using incentives in order to motivate participants to respond truthfully. Hypothetical questioning offers no opportunity for monetary consequences based on responses, as is possible in gambling tasks. Therefore, my participants might display self-reporting bias. Hence, this doctoral thesis relies on the assumption that participants know how they would behave in decision tasks and that they have no reason to disguise their true preferences.

Moreover, a lack of reality, particularly about the duration of the experimental task, is a key limitation of quasi-laboratory experiments. Studies have shown that important behavioral differences among cognitive processes occur in the short-term and in the long-term (Falk & Fehr, 2003). Loewenstein (2005) found that immediate reactions to a decision task are emphasized by "hot" decision making, while "cold" decision making is observed within the long-term. This might have an important effect on the adaptation process. Gilbert et al. (1998) showed that individuals tend to adapt to new situations over time. However, decision choices within these experiments were not carried out as interactions in the market typically would be, which go on for days, or even weeks or months.

In addition, the third study suggests that it is valuable to recruit participants outside university environments, or at least to investigate different groups and populations. This would not only lead to the increased validity of the gained findings but would also provide additional insights into differences in the cognitive processes of reference point settings. Furthermore, in all experiments, the reference point was measured in a monetary framing. Prior research results have suggested that framing around changes in salaries, advancement opportunities, promotions, and organizational change might lead to other results.

8.3 Implications

8.3.1 Theoretical implications

By using and extending the experiments of Arkes et al. (2008) and Baucells et al. (2011), this dissertation has shown these models to be highly portable and generally applicable. These methods are essential to the reference dependence literature. As highlighted in the literature review, most studies have still not directly evaluated the locations and evolution of reference points. Thus, current reference dependence theory is based on a "patchwork rug" of ideas and suggestions from different disciplines in the economics and psychological research areas without measuring the actual reference point.

As mentioned above, measuring reference points helps gain a better understanding and apply reference-dependent preferences to other models and studies. For instance, Ho et al. (2010) assumed that expectations serve as reference points in a study of behavioral operation management. The authors incorporated reference dependence into a newsvendor framework by assuming that psychological aversion to leftovers is greater than the disutility for stock-outs. Expected demands serve as reference points by which the manager evaluates the effectiveness of his/her order decisions. Hence, the findings about the location and adaptation of reference points enhance the meaning of models.

The results of empirical investigations have also highlighted the importance of considering asymmetric decision making in the domains of gains and losses. A number of theoretical models of asset pricing consider reference point adaptation (Barberis et al., 2001; Grinblatt & Han, 2005). However, in these models reference points update symmetrically to new outcomes and thus do not differentiate between the domains of gains and losses. The observed asymmetrically adaptation to gains and losses thus has important consequences for these theories of asset pricing. Therefore, further studies should always consider the domains of gains and losses by investigating their research questions to obtain a comprehensive contribution to the literature.

Furthermore, every empirical study provides further evidence for multiple and adaptive reference points. Therefore, studies considering single reference points in single period settings should be counted, as their contributions are limited. In addition, discovering further information that might serve as reference points has not yet been finalized. The identification of the factor risk suggests that several other pieces of information that exist in decision tasks are likely to be considered in decision making.

The results further encourage considering previously discussed and investigated determinants of cognitive processes in the reference-dependent preferences literature. The influence of personality traits and their effects on mental processes have already been investigated. In addition, the influence of affects on decision making has recently been discussed (e.g., Baron, 2004, 2008). However, this dissertation project investigated them in a reference-dependent preferences context for the first time. The consideration of individual differences and contextual factors is the most under-researched field of reference-dependent preferences.

8.3.2 Practical implications

As this doctoral thesis deals with basic research questions on reference-dependent preferences, there are few directly related practical implications besides those outlined in the discussion parts of each experimental investigation.

Nevertheless, I will now point out some general implications for decision makers in the economic environment.

Asymmetric reference point formation underlines the importance of every decision maker anticipating framing effects. Framing an issue as a gain rather than as a loss has enormous decision consequences on consumer decisions. An interesting example presented by Bentham (1828) and Lapidus and Sigot (2000) regarding payment schemes also demonstrates the importance of remuneration systems. Bentham suggested that a payment scheme with a high salary and fines for bad performance would work better than a low salary and bonuses for good performance, as fines are perceived as a loss, which looms larger than the equivalent gain compared with the reference point (salary).

Furthermore, asymmetric reference point adaptation is also important for investors' trading behavior. The findings of my studies are consistent with the disposition effect. Therefore, this dissertation confirms the bias that there is a positive hedonic consequence of closing mental accounts in the domain of gains, while there is a negative hedonic consequence of closing mental accounts in the domain of losses (Arkes et al., 2008). However, for investors it is irrational to hold onto stocks that have lost value for too long and be eager to sell stocks that have increased value.

The effects of reference points on any decision maker seem particularly important for consumers, investors, and negotiators. By understanding reference point formation processes and the relevant reference points, decision making can be manipulated by marketing departments, investors, and negotiation counterparts.

My findings show that expectations, historical status quos, recent status quos, and risk serve as pieces of information that constitute reference points for individuals. This enables marketing departments to define promotion campaigns more effectively. The forming of expectations over planned price increases of the product portfolio may also lead to more satisfied customers, as their consumptions are perceived as gains (consumption before vs. after price increases). With the knowledge that higher expectations or volatile decision situations lead to higher subjective reference points, thus resulting in higher prices, for instance, by which the decision maker is neutral about buying or selling a product, enables managers to enhance their profits.

In this spirit, my findings suggest that certain personality traits and affective expressions in contextual situations influence reference point formation. Based on prospect theory, setting reference points also influences the situational risk-taking of individuals. For instance, individuals who score high on need for achievement set higher reference points in the domain of gains. This implies that these individuals probably behave in a more risk-seeking manner. In negotiation contexts, each negotiation round might take into consideration the individual differences or affective states of their counterparts to assume a reference level and thus place their offers in a way that maximizes their outcomes. In human resources, applicants can be chosen depending on the organizational expectations of the necessary risk behavior of employees in decision situations.

8.4 Directions for further research

As reference-dependent preferences are still an under-researched field in behavioral economics, there are important future research directions worth considering. For instance, the experiments of this dissertation only considered a single attribute outcome – the selling of a stock or investment. A direction of future research concerns multi-attribute outcomes, in which reference points may be taken per attribute or holistically (Bleichrodt et al., 2009). Empirical efforts are limited, as the set of stimuli is limited as well. Extending the set of stimuli in empirical investigations would thus be a worthwhile endeavor. Especially for the marketing literature, the consideration of multiple attribute of products is important. Imagine the case of purchasing an automobile. In this situation, decision makers might not only have a reference point for prices but also for the power of the engine, for the branding of the car, for the leasing conditions, and so on. The buyer may have separate mental accounts for each attribute. What determinants influence which kinds of attributes? This would be an interesting topic for further research.

Currently, reference dependence theory has found its way into economic modeling (e.g., Sugden, 2003; Masatlioglu & Ok, 2005; Köszegi & Rabin, 2006). However, all these authors have highlighted that it is still necessary to find an appropriate notion of the reference point, such as the location and evolution of the reference point. Even if it is impossible to capture such intrapersonal and dynamic aspects in a metric model, it is at least necessary to develop a widely accepted experiment to measure reference points that is adaptable by discipline.

Reference point formation in a multiple relevant reference point setting is still an open field of research, too. As the third experiment demonstrated, reference point formation depends on the available information. Hence, other combinations of pieces of information that might serve as reference points would be worthwhile evaluating. Other important types of references such as aspiration levels or intermediate wealth could also constitute reference points. Because situations involving multiple reference points are abundant, there is a strong need for further research on the impact of multiple reference points on reference point formation.

Other personality traits, such as anxiousness and perceived self-efficacy, are eventually more likely to explain adaptation differences in reference point formation. Besides the direct investigations of affects on reference point formation, other determinants also seem worth exploring, namely social comparisons, differences in cognitive efforts, different contexts, and different situations and habits. Additional factors of reference point formation should be identified, weighted, and placed in a specific order of precedence to gain a comprehensive overview. Moreover, it would be interesting to investigate possible differences in reference point formation regarding individuals vs. group decision making. Several day-to-day decisions are made in groups, especially in organizations. In addition, whether the individual chooses or decides for him-/herself or for a third party may also matter.

As mentioned above, for future research it would be interesting to apply these approaches in the field. Furthermore, the results of this dissertation should be applicable not only in situations of monetary comparisons but also in situations such as advancements in key workplace attributes (Georgellis et al., 2007) or general life quality. Another interesting aspect of investigation is to consider the role of memory, for instance especially in recalling historical status quos. The time delay between the arrival of each piece of information within a decision process might also be important.

In summary, all further research approaches should strive to develop a holistic view of reference-dependent preferences by considering the factors that influence the cognitive reference formation process, the reference point formation process itself, and the information that serves as a reference point.

9 Bibliography

A

Abeler, J., Falk, A., Goette, L., & Huffmann, D. (2011). Reference points and effort Provision. *American Economic Review*, 101, 470–492.

Alba, J. W., Mela, C. F., Shimp, T. A., & Urbany, J. E. (1999). The effect of discount frequency and depth on consumer price judgments. *Journal of Consumer Research*, 26, 99–114.

Allais, M, M. (1953). Le comportement de l'homme rationnel devant le risque: critique des postulats et axiomes de l'ecole americaine, *Econometrica*, 21, 503–546.

Aiken, L. S., & West, S. G. (1991). Multiple regression: testing and interpreting interactions. Thousand Oaks, CA: Sage.

Aldrich, H. E., & Cliff, J. E. (2003). The pervasive effects of family on entrepreneurship: toward a family embeddedness perspective. *Journal of Business Venturing*, 18, 573–596.

Amihud, Y., & Lev, B. (1981). Risk reduction as a managerial motive for conglomerate mergers. *Journal of Economics*, 12, 605–618.

Anderson, R. C., & Reeb, D. M. (2003). Founding-family ownership and firm performance: evidence from the S&P 500. *The Journal of Finance*, 58, 1301–1328.

Anderson, R. C., & Reeb, D. M. (2004). Board composition: balancing family influence in S&P 500 firms. *Administrative Science Quarterly*, 49, 209–237.

Andreoni, J, & Sprenger, Ch. (2011). Uncertainty equivalents: testing the limits of the independence axiom. *Working paper*.

Annaert, J., Heyman, D., Vanmaele, M., & Van Osselaer, S. (2008). Disposition bias and overconfidence in institutional trades. *Working Paper*.

Arkes, H. R., & Blumer, C. (1985). The psychology of sunk cost. *Organizational Behavior and Human Decision Processes*, 35, 124–140.

Arkes, H. R., Hirshleifer, D., Jiang, D., & Lim, S. S. (2008). Reference point adaptation: tests in the domain of security trading. *Organizational Behavior and Human Decision Processes,* 105, 67–81.

Arkes, H. R., Hirshleifer, D. A., Jiang, D., & Lim, S. S. (2010). A cross-cultural study of reference point adaptation: evidence from China, Korea, and the US. *Organizational Behavior and Human Decision Processes,* 112, 99–111.

Aronoff, C. E., & Ward, J. L. (2000). More than family: non-family executives in the family business. *Family Business Leadership Series*. Marietta, GA: Business Ownership Resources.

Arregle, J. L., Hitt, M. A., Sirmon, D., & Very, P. (2007). The development of organizational social capital and its performance implications: insights from family firms. *Journal of Management Studies*, 44, 73–95.

Arrow, K. J. (1965). *Aspects of the theory of risk bearing*. Helsinki: Yrjö Jahnssonis Säätio.

Arrow, K. J. (1971). *Essays on the theory of risk bearing*. North-Holland, Amsterdam.

Arrow, K. J. (1982). Risk perception in psychology and economic. *Economics Inquiry*, 20, 1–9.

Asgary, A., & Levy, J. (2009). A Review of the Implications of Prospect Theory for Natural Hazards and Disaster Planning. *International Journal of Environmental Research*, 3, 379–394.

Astrachan, J. H., & Shanker, M. C. (2003). Family businesses' contribution to the U.S. economy: a closer look. *Family Business Review*, 16, 211–219.

Astrachan, J. H., Keyt, A., Lane, S., & Yarmalouk, D. (2002). Non-family CEO's in the family business: Connecting family values to business success. *Proceedings FBN-ifera Helsinki*, 183–199.

Athanassiou, N., Crittenden, W. F., Kelly, L. M., & Marquez, P. (2002). Founder Centrality effects on the Mexican family firm's top management group: firm culture, strategic vision and goals, and firm performance. *Journal of World Business*, 37, 139–150.

Atkinson, J. W., Bastian, J. R., Earl, R. W., & Litwin, G. H. (1960). The achievement motive, goal setting, and probability preferences. *Journal of Abnormal and Social Psychology*, 60, 27–36.

B

Bakan, D. (1966). The test of significance in psychological research. *Psychological Bulletin*, 66, 423–437.

Baker, M., Pan, X., & Wurgler, J. (2009). A reference point theory of mergers and acquisitions. *Working Paper*

Baltussen, G., Post, T., & Van Vliet, P. (2006). Violations of CPT and mixed gambles. *Management Science*, 52, 1288–1290.

Bandura, A. (1997). *Self-efficacy: the exercise of control.* New York: Freeman.

Barberis, N., & Thaler, R. (2003). A survey of behavioral finance. *Handbook of the Economics of Finance*, 1, 1053–1128.

Barberis, N., & Xiong, W. (2009). What drives the disposition effect? An analysis of a long-standing preference-based explanation. *Journal of Finance*, 64, 751–784.

Barberis, N., Shleifer, A., & Vishny, R. (1998). A model of investor sentiment. *Journal of Financial Economics*, 49, 307–343.

Barberis, N., Huang, M., & Santos, T. (2001). Prospect theory and asset prices. *Quarterly Journal of Economics*, 116, 1–53.

Baron, J. (1994). *Thinking and deciding*. Cambridge, England: Cambridge University Press

Baron, R. A. (2004). The cognitive perspective: a valuable tool for answering entrepreneurship's basic "why" questions. *Journal of Business Venturing*, 19, 221–239.

Baron, R. A. (2008). Role of affect in the entrepreneurial process. *Academy of Management Review*, 33, 328–340.

Barr, A. (2003). The potential benefits of an experimental approach. Center for the Study of African Economies. *Working Paper*.

Barrick, M. R., & Mount, M. K. (1991). The Big Five personality dimensions and job performance: a meta-analysis. *Personnel Psychology*, 44, 1–26.

Bartol, K. M., & Martin, D. C. (1998). Applicant referent information at hiring interview and subsequent turnover among part-time workers. *Journal of Vocational Behavior*, 53, 334–352.

Bateman, I., Munro, A., Rhodes, B., Starmer, C., & Sugden, R. (1997). A test of the theory of reference-dependent preferences. *Quarterly Journal of Economics*, 112, 479–505.

Baucells, M., & Sarin, R. K. (2010). Predicting utility under satiation and habit formation. *Management Science*, 56, 286–301.

Baucells, M., Weber, M., & Welfens, F. (2007). Reference point formation over time: A weighting function approach. Paper provided by Sonderforschungsbereich 504, Universität Mannheim, *Unpublished version*

Baucells, M., Weber, M., & Welfens, F. (2011). Reference-point formation and updating. *Management Science*, 57, 506–519.

Bazerman, M. H., & Neale, M. A. (1991). Negotiator rationality and negotiator cognition: the interactive roles of prescriptive and descriptive research. In: Young, P.H. (eds.), *Negotiation Analysis,* University of Michigan Press: Ann Arbor, MI., 109–129.

Bazerman, M. H., Magliozzi, T., & Neale, M. A. (1985). Integrative bargaining in a competitive market. *Organizational Behavior and Human Decision Processes*, 34, 294–313.

Beck, N., &, Katz J. N. (1995). What to do (and not to do) with time-series cross-section data. *American Political Science Review*, 89, 634–647.

Becker, S. W., & Siegel, S. (1958). Utility of grades: level of aspiration in a decision theory context. *Journal of Experimental Psychology*, 55, 81–85.

Becker, F., Hensoler, N., Bielstein, M., Cöllen, C., Ebel, N., Knoll, H., & Krumme, E. (2005). Fremdmanagement in Familienunternehmen, *Paper for Discussion* No. 531, University of Bielefeld, Germany.

Bell, D. E. (1983). Risk premiums for decision regret. *Management Science*, 29, 1156–1166.

Bell, D. E. (1985). Disappointment in decision making under uncertainty. *Operations Research,* 33, 1–27.

Benartzi, S., & Thaler, R. H. (1995). Myopic loss aversion and the equity premium puzzle. *Quarterly Journal of Economics*, 110, 73–92.

Bentham, J. (1828–43). The rationale of reward. In: Bowring, J. (ed.), *The Works of Jeremy Bentham*, part. VII, 189–266.

Bellmare, C., & Kröger, S. (2003). On representative trust. *Working paper.*

Bernoulli, D. (1738). Specimen theoriae novae de mensura sortis. *Commentarii academiae scientiarum imperialespetropolitanae*, 5, 175–192.

Bernoulli, D. (1954). Exposition of a new theory in the measurement of risk. *Econometrica*, 22, 23–26. (Translation of Bernoulli, D., 1738).

Blais, A. R., & Weber, E. U. (2001). Domain-specificity and gender differences in decision making. *Risk Decision and Policy*, 6, 47–69.

Bleichrodt, H. (2007). Reference-dependent utility with shifting reference points and incomplete preferences. *Journal of Mathematical Psychology*, 51, 266–276.

Bleichrodt, H., Rohde, K. I. M.., & Wakker, P. P. (2009). Non-hyperbolic time inconsistency. *Games and Economic Behavior,* 66, 27–38.

Bleichrodt, H., Pinto, J. L., & Wakker, P. P. (2001). Making descriptive use of prospect theory to improve the prescriptive use of expected utility. *Management Science*, 47, 1498–1514.

Boles, T. L., & Messick, D. M. A (1995). Reverse outcome bias: the influence of multiple reference points on the evaluation of outcomes and decisions. *Organizational Behavior and Human Decision Processes*, 61, 262–275.

Bolton, G. E., & Ockenfels, A. (2000). A theory of equity, reciprocity, and competition. *American Economic Review*, 90, 166–193.

Borkenaus, P., & Ostendorf, F. (2008). Neo-Fünf-Faktoren-Inventar nach Costa und McCrae, Handanweisung. Göttingen: Hogrefe.

Botwin, M. D., & Buss D. M. (1989). Structure of act-report data: is the Five-Factor Model of personality recaptured? *Journal of Personality & Social Psychology*, 56, 988–1001.

Bower, G. H. (1991). Mood congruity of social judgments. In: Forgas, J. P. (ed.), *Emotion and social judgments*, Oxford: Pergamon Press, 31–55.

Bowman, E. H. (1980). A risk/return paradox for strategic management. *Management Review*, 21, 17–31.

Bowman, D., Minehart, D., & Rabin, M. (1999). Loss aversion in consumption / savings model. *Journal of Economics Behavior and Organization*, 38, 155–178.

Breiter, H. C., Aharon, I., Kahneman, D., Dale, A., & Shizgal, P. (2001). Functional imaging of neural responses to expectancy and experience of monetary gains and losses. *Neuron*, 30, 619–639.

Brewer, M. B., & Kramer, R. M. (1986). Choice behavior in social dilemmas: effects of social identity, group size, and decision framing. *Journal of Personality and Social Psychology*, 50, 543–549.

Brickman, P. (1975). Adaptation level determinants of satisfaction with equal and unequal outcome distributions in skill and chance situations. *Journal of Personality and Social Psychology*, 32, 191–198.

Brockner, J. (1984). Low self-esteem and behavioral plasticity: some implications of personality and social psychology. In: Wheeler, L. (ed.), *Review of personality and social psychology*, Beverly Hills, CA: Sage, 237–271.

Bromiley, P. (1991). Testing a causal model of corporate risk taking and performance. *Academy of Management Journal*, 34, 37–59.

Brown, S. S. A., Venkatesh, V., Kuruzovich, J. & Massey A. P. (2008). Expectation confirmation: an examination of three competing models. *Organizational Behavior and Human Decision Processes*, 105, 52–66.

Bucklin, R. E., & Lattin, J . M. (1991). A two-state model of purchase incidence and brand choice. *Marketing Science*, 19, 24–39.

Buehler, R. Griffin, D., & Rposs, M. (1994). Exploring the "planning fallacy": why people underestimate their task completion times. *Journal of Personality & Social Psychology*, 67, 984–996.

Byrnes, J. P. (1998). *The Nature and Development of Decision Making*: Self-regulation model. Lawrence Erlbaum Association, Inc., Publishers, New Jersey.

C

Camerer, C. F. (1989). An experimental test of several generalizes utility theories. *Journal of Risk and Uncertainty*, 2, 61–104.

Camerer, C.F., 1995. Individual decision making. In: Kagel, J. H., & Roth, A. E. (eds.), *Handbook of Experimental Economics*, Princeton University Press, Princeton, 587–616.

Camerer, C. F. (1998). Prospect theory in the wild: evidence from the field. In: Kahneman, D. (eds), & Tversky, A. (2000). *Choices, values, and frames*, Cambridge university press, New York, 288–300.

Camerer, C. F., & Ho, T. H. (1991). Nonlinear weighting of probabilities and violations of the betweenness axiom. *Working Paper*

Camerer, C. F., & Ho, T. H. (1994). Violations if the betweenness axiom and nonlinearity in probability. *Journal of Risk and Uncertainty*, 8, 167–196.

Camerer, C. F., & Malmendier, U. (2005). *Behavioral organizational economics*. Manuscript, Caltech.

Camerer, C. F., Babcock, L., Loewenstein, G., & Thaler, R. H. (1997). Labor supply of New York cabdrivers: one day at a time. *Quarterly Journal of Economics*, 112, 407–441.

Cameron, L. A. (1999). Raising the stakes in the ultimatum game: experimental evidence from Indonesia. *Economic Inquiry*, 37, 47–59.

Card, D., & Dahl, G. B. (2010). Family violence and football: the effect of unexpected emotional cues on violent behavior. *Working Paper*.

Cardenas, J .C., & Carpenter, J. P. (2005). Three themes on field experiments and economic development. *Research in Experimental Economics*, 10, 71–123.

Carland, J. W., Hoy, F., Boulton, W. R., & Carland, J. A. (1984). Differentiating entrepreneurs from small business owners: a conceptualization. *Academy of Management Review*. 9, 354–359.

Carlsson, F., Daruvala, D., & Johansson-Stenman, O. (2005). Are people inequality-averse, or just risk-averse? *Economica*, 72, 375–396.

Carpenter, J. (2002). Measuring social capital: adding field experimental methods to the analytical toolbox. In: Isham, J., Kelly, T., & Ramaswamy S. (eds.), *Social Capital and Economic Development: Well-Being in Developing Countries*, Northampton: Edward Elgar, 119–137.

Carr, C. (2005). Are German, Japanese and Anglo-Saxon strategic decision styles still different in the context of globalization? *Journal of Management Studies*, 42, 1155–1188.

Casson, M. (1999). The economics of the family firm. *Scandinavian Economic History Review*, 17, 10–23.

Chang, O. H., & Nichols, D. R. (1987). Taxpayer attitudes toward tax audit risk. *Journal of Economic Psychology*, 8, 299–309.

Chang, E. (2001). *Introduction: optimism and pessimism and moving beyond the most fundamental question. Optimism and pessimism*, Washington, D. C.: American Psychological Association.

Chaiken, S., Liberman, A., & Eagly, A. H. (1989). Heuristic and systematic information processing within and beyond the persuasion context. In: Uleman, J., & Bargh, J. (eds.) *Unintended Thought*, Guilford, New York, 212–252.

Chapman, G. B. (2000). Preferences for improving and declining sequences of health outcomes. *Journal of Behavior Decision Making*, 13, 203–18.

Chen, H. A., & Rao, A. R. (2002). Close encounters of two kinds: false alarm and dashed hopes. *Marketing Science*, 21, 178–196.

Chrisman, J. J., Chua, J. H., & Litz, R. (2004). Comparing the agency costs of family and non-family firms: conceptual issues and exploratory evidence. *Entrepreneurship Theory and Practice*, 28, 335–354.

Chua, J. H., Chrisman, J. J., & Sharma, P. (1999). Defining the family business by behavior. *Entrepreneurship Theory and Practice*, 23, 19–37.

Chua, J. H., Chrisman, J. J., & Sharma, P. (2003). Succession and nonsuccession concerns of family firms and agency relationship with nonfamily managers. *Family Business Review*, 16, 89–107.

Clore, G. L., Schwarz, N., & Conway, M. (1994). Affective causes and consequences of social information processing. In: Wyer, R. S., & Srull, T. K. (eds.), *Handbook of social cognition*, Hillsdale, NJ: Erlbaum, 323–417.

Coles, J. L., Naveen, D. D., & Naveen, L. (2006). Managerial incentives and risk-taking. *Journal of Financial Economics*, 79, 431–468.

Combs, J. G. (2008). Commentary: the servant, the parasite, and the enigma: a tale of three ownership structures and their affiliate directors. *Entrepreneurship Theory and Practice*, 32, 1027–1033.

Cooper, A. C., & Dunkelberg, W. C. (1981). A new look at business entry: experiences of 1,805 entrepreneurs. In: Vesper, K H. (ed.), *Frontiers of entrepreneurship research*, Wellesley, MA: Babson College, 1–20.

Costa, P. T. Jr., & McCrae, R. R. (1992). Normal personality assessments in clinical practice: the personality inventory. *Psychological Assessments,* 4, 5–13.

Crocker, J., & Wolfe, C. T. (2001): Contingencies of self-worth. *Psychological Review,* 108, 593–623.

Cramer, J. S., Hartogb, J., Jonkerb, N., & Van Praag, C. M. (2002). Low risk aversion encourages the choice for entrepreneurship: an empirical test of truism. *Journal of Economic Behavior & Organization*, 48, 29–36.

Crandall, R. (1973). The measurement of self-esteem and related constructs. In J. Robinson & P. Shaver (eds.), *Measures of social and psychological attitudes*. Ann Arbor, MI: Institute for Social Research, 45–168.

Crawford, V., & Meng, J. (2011). New York City cab drivers' labor supply revisited: reference-dependent preferences with rational expectations targets for hours and income. *American Economic Review*, 101, 1912–1932.

Cronbach, L. J. (1951). Coefficient alpha and the internal structure of tests. *Psychometrika,* 16, 297–334.

Croson, R., & Sundali, J. (2005). The gambler's fallacy and the hot hand: empirical data from casinos. *Journal of Risk and Uncertainty*, 30, 195–209.

Cropanzano, R., & Wright, T. A. (1999). A 5–year study of change in the relationship between well-being and job performance. *Consulting Psychology Journal: Practices and Research*, 51, 252–265.

Crouch, E. A. C., & Wilson, R. (1982). *Risk/benefit analysis*. Ballinger, Cambridge, MA.

Crum, R., Laugghunn, D., & Payne, J. (1980). Risk preferences: empirical evidence and is implications for capital budgeting. In: Derkindren, F., & Crum, R. (eds.), *Financing Issues in Corporate Project Selection*. Boston, MA, 99–117.

Cuba, R., Decenzo, D., & Anish, A. (1983). Management practices of successful female business owners. *American Journal of Small Business*, 8, 40–45.

Cyert, R. M., & March, J. G. (1963). *A behavioral theory of the firm*. Englewood Cliffs, NJ: Prentice-Hall.

D

Damasio, A. R. (1994). *Descartes' error: Emotion, reason, and the human brain.* New York: Putnam.

Daily, C. M., & Dollinger, M. J. (1992). An empirical examination of ownership structure in family and professionally managed firms. *Family Business Review,* 5, 117–136.

Dawes, R. M. (2001). *Everyday Irrationality: how pseudo-scientists, lunatics, and the rest of us systematically fail to think rationally.* Boulder, CO: Westview Press.

DeCarlo, J. F., & Lyons, P. R. (1979). A comparison of selected personal characteristics of minority and non-minority female entrepreneurs. *Proceedings of 39th Annual Meeting of Academy of Management*, 369–373.

Deck, C., Lee, J., Reyes, J., & Rosen, C. (2008). Measuring risk attitudes controlling for personality traits. *Working Paper.*

DeFinetti, B. (1937). *La prevision: ses lois logiques, ses sources subjectives.* Annales de l'Institut Poincare, 7, 1–68.

Delquié, P., and Cillo, A. (2006). Disappointment without prior expectations: a unifying perspective on decision under risk. *Journal of Risk and Uncertainty*, 33, 197–215.

De Meza, D., & Webb, D.C. (2007). Incentive design under loss aversion. *Journal of the European Economic Association*, 5, 66–92.

Diener, E. (1984). Subjective well-being. *Psychological Bulletin*, 95, 542–575.

Diener, E., Sandvik, E., & Pavot, W. G. (1990). Happiness is the frequency, not intensity, of positive versus negative affect. In: Strack, F., Argyle, M., & Schwarz, N. (eds.), *Social psychology of subjective well-being.* Elmsford, NY: Pergamon Press, 119–139.

Digman, J. M. (1990). Personality structure: emergence of the five factor model. *Annual Review of Psychology*, 41, 417–440.

Dimitruk, P., Schermelleh-Engel, K., Kelava, A., & Moosbrugger, H. (2007). Challenges in nonlinear structural equation modeling. *Methodology*, 3, 100–114.

Dhar, R., & Zhu, N. (2006). Up close and personal: investor sophistication and the disposition effect. *Management Science*, 52, 726–740.

Dohmen, T., Falk, A., Huffman, D., Sunde, U., Schupp, J., & Wagner, G. (2005). Individual risk attitudes: new evidence from large, representative, experimentally-validated survey. *IZA Discussion Paper Series 1739*, Forschungsinstitut zur Zukunft der Arbeit.

Douglas, M., & Wildavsky, A. (1982). *Risk and culture.* University of California Press, Berkeley.

E

Eddleston, K. A., & Kellermanns, F. W. (2007). Destructive and productive family relationships: a stewardship theory perspective. *Journal Business Venturing*, 22, 545–565.

Edwards, W. (1955). Behavioral decision theory. *Journal of Experimental Psychology*, 50, 201–14.

Ellison, G., & Fudenberg, D. (1995). Word-of mouth communication and social learning. *Quarterly Journal of Economics*, 110, 95–126.

Ellsberg, D. (1961). Risk, ambiguity and the Savage axioms. *Quarterly Journal of Economics*, 75, 643–669.

Epstein, L. G. (1999). A definition of uncertainty aversion. *Review of Economic Studies*, 66, 579–608.

Eysenck, H. J. (1947). *Dimensions of personality*. London.

Eysenck, H. J. (1973). *Eysenck on extraversion.* New York: Wiley.

Eysenck, S. B. G., & Eysenck, H. J. (1977). The place of impulsiveness in a dimensional system of personality description. *British Journal of Social and Clinical Psychology*, 2, 46–55.

F

Falk, A., & Fehr, E. (2003). Why labor market experiments? *Labor Economics*, 10, 399–406.

Fehr, E., & Schmidt, K. (1999). A theory of fairness, competition and cooperation. *Quarterly Journal of Economics*, 114, 817–868.

Fellnera, G., & Maciejovsky, B. (2007). Risk attitude and market behavior: evidence from experimental asset markets. *Journal of Economic Psychology*, 28, 338–350.

Ferring, D., & Filipp, S. H. (1996). Messung des Selbstwertgefühls: Befunde zur Reliabilität, Validität und Stabilität der Rosenberg-Skala. *Diagnostica*, 3, 284–292.

Ferris, S. P., Haugen, R. A., & Makhija, A. K. (1988). Predicting contemporary volume with historic volume at differential price levels: evidence supporting the disposition effect. *Journal of Finance*, 43, 677– 697.

Fershtman, C. (1996). On the value of incumbency managerial reference points and loss aversion. *Journal of Economic Psychology*, 17, 245–257.

Fiegenbaum, A. H. T. (1990). Prospect theory and the risk-return association: an empirical examination in 85 industries. *Journal of Economic Behavior & Organization*. 14, 187–203.

Fiegenbaum, A. H. T., & Thomas, H. (1988). Attitudes toward risk and the risk return paradox: prospect theory explanations. *Academy of Management*, 31, 85–106.

Fiegenbaum, A. H. T., Stuart, H., & Schendel, D. (1996). Strategic reference point theory. *Strategic Management Journal*, 17, 219–235.

Fine, T. L. (1973). *Theories of probabilities*. New York, Academic Press.

Fisher, R. A. (1919). The correlation between relatives on the supposition of mendelian inheritance. *Transactions of the Royal Society of Edinburgh*, 52, 399–433.

Fishburn, P .C. (1986). The axioms of subjective probability. *Statistical Science*, 1, 335–358.

Fishburn, P. C., & Kochenberger, G. (1979). Two pieces von Neumann-Morgenstern utility functions. *Decision Science*, 10, 503–518.

Fleishman, J. A. (1988). The effects of decision framing and others' behavior on cooperation in a social dilemma. *Journal of Conflict Resolution*, 32, 162 180.

Forgas, J. P. (1992). Affect and social perception: research evidence and an interfrative theory. *European Review of Social Psychology*, 3, 183–223.

Forgas, J. P. (1995). Mood and judgment: the affect infusion model (AIM). *Psychological Bulletin*, 117, 39–66.

Forgas, J. P. (1999). On feeling good and being rude: affective influences on language use and request formulations. *Journal of Personality and Social Psychology*, 76, 928–939.

Forgas, J. P. (2000). *Feeling and thinking: affective influences on social cognition*. New York: Cambridge University Press.

Forgas, J. P., Lahama, S. M., & Vargas, P. T. (2005). Mood effects on eyewitness memory: affective influences on susceptibility to misinformation. *Journal of Experimental Social Psychology*, 41, 574–588.

Frazier, P. A., Tix, A. P. & Barron, K. E. (2004). Testing moderator and mediator effects in counseling psychology research. *Journal of Counseling Psychology*, 51, 115–134.

Frecka, T. J., & Lee, C. F. (1983) Generalized financial ratio adjustment processes and their implications. *Journal of Accounting Research*, 21, 308–316.

Fredrickson, J. W., & Iaquinto, A. L. (1989). Inertia and creeping rationality in strategic decision processes: extension, observations, future directions. *Academy of Management Journal*, 26, 705–732.

Friedman, M., & Savage, L. J. (1948). The utility analysis of choices involving risks. *Journal of political Economics*, 56, 279–304.

G

Galve-Górriz, C., & Sala-Fumás, V. (1996).Ownership structure and firm performance: some empirical evidence from Spain. *Managerial and Decision Economics*, 17, 587–594.

Garrod, N. & Valentincic, A. (2004). The term structure of implicit discount rates in security valuation. *Journal of Business Finance & Accounting*, 32, 1237–1274.

Gau, R., & Viswanathan M. (2008). The retail shopping experience: experience of low-literate consumers. *Journal of Research for Consumers*, 15, 1–8.

Genesove, D., & Mayer, C. (2001). Loss aversion and seller behavior: evidence from the housing market. *Quarterly Journal of Economics*, 116, 1233–1260.

Georgellis, Y., Gregoriou, A., & Tsitsianis, N. (2008). Adaptation towards reference values: a non-linear perspective. *Journal of Economic Behavior and Organization*, 67, 768–781.

George, J. M., & Brief, A. P. (1992). Feeling good-doing good: a conceptual analysis of the mood at work-organizational spontaneity relationship. *Psychological Bulletin*, 112, 310–329.

George, D., & Mallery, P. (2007). SP*SS for Windows step by step: a simple guide and references - 14.0 update*. Seventh edition, Pearson education, Boston.

Gigerenzer, G. (1991). *Rationality for mortals: risk and rules of thumb*. Oxford University Press, New York.

Gilbert, D., Pinel, E., Wilson, T., Blumberg, S., & Wheatley, T. (1998). Immune neglect: a source of durability bias in affective forecasting. *Journal of Personality and Social Psychology*, 75, 617–638.

Gill, C. M., & Hodgkinson, G. D. (2007). Development and validation of the Five-Factor Model Questionnaire (FFMQ): an adjectival-based personality inventory for use in occupational settings. *Personnel Psychology*, 60, 731–766.

Gilovich, T., Vallone, R., & Tverky, A. (1985). The hot hand in basketball: on the misperception of random sequences. *Cognitive Psychology*, 17, 295–314.

Gläser, E. L., Laibson, D., Scheinkman, J. A., & Soutter, C. L. (2000). Measuring trust. *Quarterly Journal of Economics*, 65, 811–846.

Gneezy, U. (2005). Updating the reference level: experimental evidence. In: Zwick, R. (eds.), & Rapoport, A., *Experimental Business Research*, Netherlands: Springer, 263–284.

Gómez-Mejía, L., Haynes, K., Nunez-Nichel, M., Jacobson, K., & Moyano-Fuentes, J. (2007). Socioemotional wealth and business risks in family-controlled firms: evidence from Spanish olive oil mills. *Administrative Science Quarterly*, 52, 106–137.

Goldberg, L. R. (1981). Language and individual differences. the search for universals in personality lexicons. In: Wheeler L. (ed.), *Review of Personality and Social Psychology*, Beverly Hills, CA: Sage Publications, 141–166.

Gosset, W. S. (Student) (1908). The probable error of a mean. *Biometrika*, 6, 1–25.

Greenleaf, E. A. (1995). The impact of reference price effects on the probability of price promotions. *Marketing Science*, 14, 82–104.

Greve, H. (2002). Sticky aspirations: organizational time perspective and competitiveness. *Organizational Science*, 13, 1–17.

Grinblatt, M., & Keloharju M. (2001). What makes investors trade? *Journal of Finance*, 56, 589–616.

Grinblatt, M., & Han, B. (2005). Prospect theory, mental accounting, and momentum. *Journal of Financial Economics,* 78, 311–339.

H

Hack, A., & Lammers, F. (2008). Why are entrepreneurs more risk loving? On the reference dependencies of entrepreneurial decision making. *Working paper*.

Hack, A., & Lammers, F. (2011). The role of expectations in the formation of reference points. *Working Paper*.

Hagborg, W. (1993). The Rosenberg self -esteem scale and Harter's self-perception profile for adolescents: a concurrent validity study. *Psychology in the Schools*, 30, 132–136.

Hair, J. F., Black, W. C., Babin, B. J., Anderson, R. E., & Tatham, R. L. (2006). *Multivariate data analysis*, 6th ed. Prentice Hall.

Hair, J. F., Black, W. C., Babin, B. J., & Anderson, R. E. (2010). *Multivariate data analysis – a global perspective*, 7th ed. Prentice Hall.

Handler, W. C. (1990). Succession in family firms: a mutual role adjustment between entrepreneur and next-generation family members. *Entrepreneurship Theory & Practice*, 15, 37–51.

Handa, J. (1977). Risk, probabilities, and a new theory of cardinal utility. *Journal of Political Economy*, 85, 97–122.

Harless, D. W., & Camerer, C. F. (1994). The predictive utility of generalized expected utility theories. *Econometrica*, 62, 1251–1289.

Hartman, R. S., Doane, M. J., & Woo, C. K. (1991). Consumer rationality and the status-quo. *Quarterly Journal of Economics*, 106, 141–162.

Harvey, S. J. (1999). Owner as manager, extended horizons and the family firm. *International Journal of the Economics of Business*, 6, 41–55.

Hastorf, A., & Isen, A. M. (1982). *Cognitive Social Psychology*, Elsevier, New York.

Heath, C., & Tversky, A. (1991). Preferences and belief: ambiguity and competences in choices under uncertainty. *Journal of Risk and Uncertainty*, 4, 5–28.

Heath, C., Larrick, R. P., & Wu, G. (1999). Goals as reference points. *Cognitive Psychology*, 38, 79–109.

Heckman, J, Ichimura, H., Smith, J., & Todd, P. (1999). Characterizing selection bias using experimental data. *Econometrica*, 66, 1017–1098.

Heidhues, P., & Köszegi, B. (2008). Competition and price variation when consumers are loss averse. *American Economic Review*, 98, 1245–1268.

Hennig-Thurau, T. H., Walsh, G., & Schrader, U. (2003): VHB- JOURQUAL: Ein Ranking von betriebswirtschaftlich-relevanten Zeitschriften auf der Grundlage von Expertenurteilen, in: *Zeitschrift für betriebswirtschaftliche Forschung*, 56, 520–545.

Heyman, J., Mellers, B., Tishcenko, S., & Schwartz, A. (2004). I was pleased a moment ago: how pleasure varies with background and foreground reference points. *Motivation and Emotion*, 28, 65–83.

Highhouse, S., Brooks-Laber, M. E., Lin, L., & Spitzmueller, C. (2003). What makes a salary seem reasonable? Frequency context effects on starting-salary expectations. *Journal of Occupational and Organizational Psychology*, 76, 69–81.

Hill, C. W. L., & Snell, S. (1988). External control, corporate strategy, and firm performance in research intensive industries. *Strategic Management Journal*, 9, 577–590.

Hirshleifer, D., & Subrahmanyam, A. (1998). Investor psychology and security market under- and over-reactions. *Journal of Finance*, 53, 1839–1886.

Ho, T. H., Lim, N., & Camerer, C. F. (2006). Modeling the Psychology of Consumer and Firm Behavior with Behavioral Economics. *Journal of Marketing Research*, 43, 307–331.

Ho, T-H., Lim, N., & Cui, T. H. (2010). Reference-dependence in multi-location newsvendor models: a structural Analysis. *Management Science*, 56, 1891–1910.

Hoeffler, S., Dan, S., & West, P. (2006). Path dependent preferences: the role of early experience and biased search in preference development. *Organizational Behavior and Human Decision Processes*, 101, 215–229.

Hogan, R. (1983). A socioanalytic theory of personality. *Nebraska symposium on motivation. Lincoln,* 55–89.

Hogan, J., & Ones, D. S. (1997). Conscientiousness and integrity at work. In Hogan, J., Johnson J. A., & Briggs, S. (eds.), *Handbook of personality psychology*. San Diego, CA: Academic Press, 849–870.

Hollenbeck, J. R., & Brief, A. P. (1987). The effect if individual differences and goals origin on goal setting and performance. *Organizational Behavior and Human Decision Processes*, 40, 392–414.

Holt, C. A. (1986). Reference reversals and the independence axiom. *American Economic Review*, 76, 508–515.

Holt, C. A., & Laury, S. K. (2002). Risk aversion and incentive effect. *American Economic Review*, 92, 1644–1655.

Howard, G. S. (1994). Why do people say nasty things about self-reports? *Journal of Organizational Behavior*, 15, 399–404.

I

Irwin, J. R., & McClelland, G. H. (2001). Misleading heuristics and moderated multiple regression models. *Journal of Marketing Research*, 38, 100–109.

Isen, A. M. (1993). Positive affect and decision making. In: Lewisk M., &. Haviland-Jones, J. M. (eds.), *Handbook of emotions*, Chrichester, UK, Wiley, 261–277.

Isen A. M. (2002). Missing in action in the AIM: positive affect's facilitation of cognitive flexibility, innovation, and problem solving. *Psychological Inquiry*, 13, 57–65.

J

Jackson, D. N. (1974). *Personality research form manual.* Goshen, N.Y.: Research Psychologists Press.

Jackson, D. N. (1976). *Jackson personality inventory manual.* Goshen, New York: Research Psychologists Press.

Jackson, D. N. (1994). *Jackson personality inventory – revised manual.* Port Huron, MI: Research Psychologists Press.

John, D. N. (1990). The "Big Five" factor taxonomy: dimensions of personality in the natural language and in questionnaire. In: Pervin, L. (eds.), *Handbook of personality theory and research.* New York: Guilford, 83–100.

Johnson, B. R. (1990). Toward a multidimensional model of entrepreneurship: the case of achievement motivation and the entrepreneur. *Entrepreneurship Theory and Practice*, 14, 39–54.

Johnson, E. J., & Tversky, A. (1983). Affect, generalization and the perception of risk. *Journal Personality and Social Psychology*, 45, 20–31.

Johnson, E J., Hershey, J., Meszaros, J., & Kunreuther, H. (1993). Framing, probability distortions and insurance decisions. *Journal of Risk and Uncertainty*, 7, 35–51.

Joyce, W. B. (2007). On modeling in behavioral accounting research. *Journal of Business & Economics Research*, 5, 35–46.

Jullien, B., & Salanié, B. (2000). Estimation preferences under risk: the case of racetrack bettors. *Journal of Political Economy*, 108, 503–530.

K

Kagan, J. (2007). A trio of concerns. *Perspectives on Psychological Science*, 2, 361–376.

Kahneman, D. (1992). Reference points, anchors, norms, and mixed feelings. *Organizational Behavior Human Decision Processes*, 51, 296–312.

Kahneman, D. (2003). Maps of bounded rationality: psychology for behavioral economics. *American Economic Review*, 93, 1449–1475.

Kahneman, D., & Tversky, A. (1979). Prospect theory: an analysis of decision under risk. *Econometrica,* 47, 263–292.

Kahneman, D., & Tversky, A. (1982). Variants of uncertainty. *Cognition*, 11, 143–157.

Kahneman, D., & Tversky, A. (1984). Choices, values, and frames. *American Psychologist*, 39, 341–350.

Kahneman, D., & Miller, D. T. (1986). Norm theory: comparing reality to its alternatives. Psychological Review, 93, 136–153.

Kahneman, D., & Tversky, A. (1992). Advances in prospect theory: cumulative representation of uncertainty. *Journal of Risk and Uncertainty*, 5, 297–324.

Kahneman, D., & Lovallo, D. (1993). Timid choices and bold forecasts: a cognitive perspective on risk taking. *Management Science*, 39, 17–31.

Kahneman, D., & Tversky, A. (2000). *Choices, values, and frames*. Cambridge University Press, Cambridge.

Kahneman, D., Slovic, P., & Tversky, A (eds.) (1982). *Judgment under uncertainty: heuristics and biases*. New York, Cambridge University Press

Kahneman, D., Knetsch, J. L., & Thaler, R. H. (1990). Experimental tests of the endowment effect and the coase theorem. *Journal Political Economics*, 98, 1325–1348.

Kahneman, D., Knetsch, J. L., & Thaler, R. H. (1991). Anomalies: the endowment effect, loss aversion, and status quo bias. *Journal Political Economics*, 5, 193–206.

Kahneman, D., Wakker, P. P., & Sarin, R. K. (1997). Back to Bentham? Explorations of experienced utility. *Quarterly Journal of Economics,* 112, 375–405.

Kahneman, D., Knetsch, J. T., Thaler, R. H., Kunreuther, H., Luce, R. D., Shweder, R. A. (1986). Fairness and the assumptions of economics / comments. *Journal of Business*, 59, 285–300.

Kaish, S., & Gilad, B. (1991). Characteristics of opportunities search of entrepreneurs versus executives: sources, interests, and general alertness. *Journal of Business Venturing*, 6, 45–61.

Kalyanaram, G., & Winer, R. S. (1995). Empirical generalizations from reference price research. *Marketing Science*, 14, 161–169.

Karmarkar, U. S. (1978). Subjectively weighted utility: a descriptive extension of the expected utility model. *Organizational Behavior and Human Performance,* 21, 61–72.

Kasimatis, M., & Wells, G. L. (1995). Individual differences in counterfactual thinking. In: Roese, N. J., & Olson, J. M. (eds.), *What might have been: the social psychology of counterfactual thinking*, Mahwah, NJ: Lawrence Erlbaum Associates, Inc., 81–101.

Keh, H. T., Foo, M .D., & Lim, B. C. (2002). Opportunity evaluation under risky conditions: the cognitive processes of entrepreneurs. *Entrepreneurship Theory and Practice*, 27, 125–148.

Kellermanns, F. W., & Eddleston, K. A. (2004). Feuding families: when conflict does a family firm good. *Entrepreneurship Theory and Practice,* 28, 209–228.

Kihlstrom, R. E., & Laffont, J. J. (1979). A general equilibrium theory of firm formation based on risk aversion. *Journal of Political Economy,* 87, 719–748.

Kim, N., Han, J. K., & Srivastava, R. K. (2002). A dynamic IT adoption model for the SOHO market: PC generational decisions with technological expectations. *Management Science*, 48, 222–240.

Kim, E. H., Morse, A., & Zingales, L. (2006). What has mattered to economics since 1970. *Journal of Economic Perspectives*, 20, 189–202.

Kivetz, R. (2003). The effects of effort and intrinsic motivation on risky choice. *Marketing Science*, 22, 477–502.

Klein, H. J. (1991). Further evidence on the relationship between goal setting and expectancy theories. *Organizational Behavior and Human Decision Processes,* 49, 230–257.

Knetsch, J. L. (1989). The endowment effect and evidence of nonreversible indifference curves. *American Economic Review*, 79, 1277–1284.

Knight, E. H. (1921). *Risk, uncertainty, and profit*. New York: Houghton Mifflin

Knutson, B., & Peterson, R. (2005). Neurally reconstructing expected utility. *Games and Economic Behavior*, 52, 305–315.

Kolmogorov, A. (1941). Confidence limits for an unknown distribution function. *Annals of Mathematical Statistics*, 23, 525–540.

Koop, G. J., & Johnson, J. G. (2012). The use of multiple reference points in risky decision making. *Journal of Behavioral Decision Making*, 25, 49–62.

Korman, A. K. (1970). Toward a hypothesis of work behavior. *Journal of Applied Psychology*, 54, 31–41.

Köszegi, B., & Rabin, M. (2006). A model of reference-dependent preferences. *Quarterly Journal of Economics*, 121, 1133 1165.

Köszegi, B., & Rabin, M. (2007). Reference-dependent risk attitudes. *American Economic Review*, 97, 1047–1073.

Köszegi, B., & Rabin, M. (2009). Reference-dependent consumption plans. *American Economic Review,* 99, 909–936.

Krantz, J. H., Ballard, J., & Scher, J. (1997). Comparing the results of laboratory and World- Wide Web samples on the determinants of female attractiveness. *Behavioral Research Methods, Instruments, & Computers*, 29, 264–269.

Kühberger, A. (1998). The influence of framing on risky decisions: a meta-analysis. *Organizational Behavior and Human Decision Processes*, 75, 23–55.

Kühberger, M., Schulte-Mecklenbeck, J., & Perner, J. (1999). The effects of framing, reflection, probability, and payoff on risk preference in choice tasks. *Organizational Behavior and Human Decision Processes*, 78, 204–231.

Kume, K., & Suzuki, A. (2010). Ageing, probability weighting, and reference point adaptation: experimental evidence. *Working Paper.*

Kunda, Z. (1999). *Social cognition: making sense of people.* MIT Press, Cambridge, MA.

Kuvaas, B., & Kaufmann, G. (2004). Impact of mood, framing, and need for cognition on decision makers. *Journal of Behavioral Decision Making*, 17, 59–74.

L

Lant, T. (1992). Aspiration level adaptation: an empirical exploration. *Management Science*, 38, 623–644.

Lant, T. K., & Mezias, S. J. (1990). Managing discontinuous change: a simulation study of organizational learning and entrepreneurial strategies. *Strategic Management Journal*, 11, 147–179.

Lant, T. K., & Mezias, S. J. (1992). An organizational learning model of convergence and reorientation. *Organization Science*, 3, 47–71.

Lapidus, A., & Sigot, N. (2000). Individual utility in a context of asymmetric sensitivity to pleasure and pain: an interpretation of Bentham's felicific calculus. *European Journal of the History of Economic Thought*, 7, 45–78.

Larraza-Kintana, M., Wiseman, R. M., Gómez-Mejía, L. R., & Welbourne, T. M. (2007). Distinguishing between employment and compensation risk influences on perceived risk taking. *Strategic Management Journal*, 28, 1001–1019.

Lauriola, M., & Levin, I. P. (2001). Relating individual differences in attitude toward ambiguity to risky choices. *Journal of Behavioral Decision Making*, 14, 107–122.

Le Breton-Miller, I., & Miller, D. (2006). Why do some family businesses outcompete? Governance, long-term orientations, and sustainable capability. *Entrepreneurship Theory and Practice*, 30, 731–746.

Lehner, J. M. (2000). Shifts of reference points for framing of strategic decisions and changing risk-return association. *Management Science*, 46, 63–76.

Lev, B (1969). Industry average as targets for financial ratios. *Journal of Accounting Research*, 7, 290–299.

Lewin, K., Dembo, T., Festinger, L., & Sears. P. S. (1944). Level of aspiration. In: Hunt, J. McV. (ed.), *Personality and the Behavior Disorders*, Ronald, New York, 333– 378.

Levin, I. P., & Gaeth, G.J. (1988). How consumers are affected by the framing of attribute information before and after consuming the product. *Journal of Consumer Research*, 15, 374–378.

Levin, I.P., Schneider, S.L., & Gaeth, G.J. (1998). All frames are not created equal: a typology and critical analysis of framing effects. *Organizational Behavior and Human Decision Processes*, 76, 149–188.

Levin, I. P., Johnson, R. D., Russo, C. P., & Deldin, P. J. (1985). Framing effects in judgment tasks with varying amounts of information. *Organizational Behavior and Human Decision Processes*, 36, 362–377.

Levin, I. P., Gaeth, G. J., Schreiber, J., & Lauriola, M. (2002). A new look at framing effects: distribution of effect sizes, individual differences, and independence of types of effects. *Organizational Behavior and Human Decision Processes*, 88, 411–429.

Levy, J. S. (1992a). An introduction to prospect theory. *Political Psychology*, 13, 171–186.

Levy, M., & Levy, H. (2002a). Prospect theory: much about nothing? *Management Science*, 48, 1334–1349.

Levy, H., & Levy, M. (2002b). Experimental test of the prospect theory value function. *Organizational Behavior and Human Decision Processes,* 89, 1058–1081.

Lin, C.H., Huang, W.H., & Zeelenberg, M. (2006). Multiple reference points in investor regret. *Journal of Economic Psychology*, 27, 781–792.

Linde J., & Sonnemans J. (2009). Social comparison and risky Choices. *Working Paper*

Linville, P. W., & Fischer, G. W. (1991). Preferences for separating or combining events. *Journal of Personality and Social Psychology*, 60, 5–23.

Locke, E. A. (1968). Toward a theory of task motivation and incentives. *Organizational Behavior and Human Performance*, 3, 157–189.

Locke, E. A., & Latham, G. P. (1990). *A theory of goal setting and task performance*. Englewood Cliffs, NJ: Prentice-Hall.

Locke, E. A., Shaw, K. N., Saari, L. M., & Latham, G. P. (1981). Goal setting and tasks performance: 1969–1980. *Psychological Bulletin*, 90, 125–152.

Loewenstein, G. (1988). Reference points in intertemporal choice. *Management Science*, 34, 200–214.

Loewenstein, G. (2005). Hot-cold empathy gaps and medical decision making. *Health Psychology*, 24, 49–56.

Loewenstein, G., & Kahneman, D. (1991). Explaining the endowment effect. *Working Paper*.

Loewenstein, G., & Prelec, D. (1993). Preferences for sequences of outcomes. *Psychological Review*, 100, 91–108.

Loewenstein, G., Weber, E. U., Hsee, C. K., & Welch, N. (2001). Risk as feelings, *Psychological Bulletin*, 127, 267–286.

Loomes, G., & Sugden, R. (1986). Disappointment and dynamic consistency in choice under uncertainty. *Review of Economic Studies*, 53, 271–282.

Lopes, L. L. (1987). Between hope and fear: the psychology of risk. *Advances in Experimental Social Psychology*, 20, 255–295.

Lopes, L. L., & Oden, G. C. (1999). The role of aspiration level in risky choice: a comparison of cumulative prospect theory and SP/A theory. *Journal of Mathematical Psychology*, 43, 286–313.

Luce, R. D., & von Winterfeldt, D. (1994). What common ground exists for descriptive, prescriptive, and normative utility theories? *Management Science*, 40, 263–279.

Luthans, F. (2002). The need for and meaning of positive organizational behavior. *Journal of Organizational Behavior*, 23, 695–706.

M

MacCallum, R. C., Zhang, S., Preacher, K. J., & Rucker, D. D. (2002). On the practice of dichotomization of quantitative variables. *Psychological Methods*, 7, 19–40.

Machina, M. J. (1987). Choice under uncertainty: problem solved and unsolved. *Journal of Economic Perspectives,* 1, 121–154.

Malouff, J. M., Thorsteinsson, E. B., & Schutte, N. S. (2006). The Five-Factor Model of personality and smoking: A meta-analysis. *Journal of Drug Education*, 36, 47–58.

Mano, H. & Oliver, R. (1993). Assessing the dimensionality and structure of the consumption experience. *Journal of Consumer Research*, 20, 451–466.

Mann, H., & Whitney, D. (1947). On a test of whether one of two random variables is stochastically larger than the other. *Annals of mathematical Statistics,* 18, 50–60.

Marsh, H. W., Hau, K. T., Wen, Z., Nagengast, B., & Morin, A. J. S. (in press). Moderation. In: Little, T. D. (ed.), *Oxford handbook of quantitative methods*. New York: Oxford University Press.

Marshall, G. N., Wortman, C. B., Kusulas, J. W., Hervig, L. K., & Vickers, R. R. (1992). Distinguishing optimism from pessimism: Relations to fundamental dimensions of mood and personality. *Journal of Personality and Social Psychology*, 62, 1067–1074.

March, J. G. (1988). Variable risk preferences and adaptive aspirations. *Journal of Economic Behavior and Organizations*, 9, 5–24.

March, J. G., & Shapira, Z. (1987). Managerial perspectives on risk and risk taking. *Management Science*, 33, 1404–1418.

Masatlioglu, Y, & Ok, E. A. (2005). Rational choice with status quo bias. *Journal of Economic Theory,* 121, 1–29.

Mayer, R. C., & Davis, J. H. (1999). The effect of the performance appraisal system on trust for management: a field quasi-experiment. *Journal of Applied Psychology*, 84, 123–136.

Mazumdar, T. S. P. & Jun, S. Y. (1993). Consumer evaluations of multiple versus single price change. *Journal of Consumer Research*, 20, 441–450.

Mazumdar, T. S. P., & Sinha, I. (2005). Reference price research: review and propositions. *American Marketing Associations*, 69, 84–102.

McCarthy, J. D., & Hoge, D. R. (1982). Analysis of age effects in longitudinal studies of adolescent self-esteem. *Developmental Psychology*, 18 (3), 372–379.

McClelland, D. C. (1961). *The achieving society*. Princeton, New York: Van Nostrand.

McClelland, D. C. (1972). What is the effect of achievement motivation training in the schools? *Teachers College Record*, 74, 129–146.

McClelland, D. C., & Liberman, A. M. (1949). The effect of need for achievement on recognition of need-related words. *Journal of Personality*, 18, 236–251.

McConaughy, D. L., Matthews, C. H., & Fialko, A. S. (2001). Founding family controlled firms: performance, risk and value. *Journal of Small Business Management*, 39, 31–49.

McCrae, R. R., & Costa, P. T. (1985). Updating norman's "adequate taxonomy": intelligence and personality dimensions in natural language and in questionnaires. *Journal of Personality and Social Psychology*, 49, 710–721.

McCrae, R. R., & Costa, P. T. (1989). Different points of view: self reports and ratings in the assessment of personality. In: Forgas, J. P., &. Innes, J. M (eds.), *Recent advances in social psychology: An international perspective*, Amsterdam: Elsevier, 429–439.

McCrae, R. R., & Costa, P. T. (1997). Conceptions and correlates of openness to experiences. In: Hogan, J. J., & Briggs, S. (eds.), *Handbook of Personality Psychology*, London: Academic Press, 825–847.

McElroy, T., Seta, J. J., & Waring, D. A. (2007). Reflection on the self: how a self-esteem determines decision framing and increases risk taking. *Journal of Behavioral Decision Making*, 20, 223–240.

McFarlin, D. B., & Blascovich, J. (1981). Effects of self-esteem and performance feedback on future affective preferences and cognitive expectations. *Journal of Personality and Social Psychology*, 40, 521–531.

McNeil, B. J., Pauker, S. G. Sox, H. C., & Tversky, A. (1982). On the elicitation of preferences for alternative therapies. *New England Journal of Medicine*, 306, 1259–1262.

Medvec, V. H., Madey, S. F., & Gilovich, T. (1995). When less is more: counterfactual thinking and satisfaction among Olympic medalists. *Journal of Personality and Social Psychology*, 69, 603–610.

Mellers, B., Schwartz, A., & Ritov, I. (1999). Emotion-based choice. *Journal of Experimental Psychology,* 128, 332–345.

Mellers, B. A., Schwartz, A., Ho, K., & Ritov, I. (1997). Decision affect theory: emotional reactions to the outcomes of risky options. *Psychological Science*, 8, 423–429.

Menon, G., & Raghubir, P. (2003) Ease-of-retrieval as automatic input in judgments: a mere-accessibility framework. *Journal of Costumer Research*, 30, 230–243.

Mercer, J. (2005). Prospect theory and political Science. *Annual Review of Political Science*, 8, 1–21.

Meyerowitz, B. E., & Chaiken, S. (1987). The effect of message framing on breast self-examination attitudes, intentions, and behavior. *Journal of Personality and Social Psychology*, 52, 500–510.

Mezias, S. J. (1988). Aspiration level effects: an empirical investigation. *Journal of economic behavior and organization*, 10, 389–400.

Milch, K. F., Weber, E. U., Appelt, K. C., Handgraaf, M. J. J., & Krantz D. H. (2009). From individual preference construction to group decisions: framing effects and group processes. *Organizational Behavior and Human Decision Processes,* 108, 242–255.

Miner, J. B., & Raju, N. S. (2004). Risk propensity differences between managers and entrepreneurs and between low- and high-growth entrepreneurs: a reply in a more conservative vein. *Journal of Applied Psychology*, 89, 3–13.

Mitchell, R., Morse, E., & Sharma, P. (2003). The transacting cognitions of non-family employees in the family businesses setting. *Journal of Business Venturing*, 18, 533–551.

Monroe, K. B. (1973). Buyer's subjective perception of price. *Journal of Marketing Research*, 10, 70–80.

Montier, J. (2002). *Behavioral Finance.* John Wiley & Sons Inc.

Morris, M. H., Allen, J. A., Kuratko, D. F., & Brannon, D. (2010). Experiencing family business creation: difference between founders, nonfamily managers, and founders of nonfamily firms. *Entrepreneurship Theory and Practice*, 34, 1057–1083.

Moskowitz, D. S. (1986). Comparison of self-reports, reports by knowledgeable informants, and behavioral observation data. *Journal of Personality*, 54, 294–317.

Mroczek, D. K., Spiro, A., Aldwin, C. M., Ozer, D. J., & Bosse, R. (1993). Construct validation of optimism and pessimism in older men: findings from the normative aging study. *Health Psychology*, 12, 406–409.

Myagkov, M., &. Plott, C. R (1997). Exchange economies and loss exposure: experiments exploring prospect theory and competitive equilibria in market environments. *American Economic Review*, 87, 801–828.

Myers, D. G., & Diener, E. (1995). Who is happy? *Psychological Science*, 6, 10–19.

Murray, H. A. (1938). *Explorations in personality*. New York: Oxford University Press.

N

Neale, M. A., & Bazerman, M. H. (1985). The effects of framing and negotiation overconfidence on bargaining behaviors and outcomes. *Academy of Management Journal*, 28, 34–49.

Neale, M. A., & Bazerman, M. H. (1991). *Cognition and rationality in negotiation*. New York: The Free Press.

Neale, M. A., Bazerman, M. H., Northcraft, G. B., & Alperson, C. (1986). Choice shift effects in group decisions: a decision bias perspective. *International Journal of Small Group Research*, 2, 33–42.

Novemsky, N., & Schweitzer, M. E. (2004). What makes negotiators happy? The differential effects of internal and external social comparisons on negotiator satisfaction. *Organizational Behavior and Human Decision Processes*, 95, 186–197.

Nowlis, V., & Nowlis, H. H. (1956). The description and analysis of mood. *Annals of the New York Academy of Sciences*, 65, 345–355.

Nunnally, J. (1967). *Psychometric theory*. New York: McGraw-Hill.

O

Odean, T. (1998). Are investors reluctant to realize their losses? *Journal of Finance*, 5, 1775–1798.

Oppenheim, A. N. (1966). *Questionnaire design and attitude measurement*. Free Press, New York.

Ordóñez, L. D. (1998). The effect of correlation between price and quality on consumer choice. *Organizational Behavior and Human Decision Processes*, 75, 258–273.

Ordóñez, L. D., Connolly, T., & Coughlan, R. (2000). Multiple reference points in satisfaction and fairness assessment. *Journal of Behavioral Decision Making*, 13, 329–44.

P

Palich, L., & Bagby, R. (1995). Using cognitive theory to explain entrepreneurial risk-taking: Challenging conventional wisdom. *Journal of Business Venturing*, 10, 425–438.

Park, K. M. (2007). Antecedents of convergence and divergence in strategic positioning. *Organization Science*, 18, 386–402.

Park, H. M. (2009). Linear Regression models for panel data using SAS, Stata, LIMDEP, and SPSS. *Working Paper*

Paulhus, D. L. (1991). Measurement and control of response bias. In: J. P. Robinson, P. R. Shaver, & L.S. Wrightsman (eds.), *Measures of personality and social psychological attitudes,* San Diego: Academic Press, 17–59.

Paulhus, D. L., & Vazire, S. (2007). The self-report method. In: Robins, R. W., Fraley, R. C. & Krueger, R. F. (eds.), *Handbook of research methods in personality psychology*. London: The Guilford Press, 224–239.

Payne, J. W (2005). It is whether you win or lose: the importance of the overall probabilities of winning or losing in risky choice. *Journal of Risk and Uncertainty*, 30, 5–19.

Payne, J. W., Laughhunn D. J., & Crum, R. (1980). Translation of gambles and aspiration level effects in risky choice behavior. *Management Science,* 26, 1039–1060.

Pearson, K. (1990). On the criterion that a given system of derivations from the probable in the case of a correlated system of variables is such that it can be reasonably supposed to have arisen from random sampling. *Magazine and Journal of Science*. 50, 157–175.

Peeters, G, & Czapinski, J. (1990). Positive-negative asymmetry in evaluations: the distinction between affective and informational negativity effects. *European Review of Social Psychology*, 1, 33–60.

Pennings, P., Keman, H., & Kleinnijenhuis, J. (1999). *Doing research in political Science. An introduction to comparative methods and statistics*. London: Sage.

Pennings, J. M. E., Candel, M. J. J. M., & Egelkraut, T. (2003). Behavioral decision-making modeling approach toward hedging services. *Journal of Behavioral Finance*, 4, 71–84.

Peterson, C., Seligman, M. E., & Vaillant, G. E. (1988). Pessimistic explanatory style is a risk factor for physical illness: a thirty-five-year longitudinal study. *Journal of Personality and Social Psychology*, 55, 23–27.

Pilegge, A. J., & Holtz, R. (1997). The effects of social identity on self-set goals and task performance of high and low self-esteem individuals. *Organizational Behavior and Human Decision Processes*, 70, 17–26.

Plott, C. R., & Zeiler, K. (2005). The willingness to pay-willingness to accept gap, the "endowment effect," subjective misconceptions, and experimental procedures for eliciting valuations. *American Economic Review*, 95, 530–545.

Pope, D. G., & Schweitzer, M. E. (2011). Is Tiger Woods loss averse? Persistent bias in the face of experience, competition, and high stakes. *American Economic Review*, 101, 129–157.

Post, T., Van den Assem, M .J., Baltussen, G., & Thaler, R. H. (2008). Deal or no deal? Decision making under risk in a large-payoff game show. *American Economic Review*, 98, 38–71.

Prelec, D. (1998).The probability weighting function. *Econometrica*, 66, 497–527.

Prelec, D., & Loewenstein, G. (1998). The red and the black: mental accounting of savings and debt. *Marketing Science*, 17, 4–28.

Pyszczynski, T. & Greenberg, J. (1987). Self-regulatory perseveration and the depressive self-focusing style: a self-awareness theory of reactive depression. *Psychological Bulletin*, 102, 122–138.

Q

Quiggin, J. (1982). A theory of anticipated utility. *Journal of Economic Behavior and Organization*, 3, 323–343.

R

Rabin, M. (1997). Psychology and economics. *Working paper*

Rabin, M. (2002). A perspective on psychology and economics. *European Economic Review*, 46, 657–685.

Ramsey, F. P. (1931). *The foundations of mathematics*. New York: Harcourt Brace.

Read, D. (2002). Book review: choices, values and frames. *Journal of Behavior and Decision Making*, 15, 467–73.

Rogoff, E. G., & Heck, R. K. Z. (2003). Evolving research in entrepreneurship and family business: recognizing family as the oxygen that feeds the fire of entrepreneurship. *Journal of Business Venturing*, 18, 559–566.

Rosch, R. (1975). Cognitive reference points. *Cognitive Psychology*, 7, 532–547.

Rosenberg, M. (1965). *Society and the adolescent self-image*. Princeton: Princeton University Press.

Rosenberg, M. (1979). *Conceiving the self.* New York: Basic Books.

S

Sagi, J. S. (2006). Anchored preference relations. *Journal of Economic Theory*, 130, 283–295.

Samuelson, W., & Zeckhauser, R. (1988). Status quo bias in decision making. *Journal of Risk and Uncertainty*, 1, 7–59.

Sathe, V. (2003). *Corporate entrepreneurship: top managers and new business creation*. Cambridge, UK: Cambridge University Press.

Saulsman, L. M., & Page, A. C. (2004). The Five-Factor model and personality disorder empirical literature: a meta-analytic review. *Clinical Psychology Review*, 23, 1055–1085.

Savage, L. J. (1954). The foundations of statistics. New York: Wiley.

Scheier, M. F., & Carver, C. S. (1985). Optimism, coping, and health: assessment and implications of generalized outcome expectancies. *Health Psychology*, 5, 219–247.

Scheier, M. F., & Carver, C. S. (1992). Effects of optimism on psychological and physical well-being: theoretical overview and empirical update. *Cognitive Therapy and Research*, 16, 201–228.

Schlenker, B. R., Soraci, S., & McCarthy, B. (1979). Self-esteem and group performance as determinants of egocentric perceptions in cooperative groups. *Human Relations*, 29, 1163–1176.

Schmeidler, D. (1989). Subjective probability and expected utility without additivity. *Econometrica*, 57, 571–587.

Schmidt, U. (2003). Reference dependence in cumulative prospect theory. *Journal of Mathematical Psychology*, 47, 122–131.

Schmidt, U., Starmer, C., & Sugden, R. (2008). Third generation prospect theory. *Journal Risk Uncertainty*, 36, 203–223.

Schimmack, U., & Diener, E. (1997). Affect intensity: Separating intensity and frequency in repeatedly measured affect. *Journal of Personality and Social Psychology*, 73, 1313–1329.

Schneeweiss, H. (1974). Probability and utility-dual concepts in decision theory. In: Menges, G. (ed.): *Information, inference and decision*, Holland, 113–44.

Schneider, H. (2009): Nachweis und Behandlung von Multikollinearität. In: Albers, S., Klapper, D., Konradt, U., & Walter, A. (eds.) *Methodik der empirischen Forschung*, Wiesbaden, Gabler, 221–236.

Schneider, S. L., & Lopes, L. L. (1986). Reflection in preferences under risk: who and when may suggest why. *Journal of Experimental Psychology: Human Perception and Performance*, 12, 531–548.

Schoemaker, P. J. H. (1982). The expected utility model: its variants, purposes, evidence and limitations. *Journal of Economic Literature*, 20, 529–563.

Schultze, W., & Dickinson, A. (2000). Neuronal coding of prediction errors. *Annual Review of Neuroscience*, 23, 473–500.

Schulze, W. S., Lubatkin, M. H., & Dino, M. H. (2003). Toward a theory of agency and altruism in family firms. *Journal of Business Venturing*, 18, 473–450.

Schulze, W. S., Lubatkin, M. H., Dino, M. H., & Buchholtz, A. K. (2002). Agency relationships in family firms: theory and evidence. *Organization Science*. 12, 99–116.

Schwarz, N, & Clore, G. L. (1983). Mood, misattribution, and judgments of well-being: informative and directive functions of affective states. *Journal of Personality and Social Psychology*, 45, 513–523.

Schwenk, C. R. (1988). The cognitive perspective on strategic decision making. *Journal of Management Studies*, 25, 41–55.

Schwer, K. & Yucelt, U. (1984). A study of risk-taking propensities among small business entrepreneurs and managers: an empirical evaluation. *American Journal of Small Business*, 8, 31–40.

Sharma, P., Chrisman, J. J., & Chua, J. H. (1996). A *review and annotated bibliography of family business studies*. Boston, MA: Kluwer Academic Publishers.

Shefrin, H. M., & Statman, M. (1985). The disposition to sell winners too early and ride losers too long: theory and evidence. *Journal of Finance*, 40, 777–790.

Shepperd, J. A., Quellette, J. A., & Fernandez, J. K. (1996). Abandoning unrealistic optimistic performance estimates and the temporal proximity of self-relevant feedback. *Journal of Personality and Social Psychology*, 70, 844–855.

Siegel, S. (1956). *Nonparametric statistics for behavioral science*. New York, McGraw-Hill Company.

Siegel, S. (1957). Level of aspiration and decision making. *Psychological Review*, 64, 253–262.

Simon, H. A. (1976). *Administrative behavior*. New York: Free Press.

Simon, M., Houghton, S. M., & Aquino, K. (2000). Cognitive biases, risk perception, and venture formation: how individuals decide to start companies. *Journal of Business Venturing,* 14, 113–134.

Sirmon, D. G., & Hitt, M. A. (2003). Managing resources: linking unique resources, management and wealth creation in family firms. *Entrepreneurship Theory and Practice*, 27, 339–358.

Sitkin, S. B., & Pablo, A. L. (1992). Reconceptualizing the determinants of risk behavior. *Academy of Management Review*, 17, 9–38.

Shea, J. (1995). Union contracts and the life-cycle / permanent-income hypothesis. *American Economic Review*, 85, 186–200.

Smallwood, D. E., & Conlisk, J. (1979). Product quality in markets where consumers are imperfectly informed. *Quarterly Journal of Economics*, 93, 1–23.

Smith, V. (1982). Microeconomic systems as an experimental science. *American Economic Review*, 72, 923–955.

Smith, K. G., Locke, E. A., & Barry, D. (1990). Goal setting, planning, and organizational performance: an experimental simulation. *Organizational Behavior and Human Decision Processes*, 46, 118–134.

Slovic, P., Lichtenstein, S., & Fischhoff, B. (1988). Decision making. In: Atkinson, R. C., Herrnstein, R. J., Lindzey, G., &. Luce, R. D (eds.), *Stevens' handbook of experimental psychology,* New York: Wiley, 673–738.

Slovic, P., Flynn, J. H., & Layman, M. (1991). Perceived risk, trust, and the politics of nuclear waste. *Science*, 254, 1603–1607.

Spangler, W. D. (1992). Validity of questionnaire and TAT measures of need for achievement: two meta-analyses. *Psychological Bulletin*, 112, 140–154.

Sprent, P., & Smeeton, N. C. (2000). *Applied nonparametric statistical methods*. London: Chapman and Hall/CRC.

Stanley, L. J. (2010). Emotions and family business creation: an extension and implications. *Entrepreneurship Theory and Practice*, 34, 1085–1092.

Starmer, C. (2000). Developments in non-expected utility theory: the hunt for a descriptive theory of choice under risk. *Journal of Economic Literature*, 38, 332–383.

Stata Corporation (2003). *Stata statistical software*. Release 11.0 College Station, TX: Stata Press.

Staw, B. M. (1981). The escalation of commitment to a course of action. *Academy of Management Review,* 6, 577–587.

Staw, B. M, & Barsade, S. G. (1993). Affect and managerial performance: a test of the sadder-but-wiser vs. happier-and-smarter hypothesis. *Administrative Science Quarterly*, 38, 304–331.

Stewart, W. H., & Roth, P. L. (2001). Risk propensity differences between entrepreneurs and managers: a meta-analytic review. *Journal of Applied Psychology*, 86, 145–153.

Stumpf, H., Angleitner, A., Wieck, T., Jackson, D. N., & Beloch-Till, H. (1985). *Deutsche Personality Research Form (PRF)*. Handanweisung. Göttingen: Hogrefe.

Sugden, R. (2003). Reference-dependent subjective expected utility. *Journal of Economic Theory*, 111, 172–191.

Sullivan, K, & Kida, T. (1995). The effect of multiple reference points and prior gains and losses on managers' risky decision making. *Organizational Behavior and Human Decision processes*, 64, 76–83.

Sulsky, L. M., & Day, D. V. (1992). Frame-of-reference training and cognitive categorization: an empirical investigation of rater memory issues. *Journal of Applied Psychology,* 77, 501–510.

T

Tabachnick, B. G., Fidell, L. S. (1996). *Using multivariate statistics*. 3 rd. ed. HarperCollins College Publishers, New York.

Tagiuri, R., & Davis, J. A. (1992). On the goals of successful family companies. *Family Business Review*, 5, 43–62.

Tang, T. L. P., & Sarsfield-Baldwin, L. (1991). The effect of self-esteem, task label, and performance feedback and goal setting, certainty and attributions. *Journal of Psychology*, 125, 413–418.

Thaler, R. H. (1980). Toward a positive theory of consumer choice. *Journal of Economic Behavior and Organization*, 1, 39–60.

Thaler, R. H. (1985). Mental accounting and consumer choice. *Marketing Science*, 4, 199–214.

Thaler, R. H. (1989). Anomalies: interindustry wage differentials. *Journal of Economic Perspectives,* 3, 181–193.

Thaler, R. H. (1999). Mental accounting matters. *Journal of Behavioral Decision Making*, 12, 183–206.

Thaler, R. H., & Johnson, E. J. (1990). Gambling with the house money and trying to break even: the effects of prior outcomes on risky choice. *Management Science*, 36, 643–660.

Tryon, W. W. (1994). Expectation. In: Ramachandran, V. S. (ed.), *Encyclopedia of Human Behavior*, San Diego, CA: Academic, 313–319.

Tversky, A. (1969). Intransitivity of preferences. *Psychological Review*, 76, 31–48.

Tversky, A., & Kahneman, D. (1981). The framing of decisions and the psychology of choice. *Science,* 211, 453–458.

Tversky, A., & Kahneman, D. (1986). Rational choice and the framing of decisions. *Journal of Business*, 59, 251–278.

Tversky, A., & Kahneman, D. (1991). Loss aversion in riskless choice: a reference dependent model. *Quarterly Journal of Economics*, 107, 1039–1061.

Tversky, A., & Kahneman, D. (1992). Advances in prospect theory: cumulative representation of uncertainty. *Journal of Risk and Uncertainty*, 5, 297–323.

V

Van den Bos, K., & Van Prooijen, J. W. (2001). Referent cognitions theory: the psychology of voice depends on closeness of reference points. *Journal of Personality and Social Psychology*, 81, 616–626.

Van Dijk W. W., & Van der Pligt, J. (1996). The impact of probability and magnitude of outcome on disappointment and elation. *Organizational Behavior and Human Decision Processes,* 69, 277–284.

Van Dijk W. W., Van der Pligt, J, & Zeelenberg, M (2003). Blessed are those who expect nothing: lowering expectations as a way of avoiding disappointment. *Journal of Economic Psychology,* 24, 505–516.

Van Osch, S. M. C, Stiggelbout, A. M., & Van den Hout, W. B (2006). Exploring the reference point in prospect theory: gambles for length of life. *Medical Decision Making*; 26, 38–346.

Von Neumann, J., & Morgenstern, O. (1944). *Theory of games and economic behavior*. Princeton University Press, Princeton.

Von Neumann, J., & Morgenstern, O. (1947). *Theory of games and economic behavior*. (2nd ed.) Princeton, NJ: Princeton University Press.

Vroom, V. H. (1964). *Work and motivation*. New York: Wiley.

W

Wakker, P. P. (2010). *Prospect theory for risk and ambiguity*. Cambridge University Press, Cambridge.

Walsh, J. P., & Seward, J. K. (1990). On the efficiency of internal and external corporate control mechanisms. *Academy of Management Review*, 15, 421–458.

Wang, X. T. (2008). Decision Heuristics as Predictors of Public Choice. *Journal of Behavioral Decision Making*, 2, 77–89.

Wang, X. T., & Johnson, J. G. (2009). Tri-reference point theory of risky choice. *Manuscript submitted for publication.*

Watson, D. & Tellegen, A. (1985). Toward a consensual structure of mood. *Psychological Bulletin*, 98, 219–235.

Weber, E. U. (1994). From subjective probabilities to decision weights: the effect of asymmetric loss function in the evaluation of uncertain outcomes. *Psychological Bulletin*, 115, 228–242.

Weber, E. U., & Milliman, R. A. (1997). Perceived-risk attitudes: relating risk perception to risky choice. *Management Science*, 43, 123–144.

Weber, M., & Camerer, C. F. (1998). The disposition effect in securities trading: an experimental analysis. *Journal of Economic Behavior & Organization*, 33, 167–184.

Weber, E. U., Blais, A.-R., & Betz, N. E. (2002). A fomain-specific risk-attitude scale: measuring risk perceptions and risk behaviors. *Journal of Behavioral Decision Making*, 2002, 263–290.

Weiner, B., D., & Lerman. R. D. (1979). The cognition - emotion process in achievement-related contexts. *Journal of Personality and Social Psychology*, 37, 1211–1220.

Weimer, J., & Pape, J. (1999). A taxonomy of systems of corporate governance. *Corporate Governance - An International Review*, 7, 152–166.

Weiss, H. M., & Cropanzano, R. (1996). Affective events theory: a theoretical discussion of the structure, causes and consequences of affective experiences at work. In: Staw, B. M.; & Cummings, L. L. (eds.), *Research in organizational behavior: An annual series of analytical essays and critical reviews*, 18, 1–74.

Weiss, H. M., Nicholas, J. P., & Daus, C. S. (1999). An examination of the joint effects of affective experiences and job beliefs on job satisfaction and variations in affective experiences over time. *Organizational Behavior and Human Decision Processes*, 78, 1–24.

Westhead, P., & Cowling, M. (1998). Family firm research: the need for a methodological rethink. *Entrepreneurship Theory and Practice,* 23, 31–56.

White, H. (1980), A heteroscedasticity-consistent covariance matrix estimator and a direct test for heteroscedasticity. *Econometrica*, 48, 817–838.

Wicker, F. W., Turner, J. E., Reed, J. H., McCann, E. J., & Do, S. L. (2004). Motivation when optimism declines: data on temporal dynamics. *Journal of Psychology: Interdisciplinary and Applied*, 138, 421–432.

Winer, R. S. (1985). A price vector model of demand for consumer durables: preliminary developments. *Marketing Science*, 4, 74–90.

Winer, R. S. (1986). A reference price model of brand choice for frequently purchased products. *Journal of Consumer Research*, 13, 250–256.

Wiseman, R. M., & Gómez-Mejía, L.R. (1998). A behavioral agency model of managerial risk taking. *Academy of Management Review*, 23, 133–153.

Wiseman, R. M., Gómez-Mejía, L. R., & Fugate, M. (2000). Rethinking compensation risk. In: Rynes S. L., & Gerhard, B. (eds.), *Compensation in organizations*, Josey-Bass: San Francisco, CA; 311–347.

Wilcoxon, F. (1945). Individual comparisons by ranking methods. *Biometrics Bulletin,* 1, 80–83.

Wright, P., Ferris, S., Sarin, A., & Awasthi, V. (1996). The impact of corporate insider, blockholder, and institutional equity ownership on firm risk-taking. *Academy of Management Journal*, 39, 441–463.

Wrosch, C., & Scheier, M. F. (2003). Personality and quality of life: the importance of optimism and goal adjustment. *Quality of Life Research*, 12, 59–72.

Wu, G. (1994). An empirical test of ordinal independence. *Theory and Decisions*, 9, 39–60.

Wu, G., & Markle, A. B. (2008). An empirical test of gain-loss separability in prospect theory. *Management Science,* 54, 1322–1335.

Y

Yogo, M. (2008). Asset prices under rising aspirations and reference-dependent preferences. *Journal of Business and Economic Statistics*, 26, 131–143

Z

Zahra, S. A. (2005). Entrepreneurial risk taking in family firms. *Family Business Review*, 18, 23–40.

Zeelenberg, M., Van Dijk, W. W., Manstead, A. S. R., & Van de Pligt, J. (2000). On bad decisions and disconfirmed expectancies: the psychology of regret and disappointment. *Cognition and Emotion,* 14, 521–541.

Zellweger, T. M. (2007). Time horizon, costs of equity capital, and generic investment strategies of firms. *Family Business Review*, 20, 1–15.

Zellweger, T. M., & Astrachan, J. H. (2008). On emotional value of owning a firm. *Family Business Review*, 21, 347–363.

Zellweger, T. M., Kellermanns, F. W., Chrisman, J. J., Chua, J. H. (2011). Family control and family firm valuation by family CEOs: the importance of intentions for transgenerational control. *Organization Science*, in press, published online ahead of print July 5, 2011.

Zuckerman, M. (1971). Dimensions of sensation seeking. *Journal of Consulting and Clinical Psychology*, 36, 45–52.

10 Questionnaires applied in this study

10.1 Questionnaire Experiment 1 (study 1)

Questionnaire A

Instruktionen

Bitte füllen Sie den folgenden Fragebogen vollständig aus. Lesen Sie sich die Fragen in Ruhe durch und versuchen Sie, eine möglichst wahrheitsgetreue Selbsteinschätzung vorzunehmen.

Es gibt keine richtigen und falschen Antworten, wir sind lediglich an Ihrer persönlichen Einschätzung interessiert.

Die Antworten werden anonymisiert, so dass keine Rückschlüsse auf Ihre Person gezogen werden können.

Fragenblock 1

1) Wie alt sind Sie?

☐ Jahre

2) Welches Geschlecht haben Sie? (Bitte ankreuzen)

☐ weiblich ☐ männlich

Fragenblock 2

Stellen Sie sich bitte folgende Situation vor:

Vor zwei Monaten haben Sie Aktien eines Unternehmens zu einem Kurs von **30 € je Aktie** gekauft.

Vor einem Monat waren Sie enttäuscht, als Sie von einem **Kursfall auf 24 € je** Aktie erfahren haben.

Heute entscheiden Sie sich, den Kurs der Aktie erneut zu überprüfen. Welchen Kurs müsste die Aktie heute haben, um sie **genauso traurig** zu machen, **wie Sie vor einem Monat waren**, als Sie erfahren hatten, dass der Kurs von 30 € auf 24 € gefallen war?

Bitte notieren Sie den Kurs, der Sie heute genauso traurig machen würde, hier:

☐ € je Aktie

Fragenblock 3

1) Bezüglich des Fragenblocks 2: Welchen Kurs haben Sie für heute erwartet? (hier fragen wir nach Ihren Erwartungen und nicht danach, was Sie genauso traurig machen würde)

   Bitte notieren Sie den Kurs hier: ☐ € je Aktie

2) Wie bewerten Sie das Risiko einer Anlage in Aktien? (Bitte ankreuzen)

   Sehr gering ☐—☐—☐—☐—☐—☐—☐ **Sehr hoch**

3) Wie gut können Sie generell die Entwicklung von Aktienkursen vorhersagen?

   Sehr gut ☐—☐—☐—☐—☐—☐—☐ **Sehr schlecht**

4) Haben Sie schon einmal Geld in Aktien angelegt?

☐ ja ☐ nein

→ 4a. Wie oft haben Sie Geld in Aktien angelegt?

Ständig **Sehr selten**

☐—☐—☐—☐—☐—☐—☐

4b. Wie zufrieden waren Sie mit Ihren Aktienanlagen?

Völlig zufrieden **Gar nicht zufrieden**

☐ ☐ ☐ ☐ ☐ ☐ ☐

Questionnaire B
(only differences to Questionnaire A are shown)

Fragenblock 2

Stellen Sie sich bitte folgende Situation vor:
Vor zwei Monaten haben Sie Aktien eines Unternehmens zu einem Kurs von **30 € je Aktie** gekauft.

Vor einem Monat waren Sie enttäuscht, als Sie von einem Kursfall auf **24 € je Aktie** erfahren haben. Ebenfalls vor einem Monat haben Sie erfahren, dass diesen Monat der Aktienpreis **erwartungsgemäß** innerhalb **der Spanne 10 € und 30 €** liegen wird und dass jeder Preis innerhalb dieses Intervalls mit gleicher Wahrscheinlichkeit eintreten kann.

Heute entscheiden Sie sich, den Kurs der Aktie erneut zu überprüfen. Welchen Kurs müsste die Aktie heute haben, um sie **genauso traurig** zu machen, **wie Sie vor einem Monat waren**, als Sie erfahren hatten, dass der Kurs von 30 € auf 24 € gefallen war?

Bitte notieren Sie den Kurs, der Sie heute genauso traurig machen würde, hier:

[ ] € je Aktie

Questionnaire C
(only differences to Questionnaire A are shown)

Fragenblock 2

Stellen Sie sich bitte folgende Situation vor:

Vor zwei Monaten haben Sie Aktien eines Unternehmens zu einem Kurs von **30 € je Aktie** gekauft.

Vor einem Monat waren Sie enttäuscht, als Sie von einem Kursfall auf **24 € je Aktie** erfahren haben. Ebenfalls vor einem Monat haben Sie erfahren, dass diesen Monat der Aktienpreis **erwartungsgemäß** innerhalb **der Spanne 15 € und 35 €** liegen wird und dass jeder Preis innerhalb dieses Intervalls mit gleicher Wahrscheinlichkeit eintreten kann.

Heute entscheiden Sie sich, den Kurs der Aktie erneut zu überprüfen. Welchen Kurs müsste die Aktie heute haben, um sie **genauso traurig** zu machen, **wie Sie vor einem Monat waren**, als Sie erfahren hatten, dass der Kurs von 30 € auf 24 € gefallen war?

Bitte notieren Sie den Kurs, der Sie heute genauso traurig machen würde, hier:

[ ] € je Aktie

Questionnaire D
(only differences to Questionnaire A are shown)

Fragenblock 2

Stellen Sie sich bitte folgende Situation vor:

Vor zwei Monaten haben Sie Aktien eines Unternehmens zu einem Kurs von **30 € je Aktie** gekauft.

Vor einem Monat waren Sie enttäuscht, als Sie von einem Kursfall auf **24 € je Aktie** erfahren haben. Ebenfalls vor einem Monat haben Sie erfahren, dass diesen Monat der Aktienpreis **erwartungsgemäß** innerhalb **der Spanne 5 € und 25 €** liegen wird und dass jeder Preis innerhalb dieses Intervalls mit gleicher Wahrscheinlichkeit eintreten kann.

Heute entscheiden Sie sich, den Kurs der Aktie erneut zu überprüfen. Welchen Kurs müsste die Aktie heute haben, um sie **genauso traurig** zu machen, **wie Sie vor einem Monat waren**, als Sie erfahren hatten, dass der Kurs von 30 € auf 24 € gefallen war?

Bitte notieren Sie den Kurs, der Sie heute genauso traurig machen würde, hier:

	€ je Aktie

10.2 Questionnaire Experiment 2 (study 2)

Questionnaire Aa – gain domain

Instruktionen

Bitte füllen Sie den folgenden Fragebogen **vollständig** aus. Lesen Sie sich die Fragen in Ruhe durch und versuchen Sie, eine möglichst wahrheitsgetreue Selbsteinschätzung vorzunehmen.

Es gibt keine richtigen und falschen Antworten, wir sind lediglich an Ihrer persönlichen Einschätzung interessiert.

Die Antworten werden anonymisiert, so dass **keine Rückschlüsse auf Ihre Person** gezogen werden können.

Fragenblock 1

1) Wie alt sind Sie?

☐ Jahre Jahre

2) Welches Geschlecht haben Sie? (Bitte ankreuzen)

☐ weiblich ☐ männlich

Fragenblock 2

Stellen Sie sich bitte folgende Situation vor:

Vor 2 Monaten haben Sie Aktien eines Unternehmens zu einem Kurs von **30 € je Aktie** gekauft.

Vor einem Monat konnten Sie sich über einen Kursanstieg auf **36 € je Aktie** freuen.

Heute entscheiden Sie sich, den Kurs der Aktie erneut zu überprüfen. Welchen Kurs müsste die Aktie heute haben, um Sie **genauso glücklich** zu machen, **wie Sie vor einem Monat waren**, als Sie erfahren hatten, dass der Kurs von 30 € auf 36 € gestiegen war?

Bitte notieren Sie den Kurs, der Sie heute genauso glücklich machen würde, hier:

☐ € je Aktie

Fragenblock 3

1) Bezüglich des Fragenblocks 2: Welchen Kurs haben Sie für heute **erwartet**? (hier fragen wir nach Ihren Erwartungen und nicht danach, was Sie genauso traurig machen würde)

   Bitte notieren Sie den Kurs hier: ☐ € je Aktie

2) Wie bewerten Sie das Risiko einer Anlage in Aktien? (Bitte ankreuzen)

   Sehr gering ☐ ☐ ☐ ☐ ☐ ☐ ☐ **Sehr hoch**

3) Wie gut können Sie generell die Entwicklung von Aktienkursen vorhersagen?

   Sehr gut ☐ ☐ ☐ ☐ ☐ ☐ ☐ **Sehr schlecht**

4) Haben Sie schon einmal Geld in Aktien angelegt?

☐ **ja** ☐ nein

→ 4a. Wie oft haben Sie Geld in Aktien angelegt?

Ständig **Sehr selten**

☐ ☐ ☐ ☐ ☐ ☐ ☐

4b. Wie zufrieden waren Sie mit Ihren Aktienanlagen?

Völlig zufrieden **Gar nicht zufrieden**

☐ ☐ ☐ ☐ ☐ ☐ ☐

Fragenblock 4

Bitte lesen Sie jede der folgenden Aussagen aufmerksam durch und überlegen Sie, ob diese Aussagen auf Sie persönlich zutrifft oder nicht. Kreuzen Sie bitte als Antwort die Kategorie an, die Ihre Sichtweise am Besten ausdrückt.

Bitte bewerten Sie die Aussagen so wahrheitsgemäß wie möglich, arbeiten Sie sowie zügig, aber sorgfältig. Lassen Sie keine Aussage aus. Wenn Sie sich nicht ganz sicher sind, kreuzen Sie bitte die Antwort an, die am ehesten auf Sie zutrifft. (Bitte in jeder Zeile eine Möglichkeit ankreuzen!)

Aussagen	**Starke Ableh-leh-nung**	**Ab-leh-nung**	**Neu-tral**	**Zu-stim-mung**	**Starke Zustim-mung**
1. Ich bin **nicht** leicht beunruhigt.					
2. Ich mag meine Zeit **nicht** mit Tagträumereien verschwen-den.					
3. Ich halte meine Sachen ordentlich und sauber.					
4. Ich fühle mich anderen oft unterlegen.					
5. Ich finde philosophische Dis-kussionen langweilig.					
6. Ich kann mir meine Zeit recht gut einteilen, so dass ich mei-ne Angelegenheiten rechtzeitig beende.					
7. Wenn ich unter starkem Stress stehe, fühle ich mich manch-mal, als ob ich zusammen-bräche.					
8. Mich begeistern die Motive, die ich in der Kunst und in der Na-tur finde.					
9. Ich bin **kein** sehr sympathisch vorgehender Mensch.					
10. Ich fühle mich **selten** einsam und traurig.					
11. Ich glaube, dass es Schüler oft nur verwirrt und irreführt, wenn man sie Rednern zuhören lässt, die kontroverse Stand-punkte vertreten.					
12. Ich versuche, alle mir übertra-genen Aufgaben sehr gewis-senhaft zu erledigen.					
13. Ich fühle mich oft angespannt und nervös.					
14. Poesie beeindruckt mich wenig oder gar nicht.					

Aussagen	Starke Ableh-lehnung	Ab-lehnung	Neu-tral	Zu-stim-mung	Starke Zustim-mung
15. Ich habe eine Reihe von klaren Zielen und arbeite systematisch auf sie zu.					
16. Manchmal fühle ich mich völlig wertlos.					
17. Ich probiere oft neue und fremde Speisen aus.					
18. Ich vertrödele eine Menge Zeit, bevor ich mit meiner Arbeit beginne.					
19. Ich empfinde selten Furcht oder Angst.					
20. Ich nehme nur selten Notiz von den Stimmungen oder Gefühlen, die verschiedene Umgebungen hervorrufen.					
21. Ich arbeite hart, um meine Ziele zu erreichen.					
22. Ich ärgere mich oft darüber, wie andere Leute mich behandeln.					
23. Ich glaube, dass wir bei ethischen Entscheidungen auf die Ansichten unserer religiösen Autoritäten achten sollten.					
24. Wenn ich eine Verpflichtung eingehe, so kann man sich auf mich bestimmt verlassen.					
25. Zu häufig bin ich entmutigt und will aufgeben, wenn etwas schief geht.					
26. Wenn ich Literatur lese oder ein Kunstwerk betrachte, empfinde ich manchmal ein Frösteln oder ein Welle der Begeisterung.					

Aussagen	**Starke Ableh-lehnung**	**Ab-leh-nung**	**Neu-tral**	**Zu-stim-mung**	**Starke Zustim-mung**
27. Manchmal bin ich **nicht** so verlässlich oder zuverlässig, wie ich sein sollte.					
28. Ich bin selten traurig oder deprimiert.					
29. Ich habe wenig Interesse, über die Natur des Universums oder die Lage der Menschheit zu spekulieren.					
30. Ich bin eine tüchtige Person, die ihre Arbeit immer erledigt.					
31. Ich fühle mich oft hilflos und wünsche mir eine Person, die meine Probleme löst.					
32. Ich bin sehr wissbegierig.					
33. Ich werde niemals fähig sein, Ordnung in mein Leben zu bringen.					
34. Manchmal war mir etwas so peinlich, dass ich mich am liebsten versteckt hätte.					
35. Ich habe oft Spaß daran, mit Theorien oder abstrakten Ideen zu spielen.					
36. Bei allem, was ich tue, strebe ich nach Perfektion.					

Fragenblock 5

Bitte geben Sie an, ob die folgenden Aussagen auf Sie zutreffen („Richtig“) oder nicht zutreffen („Falsch“). Geben Sie zu jedem Satz entweder „Richtig“ oder „Falsch“ als Antwort an; wenn Sie sich nicht ganz sicher sind, kreuzen Sie bitte die Antwort an, die am ehesten auf Sie zutrifft. (Bitte in jeder Zeile eine Möglichkeit ankreuzen!) Bitte bearbeiten Sie alle Aussagen zügig, aber sorgfältig, und halten Sie sich nicht zu lange an einzelnen Sätzen auf.

Aussage	Richtig	Falsch
1. Ich ärgere mich über mich selbst, wenn ich etwas nicht gründlich gelernt habe.		
2. Ich arbeite, weil ich arbeiten muss, und nur deswegen.		
3. Ich arbeite an Problemen weiter, bei denen andere schon aufgegeben haben.		
4. Ich versuche, nur soviel zu arbeiten, dass ich mein Auskommen habe.		
5. Ich setze mir oft schwer erreichbare Ziele.		
6. Ich würde lieber eine leichtere Arbeit ausführen als eine, bei der Schwierigkeiten zu überwinden sind.		
7. Ich habe mir vorgenommen, wenigstens etwas mehr zu leisten als irgendjemand vor mir.		
8. Harte Arbeit gefällt mir nicht.		
9. Ich werde lieber nach Arbeitsleistung als nach Arbeitszeit bezahlt.		
10. Im Rahmen meines Berufs habe ich für meine Fortbildung selten zusätzliche Arbeit aufgewendet.		
11. Es macht mir nichts aus zu arbeiten, während andere Leute sich amüsieren.		
12. Es ist mir an sich ziemlich gleichgültig, ob ich einer der Besten in meinem Arbeitsgebiet werde.		
13. Manchmal sagt man mir nach, ich vernachlässige andere wichtige Seiten meines Lebens, weil ich so viel arbeite.		
14. Sicherlich denken die Leute, dass ich nicht viel Energie habe.		
15. Ich arbeite lieber, als dass ich spiele.		
16. Wenn niemand zu sehen bekommt, was ich mache, tue ich oft nicht mein Bestes.		

Fragenblock 6

Bitte geben Sie an, inwieweit Sie mit den folgenden Aussagen übereinstimmen! (Bitte in jeder Zeile nur eine Möglichkeit ankreuzen!)

Aussage	**trifft aus-gespro-chen zu**	**trifft etwas zu**	**teils / teils**	**trifft kaum zu**	**trifft über-haupt nicht zu**
1. Auch in ungewissen Zeiten erwarte ich normalerweise das Beste.					
2. Wenn bei mir etwas schief laufen kann, dann tut es das auch.					
3. Meine Zukunft sehe ich optimistisch.					
4. Ich sehe immer das Positive in den Din-gen.					
5. Ich glaube an den Grundsatz, dass auf jeden Regen auch Sonnenschein folgt.					
6. Fast nie entwickeln sich die Dinge nach meinen Vorstellun-gen.					
7. Alles in allem erwar-te ich, dass mir mehr gute als schlechte Dinge widerfahren.					
8. Ich zähle selten darauf, dass mir et-was Gutes wider-fährt.					

Fragenblock 7

1) Bitte geben Sie an, ob die folgenden Aussagen auf Sie zutreffen („Richtig“) oder nicht zutreffen („Falsch“). Geben Sie zu jedem Satz entweder „Richtig“ oder „Falsch“ als Antwort; wenn Sie sich nicht ganz sicher sind, kreuzen Sie bitte die Antwort an, die am ehesten auf Sie zutrifft. (Bitte in jeder Zeile ei-ne Möglichkeit ankreuzen!)

Bitte bearbeiten Sie alle Aussagen zügig, aber sorgfältig, und halten Sie sich nicht zu lange an einzelnen Sätzen auf.

Aussage	**Richtig**	**Falsch**
1. Ich würde gern Seiltanzen lernen.		
2. Ich würde **niemals** allein in ein fremdes Land reisen, aus Furcht, dass mir dort etwas zustoßen könnte.		
3. Ich bin fast immer bereit, ein Wagnis einzugehen.		
4. Ich kann mir **nicht** vorstellen, als Fallschirmspringer aus einem Flugzeug zu springen.		
5. Ich habe das Gefühl von Geschwindigkeit gern.		
6. Ich betreibe manche Sportarten und Hobbys **nicht**, weil sie zu gefährlich sind.		
7. Ich hätte meine Freude daran, in einem offenen Fahrstuhl auf die Spitze eines sich noch im Bau befindlichen Hochhauses zu fahren.		
8. Ich versuche, Arbeiten zu umgehen, die mit gefährlichen Werkzeugen und Maschinen durchgeführt werden müssen.		
9. Es würde mir nichts ausmachen, in unbekannten Gewässern zu schwimmen.		
10. Ich ziehe ein ruhiges, sicheres Leben einem abenteuerlichen vor.		
11. Es wäre ein wunderbares Abenteuer für mich, im Segelboot den Ozean zu überqueren.		
12. Ich gehe **nie** in Stadtviertel, die als unsicher gelten.		
13. Ich würde gerne ein altes verlassenes Haus bei Nacht erkunden.		
14. Wellenreiten wäre mir zu gefährlich.		
15. Ich würde gern ein Motorrad fahren.		
16. Ich möchte auf keinen Fall beruflich bei der Bekämpfung von Waldbränden eingesetzt werden.		

2) Sie können kostenlos an einer der folgenden zwei Lotterien teilnehmen. Welche Lotterie wählen Sie? (Bitte ankreuzen)

- ☐ Lotterie A: 4.000 € mit 80% Wahrscheinlichkeit **gewinnen**
- ☐ Lotterie B: 3.200 € mit Sicherheit **gewinnen**

3) Sie können kostenlos an einer der folgenden zwei Lotterien teilnehmen. Welche Lotterie wählen Sie? (Bitte ankreuzen)

- ☐ Lotterie A: 15.000 € mit 20% Wahrscheinlichkeit **gewinnen**
- ☐ Lotterie B: 3.000 € mit Sicherheit **gewinnen**

4) Sie können kostenlos an einer der folgenden zwei Lotterien teilnehmen. Welche Lotterie wählen Sie? (Bitte ankreuzen)

- ☐ Lotterie A: 2.000 € mit 90% Wahrscheinlichkeit **gewinnen**
- ☐ Lotterie B: 1.800 € mit Sicherheit **gewinnen**

5) Sie können kostenlos an einer der folgenden zwei Lotterien teilnehmen. Welche Lotterie wählen Sie? (Bitte ankreuzen)

- ☐ Lotterie A: 16.000 € mit 10% Wahrscheinlichkeit **gewinnen**
- ☐ Lotterie B: 1.600 € mit Sicherheit **gewinnen**

6) Sie können kostenlos an einer der folgenden zwei Lotterien teilnehmen. Welche Lotterie wählen Sie? (Bitte ankreuzen)

- ☐ Lotterie A: 5.000 € mit 50% Wahrscheinlichkeit **gewinnen**
- ☐ Lotterie B: 2.500 € mit Sicherheit **gewinnen**

Fragenblock 8

Bitte geben Sie an, inwieweit Sie mit den folgenden Aussagen übereinstimmen! Auch wenn Ihnen einmal die Entscheidung schwer fallen sollte, kreuzen Sie trotzdem immer eine Antwort an, und zwar die, welche noch am ehesten auf Sie zutrifft. (Bitte in jeder Zeile nur eine Möglichkeit ankreuzen!)

Aussage	**trifft gar nicht zu**	**trifft eher nicht zu**	**trifft eher zu**	**trifft voll und ganz zu**
1. Alles in allem bin ich mit mir selbst zufrieden.				
2. Hin und wieder denke ich, dass ich gar nichts tauge.				
3. Ich besitze eine Reihe guter Eigenschaften.				
4. Ich besitze die gleichen Fähigkeiten wie die meisten anderen Menschen auch.				
5. Ich fürchte, es gibt nicht viel, worauf ich stolz sein kann.				
6. Ich fühle mich von Zeit zu Zeit richtig nutzlos.				
7. Ich halte mich für einen wertvollen Menschen, jedenfalls bin ich nicht weniger wertvoll als andere auch.				
8. Ich wünsche ich könnte vor mir selbst mehr Achtung haben.				
9. Alles in allem neige ich dazu, mich für einen Versager zu halten.				
10. Ich habe eine positive Einstellung zu mir selbst gefunden.				

Questionnaire Ab – gain domain
(only differences to Questionnaire Aa are shown)

Fragenblock 2

Stellen Sie sich bitte folgende Situation vor:

Vor zwei Monaten haben Sie Aktien eines Unternehmens zu einem Kurs von **30 € je Aktie** gekauft.

Vor einem Monat konnten Sie sich über einen Kursanstieg auf **36 € je Aktie** freuen.

Heute entscheiden Sie sich, den Kurs der Aktie erneut zu überprüfen. Welchen Kurs müsste die Aktie heute haben, um Sie **genauso glücklich** zu machen, **wie Sie vor einem Monat waren**, als Sie erfahren hatten, dass der Kurs von 30 € auf 36 € gestiegen war?

Bitte notieren Sie den Kurs, der Sie heute genauso glücklich machen würde, hier:

[ ] € je Aktie

Questionnaire Ac – gain domain
(only differences to Questionnaire Aa are shown)

Fragenblock 2

Stellen Sie sich bitte folgende Situation vor:

Vor zwei Monaten haben Sie Aktien eines Unternehmens zu einem Kurs von **30 € je Aktie** gekauft.

Vor einem Monat konnten Sie sich über einen Kursanstieg auf **36 € je Aktie** freuen.

Heute entscheiden Sie sich, den Kurs der Aktie erneut zu überprüfen. Welchen Kurs müsste die Aktie heute haben, um Sie **genauso glücklich** zu machen, **wie Sie vor einem Monat waren**, als Sie erfahren hatten, dass der Kurs von 30 € auf 36 € gestiegen war?

Bitte notieren Sie den Kurs, der Sie heute genauso glücklich machen würde, hier:

	€ je Aktie

Questionnaire Ba - Loss domain
(only differences to Questionnaire Aa are shown)

Fragenblock 2

Stellen Sie sich bitte folgende Situation vor:

Vor zwei Monaten haben Sie Aktien eines Unternehmens zu einem Kurs von **30 € je Aktie** gekauft.

Vor einem Monat waren Sie enttäuscht, als Sie von einem Kursfall auf **24 € je Aktie** erfahren haben.

Heute entscheiden Sie sich, den Kurs der Aktie erneut zu überprüfen. Welchen Kurs müsste die Aktie heute haben, um sie **genauso traurig** zu machen, **wie Sie vor einem Monat waren**, als Sie erfahren hatten, dass der Kurs von 30 € auf 24 € gefallen war?

Bitte notieren Sie den Kurs, der Sie heute genauso traurig machen würde, hier:

[ ] € je Aktie

Questionnaire Bb - Loss domain
(only differences to Questionnaire Aa are shown)

Fragenblock 2

Stellen Sie sich bitte folgende Situation vor:

Vor zwei Monaten haben Sie Aktien eines Unternehmens zu einem Kurs von **30 € je Aktie** gekauft.

Vor einem Monat waren Sie enttäuscht, als Sie von einem Kursfall auf **24 € je Aktie** erfahren haben.

Heute entscheiden Sie sich, den Kurs der Aktie erneut zu überprüfen. Welchen Kurs müsste die Aktie heute haben, um sie **genauso traurig** zu machen, **wie Sie vor einem Monat waren**, als Sie erfahren hatten, dass der Kurs von 30 € auf 24 € gefallen war?

Bitte notieren Sie den Kurs, der Sie heute genauso traurig machen würde, hier:

[ ] € je Aktie

Questionnaire Bc - Loss domain
(only differences to Questionnaire Aa are shown)

Fragenblock 2

Stellen Sie sich bitte folgende Situation vor:

Vor zwei Monaten haben Sie Aktien eines Unternehmens zu einem Kurs von **30 € je Aktie** gekauft.

Vor einem Monat waren Sie enttäuscht, als Sie von einem Kursfall auf **24 € je Aktie** erfahren haben.

Heute entscheiden Sie sich, den Kurs der Aktie erneut zu überprüfen. Welchen Kurs müsste die Aktie heute haben, um sie **genauso traurig** zu machen, **wie Sie vor einem Monat waren**, als Sie erfahren hatten, dass der Kurs von 30 € auf 24 € gefallen war?

Bitte notieren Sie den Kurs, der Sie heute genauso traurig machen würde, hier:

[ ] € je Aktie

10.3 Questionnaire Experiment 3 (study 3)

Instruktionen

Verehrte Unternehmer und Führungskräfte,

im Rahmen meiner Doktorarbeit am Institut für Familienunternehmen der **WHU – Otto Beisheim School of Managemen**t zum Thema

Entscheidungsverhalten von Fremdmanagern und Familienunternehmern

möchten wir Sie um Ihre Mithilfe bitten.

Nur eine großzahlige Studie kann valide Ergebnisse liefern und Handlungsempfehlungen für die Praxis ermöglichen. Daher wenden wir uns als Forschungsteam heute mit der Bitte an Sie, unser Forschungsvorhaben durch die Beantwortung dieses Fragebogens zu unterstützen. Der Fragebogen hat scheinbar wiederholende Inhalte, dies ist jedoch aus wissenschaftlicher Sicht für diese Studie notwendig - nur voll ausgefüllte Fragebögen sind für uns auswertbar. Die Beantwortung wird ca. 20 Minuten Ihrer Zeit in Anspruch nehmen.

Die Antworten werden anonymisiert, so dass keine Rückschlüsse auf Ihre Person oder auf Ihr Unternehmen gezogen werden können.

Als **Dankeschön** verlosen wir unter den Teilnehmern **zwei Tickets für eine Konferenz** an der WHU im Wert von jeweils 890 Euro und **3 Amazon-Gutscheine** im Wert von jeweils 50 Euro. Ebenso stellen wir Ihnen bei Interesse selbstverständlich gerne die Ergebnisse dieser Untersuchung zur Verfügung.

Vielen Dank im Voraus für Ihre Zeit!

Freundliche Grüße

Dipl.-Kffr.
Evelyn Stommel

Prof. Dr.
Andreas Hack

Prof. Dr.
Franz W. Kellermanns

Fragenblock 1

Allgemeine Fragen zur Person

1) Wie alt sind Sie?

☐ Jahre

2) Welches Geschlecht haben Sie?

□ Weiblich

□ Männlich

3) Welche Position haben Sie im Unternehmen?

□ Sprecher der Geschäftsführung (Vorstandsvorsitzender, CEO)

□ Mitglied der Geschäftsführung (Vorstand, Geschäftsführer)

□ Sprecher des Kontrollgremiums (Aufsichtsratsvorsitzender, Beiratsvorsitzender, o. ä.)

□ Mitglied des Kontrollgremiums (Beirat, Aufsichtsrat, o. ä.)

Sonstige ____________________

4) Halten Sie persönlich Anteile an Ihrem Unternehmen?

□ Ja

□ Nein

5) Wenn ja, wie viel Prozent des Eigenkapitals besitzen Sie?

☐ Prozent

6) Welcher Generation bzw. welchen Generationen der Familie gehören die aktuell tätigen Familienmitglieder im Top Management Team an?

□ 1. Generation

□ 2. Generation

□ 3. Generation

□ 4. Generation

□ 5. oder spätere Generation

7) Zu welcher Generation der Familie gehören Sie?

___ Generation

Fragenblock 2

Allgemeine Fragen zum Unternehmen

8) Bitte geben Sie die folgenden Kennzahlen Ihres Unternehmens für das Geschäftsjahr 2010 an.

- Umsatz (Euro):
- Mitarbeiter (Anzahl):
- Eigenkapitalquote (Prozent)
- Fremdkapitalquote (Prozent)

9) Wann wurde Ihr Unternehmen gegründet?

☐ Jahr

10) Zu welcher Branche würden Sie Ihr Unternehmen zählen?

☐ Automobilindustrie
☐ Baustoffe/Metallerzeugung
☐ Chemie/Pharma
☐ Elektronik/Mechatronik
☐ Energie/Versorgung/Öl/Gas
☐ Handel / Konsumgüter
☐ Maschinen- und Anlagenbau
☐ Transport/Verkehr/Logistik
☐ Bank/Versicherungen
☐ Sonstige

Fragenblock 3

A.1 Generelle Instruktionen zum Experiment

Das Experiment besteht aus mehreren Aufgaben, welche Sie nacheinander bearbeiten. Insgesamt ist das Experiment auf eine Dauer von ca. 15-20 Minuten angelegt (inkl. der Zeit zum Durchlesen der Instruktionen und dem anschließenden Beantworten eines kurzen Fragebogens).

Lesen Sie die Anmerkungen am Bildschirm in Ruhe durch und versuchen Sie, eine möglichst wahrheitsgetreue Selbsteinschätzung vorzunehmen. Bitte bearbeiten Sie alle Fragen zügig, aber sorgfältig, und halten Sie sich nicht zu lange an einzelnen Aufgaben und Fragen auf.

Es gibt keine richtigen oder falschen Antworten, wir sind lediglich an Ihrer persönlichen Einschätzung interessiert. Die Antworten werden anonymisiert, so dass keine Rückschlüsse auf Ihre Person gezogen werden können.

A.2 Experiment

<...>

A.3 Nach Beenden der experimentellen Aufgaben

Welcher Referenzpreis war für Ihre Entscheidung ausschlaggebend?

- Investitionskosten
- Letzter Preis
- Durchschnittspreis
- Höchster Preis
- Niedrigster Preis

Waren die Instruktionen für sie verständlich?
Sehr verständlich / gut verständlich / verständlich / nicht verständlich / überhaupt nicht verständlich

Fragenblock 4

Man kann sich in verschiedenen Bereichen ja auch unterschiedlich verhalten. Wie würden Sie Ihre Risikobereitschaft in Bezug auf die folgenden Bereiche einschätzen?

(0 = gar nicht risikobereit bis 10 = sehr risikobereit)

☐ bei Geldanlagen?
☐ bei Ihrer beruflichen Karriere?
☐ bei Ihrer Gesundheit?

Sie sind nun am Ende des Fragebogens angelangt. Vielen Dank für Ihre Teilnahme an der Umfrage!

Sollten Sie noch weitere Fragen zu diesem Dissertationsprojekt haben, so wenden Sie sich bitte an:

Dipl.-Kffr. Evelyn Stommel
WHU - Otto Beisheim School of Management
Institut für Familienunternehmen
Burgplatz 2
56179 Vallendar

Wenn Sie einen Überblick über die Ergebnisse der Studie erhalten möchten, dann geben Sie bitte hier Ihre Emailadresse an:

____

Wenn Sie an der Verlosung teilnehmen möchten, tragen Sie bitte hier Ihre aktuelle E-Mail-Adresse ein:

____

Im Falle eines Gewinns werden wir über die angegebene E-Mail-Adresse mit Ihnen Kontakt aufnehmen. Der Rechtsweg ist ausgeschlossen. Ihre E-Mail-Adresse wird nicht zusammen mit Ihren Antworten abgespeichert. Wir garantieren die Anonymität Ihrer Daten. Alle Angaben unterliegen den Datenschutzrichtlinien und werden ausschließlich in anonymisierter Form ausgewertet. Ihre Antworten werden ausschließlich zu wissenschaftlichen Zwecken genutzt.

MIX
Papier aus verantwortungsvollen Quellen
Paper from responsible sources
FSC® C105338

If you have any concerns about our products,
you can contact us on
ProductSafety@springernature.com

In case Publisher is established outside the EU,
the EU authorized representative is:
Springer Nature Customer Service Center GmbH
Europaplatz 3, 69115 Heidelberg, Germany

Printed by Libri Plureos GmbH
in Hamburg, Germany